Herodotus, Explorer of the Past

Herodotus, Explorer of the Past

THREE ESSAYS

J.A.S. Evans

PRINCETON UNIVERSITY PRESS

PRINCETON, NEW JERSEY

Library of Congress Cataloging-in-Publication Data

Evans, J.A.S. (James Allan Stewart), 1931-
Herodotus, explorer of the past : three essays / J.A.S. Evans.
p. cm.
Includes bibliographical references and index.
1. Herodotus. 2. Herodotus. History. 3. History, Ancient—
Historiography. 4. Historiography—Greece. 5. Biography—To 500.
6. Imperialism—Historiography. I. Title.
D56.52.H45E93   1991
938'.007202—dc20   90-8734   CIP

ISBN 0-691-06871-2 (acid-free paper)

To Eleanor

CONTENTS

PREFACE

INEVITABLY, there is a lag between the completion of a manuscript and its appearance in print. Although Princeton University Press has been admirably prompt, while *Herodotus, Explorer of the Past* was still in the throes of publication, two books have appeared that would have figured in my bibliography had I been able to read them sooner. One is Rosalind Thomas' *Oral Tradition and Written Record in Classical Athens* (Cambridge, 1989); the other is Donald Lateiner's *The Historical Method of Herodotus* (Toronto, 1989). Both are estimable books. I already had some inkling of the contents of the latter, for I have read and admired a large number of Professor Lateiner's articles over the years, and readers of this book will note that I have profited from them. Rosalind Thomas' publication came as a new discovery. I should have found both these books useful had they been available to me, but they would not have significantly influenced the writing of this book.

Valuable as it is, Rosalind Thomas' book is one that Herodotean scholars should use with discretion. Herodotus did his research in an intellectual climate that was still adjusting to literacy, whereas the fourth century orators, on whom Miss Thomas relies heavily for her evidence, lived in a world not unlike our own, except for a vastly changed communications technology. That is to say, oral and written history in the late fifth and fourth centuries existed side by side, but each had found its own province. Coherent accounts of the past belonged to the realm of written history, which was now well and truly established by Herodotus and Thucydides. Attitudes toward the past still belonged to the oral tradition, and were shaped by the orators and the theater. Thus, Athenian funeral orations helped mold Athenian perceptions of their past in the same way as Fourth of July speeches and Hollywood movies have helped to shape American impressions of theirs. I would not for a moment argue that written history in Greece was unaffected by oral perceptions of this sort, but Herodotus does not seem to me to have been greatly influenced by them. On the whole, however, Miss Thomas' conclusions about the nature of oral tradition in classical Athens differ little from my own, and they serve to emphasize how far Herodotus is from a simple narrator of oral tradition.

But I propose a somewhat different hypothesis. It is that in the archaic Greek world there were specialists who claimed to have a coherent purview of the past. They did not merely nurture a perception of it. Their medium was oral and they passed on their traditions by oral means. Yet there may never have been a time when the *logioi* of archaic Greece were completely free of the influence of literacy. Greece had once been literate in the Bronze Age, in the sense that an elite could read and write Linear B, and in the "Dark Ages" that intervened between the end of the Mycenaean world and the adoption of the Greek alphabet, Greece still had neighbors in the East Mediterranean area that were literate, and possibly she herself had memories of literacy. The antithesis between oral and literate cultures that colors modern research into the oral tradition may never have been valid in Greece. Certainly it did not exist in the world that Herodotus knew.

This book has had a long gestation period. Some of the ideas that appear in it began to germinate years ago, in a graduate seminar at Yale University with Professor Henry Immerwahr. My research has since wandered far afield from Herodotus, to Procopius of Caesarea in the sixth century, who imitated Herodotus' style (but not much else), and Father J.-F. Lafitau, who took Herodotus as his exemplar for his exploration of Iroquois customs in eighteenth-century New France. My scholarly peregrinations have not been entirely of my own volition, for it is not easy to become a specialist in a university where one's teaching must range over the broad field of classical studies. I owe a debt of gratitude to Alexander G. McKay of McMaster University who, as president of the Classical Association of Canada almost fifteen years ago, invited me to address an annual meeting on a topic that was controversial and would take about an hour to expound, and thus moved me to produce a paper on the oral background of Herodotus' *Histories*. Thanks are due as well to Oswyn Murray who was patient with my queries, and to my wife Eleanor, to whose encouragement I owe more than I can express. I should also express thanks to the Isaac Walton Killam Foundation, which has twice awarded me a fellowship, and as a result of one of these, I am enjoying a sabbatical while I am writing these words.

March 22, 1990
Vancouver, Canada

ABBREVIATIONS USED IN CITATIONS

AC	*Antiquité classique*
AJA	*American Journal of Archaeology*
AJPh	*American Journal of Philology*
AncW	*The Ancient World*
ANET	James B. Pritchard, *Ancient Near Eastern Texts Relating to the Old Testament*. Princeton, 1969.
AnSoc	*Ancient Society*
ASNP	*Annali della scuola normale superiore di Pisa*
BICS	*Bulletin of the Institute of Classical Studies*
CII	*Corpus Inscriptionum Iranicarum*
CJ	*Classical Journal*
CP	*Classical Philology*
CQ	*Classical Quarterly*
Diels-Kranz	Hermann Diels and Walther Kranz, *Die Fragmente der Vorsokratiker*. Zurich, 1952.
FGrHist	F. Jacoby, *Die Fragmente der griechischen Historiker*. Leiden, 1957.
GRBS	*Greek, Roman and Byzantine Studies*
HSCP	*Harvard Studies in Classical Philology*
ILS	*Illinois Classical Studies*
JHI	*Journal of the History of Ideas*
JHS	*Journal of Hellenic Studies*
LCM	*Liverpool Classical Monthly*
M-L	R. Meiggs and D. Lewis (eds.) *A Selection of Greek Historical Inscriptions* (Oxford, 1969).
MusHelv	*Museum Helveticum*
PCPS	*Proceedings of the Cambridge Philological Society*
QS	*Quaderni di storia*
QUCC	*Quaderni Urbinati di Cultura Classica*
RFIC	*Rivista di Filologia et d'Istituto Classica*
RhMus	*Rheinisches Museum für Philologie*
WS	*Wiener Studien*
YCS	*Yale Classical Studies*

Herodotus, Explorer of the Past

INTRODUCTION

THIS BOOK is the product of two disparate ideas that eventually inter-
meshed. The first developed out of an old question: What is the precise
meaning of Herodotus' opening sentence? It is not easy to translate without tripping over an anachronism, for the words cannot always mean what
they seem. *"Histories apodeixis"* cannot be a "publication of history," for
although we may believe that Herodotus wrote history, and Cicero recognized him as the "Father of History," Herodotus would not have com-
prehended the term with the connotation we give it, for he worked before
anthropology, history, and geography had been hived off into separate de-
partments. And *"apodeixis"* is better taken as a "public exposition" than a
"publication" as we understand it. But it is the words that conclude the
sentence that are particularly difficult: "for what *aitie* they fought one another."

The question seems to be, who or what was at fault for the war? Enoch
Powell took *aitie* here to mean "the reason why," and so does David Grene
in his recent translation. Mabel Lang renders it simply as "the way they
came into conflict."[1] Twenty years ago, I thought that causation was the
key to understanding Herodotus. I am much less certain now. Herodotus
seems about to launch into *dissoi logoi* on the guilty party responsible for
the war between Greece and Persia, but having presented the views of the
Persian *logioi*, with a Phoenician gloss, he abandons that tack and introduces Croesus, "the first of the barbarians we know" to subject Greeks to
tribute. Before his *arche*, all Greeks were free (1.6.2–3). Afterward, some
part of the Greek world was always subject to tribute, down to Herodotus'
own day.

And with that, Herodotus abandoned the search for the guilty party,
which treated the war as if it were a vendetta that escalated beyond all
proportion. Instead, he set up a new approach to the whys and wherefores
of the war. His method would be to examine the growth of empire, or to
be more correct, empires (for the Persian Empire had antecedents), and to
ask what actuated their development. He saw no point in looking for a
guilty party, for the Persians had invaded Greece because theirs was an
expanding empire, and the Greek world was next on the agenda. It shared
a frontier with an imperialist despotate. The right question to ask was why
the *arche* of the Persians developed this proclivity to expand the boundaries
of their realm. In other words, what was the motive force of imperialism?

---

[1] David Grene, *The History of Herodotus* (Chicago, 1987); M. L. Lang, *Herodotean Narrative and Discourse* (Cambridge, Mass., 1984), 3.

And who were the men who played roles in the imperial advance of
Persia, and her ultimate defeat in Greece? The question brings us to individuals in the *Histories*. Biography was to wait longer than history to become a separate genre, but Herodotus discovered the beginnings of it. The
biographical vignettes of Histiaeus and Aristagoras are masterly, and Xerxes might have been an Aeschylean tragic king illustrating the dangers of
excessive preeminence, except that the calamity falls, not on Xerxes, but on
those around him, and Xerxes learned nothing from the experience. At
least that seems to be the import of the *Histories*. But on the Greek side,
there were no paladins, and on the Persian, no ogres. Herodotus seems
reluctant to pass moral judgments. At least, he wastes no time on moraliz-
ing. The Xerxes of Herodotus is not the Xerxes of Aeschylus. The traditional association of disaster with wealth and prosperity is to be found, but
Aeschylus' *Persians* is a tragedy in black and white; the Xerxes of Herodotus is not.

There are frequently tragic elements to be found, borrowed in particular
from Aeschylus and to a lesser extent, from Sophocles, but on reflection, I
began to wonder that they were not more marked than they are. The story
of Croesus is the story of a tragic fall, and the maxim of Solon which it
illustrates—that no one should call a man happy until he is dead—is repeated in all three tragedians,[2] but surely this was an aphorism that belonged to the public domain; it is not peculiar to tragedy. Both Pausanias
and Xerxes came to tragic ends—after 479 B.C., to be sure, and thus outside the segment of the past that Herodotus chose for his research; but he
recognized no interdict preventing him from making references to the later
period. He did, in fact, mention the alleged medism of Pausanias, and he
left himself an opening (which he did not take), to refer to Xerxes' assassination. But he made no deliberate effort to portray either of them as tragic
figures. Instead, he accords them a handling in time which is closer to that
of Achilles in the *Iliad*, who dies after the epic ends: we know that he will
die if he chooses to fight on at Troy, but Homer has assigned his tragic end
to a separate segment of the past.

Yet, even if Xerxes himself is an undeveloped tragic figure, his expedition
should have provided the stuff of tragedy: Phrynichus and Aeschylus had
already exploited it. The flogging of the Hellespont had become a paradigm of *hybris* by the time Herodotus wrote. But it has been often noted
how nicely he drew the parallels with the Scythian Expedition of Darius:
Darius yoked the Bosporus and the Danube, overstepped the boundary of
Asia into Europe, but avoided tragedy, admittedly by the choice of the
Ionians guarding the Danube bridge behind him. Two kings follow similar

---

[2] Aeschylus, *Agamemnon*, 928–29; Sophocles, *Oedipus Tyrannus*, 1528–30; Euripides, *An-
dromache*, 100–101.

patterns and have different ends. Did Xerxes' *hybris* consist of the fact that his expedition was an exaggeration of his father's? That Darius built one bridge across the Bosporus, but Xerxes built twin bridges across the Hellespont, and in addition, flogged the waters and put them in chains, at least symbolically? Herodotus has suggested the question, but left it unanswered. It seems that he borrowed tragic elements when it suited his dramatic purposes, but they were literary devices designed to catch his audience; they did not inform his historical vision. Darius' *hybris* may have been less pronounced than his son's, but he avoided tragedy for a quite different reason: at the strategic moment, the Ionians guarding the Danube bridge chose to remain loyal to him.

Epic is another matter. His language, his form and structure, and his characters all testify to the pervasive influence of the Greek epic. The jump from the historical epic to prose chronicle was a short one. Herodotus' uncle, Panyassis, wrote historical epics: his *Ionika* was probably based on local traditions that were current among the Ionian cities. Moreover, the example of the Presocratic philosophers must have made an impression, for the thought-world that these *logioi* helped create was the first and longest-lasting influence on Herodotus. The late Eric Havelock[3] pointed out more than twenty years ago that the presocratics also worked within epic literary forms and traditions. Both Xenophanes and Parmenides saw themselves as itinerant reciters, moving from city to city and giving public exhibitions of their *logoi*. Heraclitus always refers, not to his readers but to his listeners, in his extant fragments, and to himself as listening to the *logoi* of others. The oral bards are both their exemplars and their competitors. And that brings me to my second disparate idea about Herodotus, who was also a teller of *logoi*.

This idea began with a paper that I presented to a joint session of the Classical Association of Canada and the Canadian Historical Association, which held their annual meetings that year at London (Ontario). I spoke on the very comprehensive topic of Herodotus as an oral historian. The first part of the paper dealt with the sort of oral sources a field-worker in fifth-century Greece might have expected to find, and I turned to other cultures for analogies, particularly the African kingdoms of the sub-Sahara. The second half was an attempt to apply a structuralist approach borrowed from Claude Lévi-Strauss to the *logoi* of Herodotus, with the Croesus-*logos* as my prime example. I later published a shortened version of the first half of this paper in an early volume of the *Canadian Journal of Oral History*; the attempt to find binary oppositions in Herodotus and to relate them to

---

[3] "Pre-Literacy and the Pre-Socratics," *BICS* 13 (1966), 44–67, repr. in *The Literate Revolution in Greece and its Cultural Consequences* (Princeton, 1982), 220–60.

preliterate modes of thought has since gathered dust. But the nature of Herodotus' epichoric sources has continued to fascinate.

Africa is a splendid laboratory for the researcher in the field of oral history. It provides examples of preliterate societies that made organized efforts to remember their past, as well as examples of societies that made no such effort. For them, traditions of the past were tales told around the campfire, and memories did not generally stretch beyond the span of three generations: that is, from the youngest of one generation to the youngest three generations on, or about a century and a quarter. But Africa also teaches us caution. When Jan Vansina, the doyen of Africanists working with oral traditions, did research for his dissertation on the Kuba of Zaire (who have a passion for history), he got what classicists would call the "local chronicle" from an official spokesman, who first checked his account with the leaders of the community, and Vansina was impressed by its exactitude. Twenty years later, sadder but wiser, he concluded that these Kuba traditions were what the Kuba had chosen to believe, not what actually happened.[4] Jack Goody[5] has argued that keeping lists is an unnatural mental activity for preliterate societies, and if he is right, it means that lists we have accepted as products of oral traditions are in fact symptoms of the beginnings of literacy. I think Goody goes too far, but that is an argument that falls outside the scope of this book.

But Africa, with all its pitfalls, does help us to understand the sort of milieu in which Herodotus worked. When he attributed traditions to various epichoric groups, such as the Spartans, the men of Cyrene, or the like, he was not fabricating a citation. He was quoting the sort of tradition that a *logios* might recite in Sparta or Cyrene, and if there was any fabrication, it was not by Herodotus. What Herodotus learned by questioning individual informants might differ from the tradition that had the general consensus of the community, or it might amplify it or simply agree with it. But the story of the past was a collection of local traditions kept by *logioi*, if there were any (Scythia had none), or if there were not, by myths and legends passed on from parents to their children. A *logios* was simply a man versed in *logoi*: the term embraced local chroniclers, but was not limited to them: even Heraclitus referred to his teachings as a *logoi*. Herodotus was both a *logios* himself, and a collector of *logoi*: probably a fairly indiscriminate one at first, but as time went on, the *logoi* began to relate to a central theme.

Here is where the two disparate ideas began to intermesh. At some point, Herodotus put his *logoi* together into a work comparable in bulk

---

[4] "Comment: Traditions of Genesis," *Journal of African History* 15 (1974), 317–22; cf. Ruth Finnegan, "Oral Tradition and Historical Evidence," *History and Theory* 9 (1970), 195–201.

[5] *The Domestication of the Savage Mind* (Cambridge, 1977), 74–111.

only to the *Iliad* and the *Odyssey*. To do that, he needed a structure and a central theme around which to build the structure. The theme was the aggressive expansion of the *arche* of Persia, its clash with Hellas, which represented its antithesis, and its retreat. The work began at one specified point in time, and ended with another: it thus appropriated a segment of the past that started with Greeks losing their freedom to an *arche*, and ended with them regaining their freedom.

Thus, Herodotus the *logios* became Herodotus the Father of History. What matters in the end is the work that we possess, not its prepublication life as disparate *logoi*. At some point, probably toward the end of his life, Herodotus put his *logoi* into their present form and introduced them to the reading public. He probably started at the beginning and worked steadily toward the end, following a preconceived plan, for the circumstances of writing on a succession of papyrus scrolls in ancient Greece offered limited opportunities for back-checking and cross-referencing. The catalyst that animated him was, I suspect, the outbreak of the Peloponnesian War. I cannot prove that suspicion, nor, I think, can anyone else; otherwise the pronouncement of Eduard Meyer[6] on the subject at the end of the last century would have stood unchallenged. Nor do I imagine that Herodotus wrote with a single motive. But among his purposes, there was one that was of paramount importance, or so I suspect. The defeat of Persia had been followed by a new *arche*, and now the leading states of Hellas, which had united against the barbarian, were locked in a struggle against each other.

We have a number of small cues that indicate that Herodotus wrote his history of the Persian Wars against the background of the Peloponnesian War and its preliminaries. Imperial Persia showed the same restless ambition as imperial Athens. Pericles could urge the Athenians not to fall below the standard of their fathers who built their empire, and to warn them that they could not give it up without peril.[7] Both Darius and Xerxes were driven on to be no lesser men than their predecessors, and Xerxes found that he could not rescind the project of invading Greece without danger to his throne. The Pausanias portrayed by our historian challenges his portrayal in Athenian propaganda as an arrogant, treacherous leader who alienated the Ionians, and made them willing confederates of Athens. The tactic of seizing Cythera, which Demaratus recommended to Xerxes,[8] was

---

[6] *Forschungen zur Alten Geschichte*, I (Halle, 1892), 154: "All die zahlreichen und meist recht unfruchtbaren Untersuchungen über die Entstehungszeit der herodotischen Geschichtswerke haben nur ein sicheres Resultat ergeben: dass die letzten Bücher in der Form wie wir sie haben, in den ersten Jahren des peloponnesischen Krieges niedergeschrieben sind."

[7] Thuc. 2.62–63.

[8] Hdt. 7.235. We need not believe that this passage was written after the Athenians occupied Cythera in 424 B.C.: see W. W. How and J. Wells, *A Commentary on Herodotus*[2], vol. 2

aired at the beginning of the Archidamian War. And finally, there is Herodotus' joyless outlook on war that reflects the suffering it brings. Croesus' comment to Cyrus expresses it most vividly: "No one is so foolish as to prefer war to peace; for in peace, children bury their fathers, but in war, fathers their children."[9]

It would appear that Herodotus did not merely want to remind the Greeks of the great deeds some of them had done when they resisted the advance of Persia. He also wanted to remind them, as a new war with its concomitant suffering split them apart, of the common patriotism that had once animated *to Hellenikon*: not a nation-state, but a nation in the root sense of the word, with a common tongue, common blood, and common shrines and rituals for their gods.[10] He also wanted to show what imperialism was: how it began, developed, and retreated. In other words, he was putting the cycle of history present into the perspective of the cycle of history past, and I suspect that he considered such an undertaking germane to the contemporary situation.

(Oxford, 1928), 233. Thuc. 1.142 shows that the tactic *epiteichismos* was in the air at the beginning of the war.

[9] Hdt. 1.87.4.

[10] Cf. Hdt. 8.144.4, where the definition of *to Hellenikon* is put into the mouths of the Athenians.

THE IMPERIALIST IMPULSE

NINE YEARS after their defeat at Marathon, the Persians were ready once again to invade Greece. The Greeks owed a debt of gratitude to Egypt for the delay. For three years after the defeat, Darius had prepared a new assault to wipe out the disgrace, but then Egypt had risen in revolt, and in 486 B.C., Darius died; Xerxes succeeded him and the rebellion was not crushed until 484. Then Xerxes called a synod of the Persian magnates. It was a congress that Herodotus recreated with imaginative skill, but there may be a solid morsel of tradition behind it: in the romance of Esther, King Ahasuerus (Xerxes) summoned his nobles to a great festival in the third year of his reign, but in the Hebrew tradition these festivities were merely a backdrop for the fall of Vashti and the elevation of the Jewish heroine Esther in her place. For Herodotus, the feasting and the pageantry that must have accompanied a congress of this sort were of no importance: the synod is treated merely as a bit of theater for a remarkable exposition of the motive force behind Persian imperialism. Herodotus has undertaken to explain the reasons why Xerxes chose to invade Greece.

Persian despots were not given to parliamentary procedures. Herodotus reported in another context that the Persians debated questions drunk, and reconsidered them sober, or vice versa, as the case may be, but he portrayed no councils of the sort for his readers. He made short shrift of the debate that took place before Darius' Scythian expedition. "While Darius was making ready his invasion of Scythia and dispatching messengers round about with orders to some to raise troops, to others to supply ships and still others to build a bridge over the Thracian Bosporus, Artabanus, son of Hysptaspes, Darius' brother, urged him strongly not to make the expedition against the Scyths, on the ground that Scythia was a difficult objective. But good as his advice was, he failed to convince and he ceased." So much for the counsel that Darius was willing to accept before he set out against the Scyths. Cyrus did better before he advanced across the river Araxes against the Massagetae: he called a council of his "first men," and all but one advised him to allow the queen of the Massagetae to move into Persian territory and fight a decisive battle there.[1] The exception was Croesus, who had lost the throne of Lydia and taken over the persona of a wise adviser instead.[2] He argued that to advance was both safer and more ap-

---

[1] Hdt. 1.133.4; 1.206–8.
[2] Cf. R. Lattimore, "The Wise Adviser in Herodotus," *CP* 34 (1939), 24–35, esp. 31.

propriate for a Persian king: therefore Cyrus should move forward into the queen's territory and use trickery to defeat the Massagetae on their soil. The result of this strategy was, first, the capture and suicide of the queen's son, and then the death of Cyrus himself in battle. There is nothing approaching the cut-and-thrust of a full-scale debate here, but only a *topos* that provided an opening for a wise adviser to make a point, and for the hero of the tale, Cyrus, to make an existential choice.

In fact, if we except the famous debate of the Persian grandees on the question of the proper constitution for Persia, which is more influenced by the sophists (particularly Protagoras)[3] than anything in the Persian tradition, there is only one other assembly in the *Histories* which is comparable. That is the council at Phaleron before the battle of Salamis. There the king took his seat; then the various princelings and squadron commanders took theirs in order of rank: the king of Sidon first, next the king of Tyre, and so on in order. Mardonius went around to each to put the question whether or not to fight. All voted for battle, except the irrepressible Artemisia, the only commander in the Persian force with an intelligence comparable to Themistocles', who delivered a brief address to Mardonius, and he in turn reported it to Xerxes. Dissent was handled with courtesy and decorum, and then dismissed: a stark contrast with the councils of the Greek admirals before Salamis. Xerxes accepted a majority verdict which, not surprisingly, agreed with his own inclination, and chose the wrong course of action, whereas the Greeks did otherwise.

This Persian council was the inverse counterpart of the conclaves of the Greek admirals, and it was hardly more than a little showcase that Herodotus used to parade the might-have-beens of history before his readers' eyes. He chose as his mouthpiece Artemisia, a woman, and therefore an outsider in this masculine assembly.[4] But the speeches of Xerxes, Mardonius, and Artabanus before the Persian magnates at the king's levee are intended to reveal something of the substance of Persian imperialism as Herodotus understood it.

The king at first had not possessed any great wish to invade Greece. He did not initially feel the weight of Persia's imperial tradition, or the obligation to expand the frontiers of the empire. The chief instigator of the war was Mardonius, son of Gobryas, who had taken command of Persia's Aegean front in 494 B.C.; Herodotus implied that he owed his elevation then, at a young age, to his "recent" marriage to Artazostra, Darius' daugh-

---

[3] Cf. K. F. Stroheker, "Zu den Anfängen der Monarchischen Theorie in der Sophistik," *Historia* 2 (1953/54), 381–412; François Lasserre, "Hérodote et Protagoras: La debat sur les constitutions," *MusHelv* 33 (1976), 65–84.

[4] Hdt. 8.67–69; cf. Carolyn Dewald, "Women and Culture in Herodotus' *Histories*," in Helen F. Foley, ed., *Reflections on Women in Antiquity* (New York, 1981), 91–125, esp. 109.

ter.[5] He had advanced into Europe as far as Mt. Athos, where he had lost three hundred ships and twenty thousand men in a tempest, and was wounded himself in a night attack on his camp by a local tribe, the Brygoi. Not a glorious achievement overall.

But Mardonius had not returned home before conquering the Brygoi, his wound notwithstanding, and his influence with the new king was paramount. Convinced of Persian superiority, and quite without any comprehension of the Greeks, he was to be the spokesman for aggressive imperialism, who still believed that no Greek would dare "look without flinching at Persian dress and the men who wore it," to take a phrase from Herodotus,[6] who wrote that, before the battle of Marathon, a Greek would not have summoned the courage to do any such thing. "Indeed my lord, who will oppose you and offer war, when you bring with you the host of Asia and all your ships?" he asked.

Events are to change his mind not one iota. In his last speech before his death, he was to gloat that the retreat of the Spartans on the battlefield of Plataea demonstrated their inferiority.[7] He pressed his advice upon the new king. Athens, he argued, had committed great crimes, and had to be punished. She had helped the king's Ionian subjects to rebel, and then at Marathon, she had humiliated Datis and Artaphrenes. Vengeance was necessary for the sake of security: Athens had to be punished so that no one in the future would dare invade the Great King's dominions.

But that was not all. Europe was beautiful: a fertile land with trees of every kind. Mardonius stood the truth as the Greeks perceived it on its head, for the contrast between Persian wealth and Greek poverty was commonplace in classical Greece. Pausanias, son of Cleombrotus, staged a tableau to illustrate this after the victory at Plataea, and at the end of the century, Xenophon was to tell his ten thousand mercenaries that they must get back to Greece to tell their friends and relatives that they were poor by their own choice, for if they migrated to Persia, they could live in luxury.[8] Mardonius reversed the polarity that the Greeks accepted as conventional wisdom. But Mardonius also harbored an ulterior motive: he wanted to be governor of Greece himself.

He had assistance in this endeavor. The pro-Persian Aleuad family, dynasts of Larissa in Thessaly, seconded his efforts; in 479 B.C., after the defeat at Salamis, they were still to urge the Persians on to their ultimate

[5] The marriage was not recent in 492 B.C.: J. M. Cook, *The Persian Empire* (London, 1983), 245n.10; J.A.S. Evans, *AJPh* 107 (1986), 382–84; D. M. Lewis, "Persians in Herodotus," in M. H. Jameson, ed., *The Greek Historians. Literature and History. Papers Presented to A. E. Raubitschek* (Saratoga, Calif., 1985), 101–17, esp. 110–11.
[6] 6.112.3. *Thesis Herodotus*, Book 6.
[7] Hdt. 9.82.1–3.
[8] Ibid.; Xen. *Anab.*, 3.2.26.

defeat at Plataea. The deposed Pisistratid tyrant Hippias had guided the
Persians to Marathon in 490 B.C., and died soon thereafter; who the new
pretenders were, we do not know, but Herodotus considered the Pisistratid lobby still effective at the Persian court, and it included a *kresmologos*,
Onomakritos, a collector and editor of oracles who provided a selection of
prophecies predicting Persian success. Xerxes let himself be persuaded by
a team made up of an ambitious courtier, self-interested Thessalian aristo-
crats, and the lobby for a discredited dynastic family driven from Athens
three decades before.

Thus far, the new king of Persia had appeared in the *Histories* as a shallow
prince, the victim of his own naivety, but no great imperialist. He was, in
fact, in his mid-thirties when he came to the throne, and he had already
shown himself to be more ruthless and bigoted than his father,[9] but his
portrayal by Herodotus is otherwise. Yet his speech to the Persian magnates presents a new dimension, for he proceeded to enunciate the principles of imperialism that actuated the empire which he had inherited.

First, expansionism was a Persian *nomos*, and not a new one. "I learn
from our elders that we have never remained inactive since we took over
this sovereign power from the Medes, when Cyrus deposed Astyages."[10] It
was a *nomos* sanctioned by Heaven, and it brought Persia greatness and
prosperity. Second, there was the example of Xerxes' predecessors who had
followed this *nomos*. Cyrus, Cambyses, and Darius had added to the empire, and so must Xerxes too. Greece still remained outside it, and, echoing
Mardonius' misrepresentation of the truth, Xerxes pronounced Greece as
large and as rich as Persia itself: the intended victim of Persian aggression
was Persia's equal. Last, there was the motive of revenge. Athens should
be punished for the wrongs she had inflicted on Persia. Yet vengeance
seems a secondary cause, for Xerxes' ambitions went far beyond Athens. If
Europe and Asia were yoked, Xerxes could make them one country. The
world would have one monarch. There would be no limits to the realm of
the Great King, and hence, we may note, no boundaries left to transgress.[11]
Thus, said Xerxes, downgrading the guilt of Athens as a motive, those who

[9] The extent to which Xerxes altered the Achaemenid policy of religious toleration, if at all,
is disputed: cf. Gerold Walser, *Hellas und Iran* (Darmstadt, 1984), 49–52. Herodotus
(1.183.6–7) refers to his ruthless suppression of the Babylonian revolt in 482 B.C., and at
7.7, mentions his harsh suppression of Egypt. See in general, Richard N. Frye, *The Heritage
of Persia* (Cleveland, 1963, repr. Mentor Books, New York, 1966), 149; id., *The History of
Ancient Iran* (Munich, 1984), 126; J. Duchesne-Guillemin, "Réligion et politique de Cyrus
à Xerxes," *Persica* 3 (1967–68), 1–9, esp. 7–9.

[10] Hdt. 7.8.1.

[11] On the concept of "limit" in the *Histories*, see Donald Lateiner, "Limit, Propriety and
Transgression in the *Histories* of Herodotus," in Jameson, ed., *The Greek Historians*, 87–100;
cf. Alan B. Lloyd, *Historia* 37 (1988), 28–29.

were *aitioi* and those who were not would both be enslaved. With that, Xerxes invited debate.

The dialectic that follows is uneven. Mardonius was outclassed by the king's uncle, Artabanus, whose role as a wise adviser urging caution has already been foreshadowed: he had tried similarly to dissuade Darius from his Scythian expedition. Mardonius has less to say; his points are comments on the king's speech, and his purpose was to soften its rough edges. The Ionians living in Europe could not be allowed to make fools of the Persians: the outrages committed at Sardis and Marathon had to be avenged. Yet, Mardonius pointed out that vengeance had played no role in Persia's expansion thus far. Persia's previous victims had done her no wrong. But that made the argument for invading Greece all the stronger, for now that Persia did have a just cause for war, it would be extraordinary if she failed to exploit it. In any case, the Greeks were poor fighters and their knowledge of military tactics puerile. They would not resist, but if they did, they would discover that the Persians were the best soldiers in the world. With that, Mardonius concluded with a wry note of irony: he gave Xerxes the conventional warning against overconfidence.

One of these arguments we have met before. Aristagoras of Miletus, who was also a fomenter of war, had tried the inverse of it on the Spartans: the Persians, he said, were not valiant men, and their weapons and armor were inadequate. It was a war hawk's standard argument. Herodotus himself, on the first point, granted the Persians valor equal to the Greeks, but on the second point, he agreed with Aristagoras.[12]

Yet a new overtone has emerged. Herodotus' judgment on the Ionians was unflattering, though we should not overemphasize, for he makes exceptions.[13] Yet his general assessment is explicit. Of all the Hellenes, the Ionians were the weakest. Their only city of importance was Athens, and she did not like to be called "Ionian." Cleisthenes, whose reforms had started the growth of Athens to power, had established new tribes that had no counterpart among the Ionians out of contempt for them.[14] The reason for Herodotus' assessment is another story; here we should note merely that the Persian miscalculation of the Greek will to resist was founded on their familiarity with those Greeks under Persian dominion. This included not merely the Ionians but the Dorians and Aeolians as well, though to the Persians they were all *Yauna*,[15] nor did Herodotus himself think it always

---

[12] Hdt. 5.49.3; 9.62.2–3.

[13] C. J. Emlyn-Jones, *The Ionians and Hellenism* (London, 1980), 168–70; J. Alty, "Dorians and Ionians," *JHS* 102 (1982), 1–14; esp. 11–14. Herodotus' assessment of Ionian weakness reflects the conventional wisdom of the fifth century; in contrast, Thucydides (1.16) noted the great advance of Ionia before the Persian conquest.

[14] Hdt. 1.143.1; 5.66.1; 5.69.1–2.

[15] Cf. Aristophanes, *Acharn.* 104; D. M. Lewis, "Persians in Herodotus," 107–8.

necessary to differentiate. They were a quarrelsome lot: those benefitting from Persian rule had been forced after the Ionian Revolt to settle their differences by arbitration rather than war,[16] but the free Greeks settled theirs by choosing a level parcel of ground and fighting it out. In any event, Xerxes had no fears that the Ionians would be anything but obedient subjects until his defeat at Salamis, after which it occurred to him that they might instigate the Greek fleet to sail to the Hellespont and destroy the bridges there. The stature of the Ionians led the Persians to underestimate all the Greeks. In any assessment of the causes of Xerxes' invasion, the poor reputation of the Ionians had something to answer for.

Only one Persian dared to present the opposing view: the king's uncle, Artabanus. He is a dramatic figure whose ultimate archetype is Cassandra. More than a wise adviser, he is almost a seer whose accurate vision of the future introduced a note of dramatic irony. The Greeks were valorous, he said, shifting the gaze of the magnates from the subject Ionians to Athens: at Marathon, the Athenians alone had vanquished the great army of Datis and Artaphrenes. Suppose the Greeks defeated the Persians on sea and then destroyed the bridge over the Hellespont? He cited Darius' Scythian expedition as a parallel: when Darius was forced to retreat, all that stood between him and disaster was the resolve of one Greek, Histiaeus of Miletus: for a few hours, the future of Persia had rested upon the shoulders of this one man. Therefore Xerxes should not act rashly; he should reflect at leisure, and Artabanus seemed confident that reflection would result in inaction.

He went on, developing an argument that Solon had put to Croesus at the height of his power. "My lord Croesus," Solon had said, "I know that all Heaven is jealous, and loves to create mischief and *you* ask me about the fortunes of men!"[17] Heaven loved to smite the great, warned Artabanus, unconsciously drawing the parallel with the Lydian king, and God endured presumption in no one but Himself. He concluded with nothing less than a confident wager on a Persian defeat: let him and Mardonius both stake their children's lives on the outcome of the expedition! If it was a success, Artabanus' line would be wiped out.

The king replied wrathfully, full of dynastic pride. The war was a necessity; vengeance *had* to be exacted from the Athenians. "I know well that if we remain at peace, they will not; they are sure to invade our country!" The expedition had become a preemptive strike: Persia must attack or herself be attacked. There was still, of course, the example of the past, though Xerxes dredged Greek mythology for a specious parallel: if Pelops the Phrygian could conquer Greece, could not the Great King too, who counted the Phrygians among his slaves?

The story is quickly concluded. At night, Xerxes did rethink, and de-

---

[16] Hdt. 6.42.1.
[17] Hdt. 1.32.1.

cided that Artabanus was right. His anger, as he was to explain to the Persian council the next day, was the hot temper of youth. Then Xerxes was visited twice in dreams by a phantom: a tall, handsome man, who also visited Artabanus. The message was always the same: Xerxes would countermand the expedition at his peril. The penalty for remaining at peace would be the loss of his royal status. "Be, then, very sure of this," said the phantom, on its second visit, "if you do not launch your war at once, this shall be the outcome: just as a brief span of time raised you to be great and mighty, so shall you speedily become humble again."[18] The reader may note that the apparition failed to promise victory, though even Artabanus imagined that a successful outcome was implied. But the message was unavoidable: Xerxes had to invade Greece or face an unpleasant alternative.

Years ago, Macan remarked that the analogy between Xerxes' dream and the deceitful dream sent to Agamemnon in the *Iliad* has "often been pointed out."[19] But though Herodotus has borrowed the literary device, he has shifted the emphasis. The dream in the *Iliad* is a simple case of a mischievous god playing with the overconfident Agamemnon, exploiting a weak point in his character by promising him victory without Achilles' help. The dream of Xerxes was not explicitly deceitful, for it did not presage a Greek defeat, though it left that impression.[20] Instead it emphasized the danger of trying to reverse what was destined to be. It was Xerxes' position as king of Persia, the descendant of a line of Achaememid imperialists who had increased the size of the empire during their several reigns, that circumscribed his freedom of action. All the reasons Mardonius had given for invading Greece and Artabanus' rebuttals did not matter. Xerxes seems to be caught, all unknowing, in a dilemma of fate and free will, quite as much as the protagonist of Sophocles' *Oedipus Tyrannus*. Xerxes was intended to invade Greece, and the dream intervened when he seemed on the point of falling short of what Bernard Knox,[21] in his study of Oedipus, calls "the divine intention." But it is fair to ask why there should be any such "divine intention" at all. What forces were there at work that forestalled Xerxes' impulse to draw back from disaster?

THE NECESSITY OF REVENGE

One thinks naturally of vengeance and retribution. The concept appears frequently in the *Histories*. Retribution (*tisis*) was a way of evening up the score, or paying off someone to whom an obligation was due, and it served the function of enforcing a kind of equilibrium in a macrocosm of contrapositions. Its near synonym, *timoria*, could mean "assistance" as well; in

---

[18] Hdt. 7.14.2.

[19] R. W. Macan, *The Seventh, Eighth and Ninth Books*, I.1 (London, 1908), 22.

[20] Cf. Hdt. 7.18.5. Similarly, the Delphic oracle left Croesus under the impression that he would defeat Cyrus, but it did not explicitly utter an untruth.

[21] *Oedipus at Thebes* (New Haven, 1957), 33–42.

the Hippocratic writings, it might mean simply "medical aid."[22] Xerxes told the assembled magnates that *tisis* and *timoria* were among the by-products of his expedition; the mention is casual, but as he went on, he elaborated. The vengeance-motive centered around the twenty ships that Athens sent to help the Ionians in their revolt against Persia; Herodotus[23] calls them the "beginnings of evils for the Greeks and the barbarians." The phrase has the Homeric echo that Herodotus liked to evoke, but it was almost a cliché,[24] and we should not give it undue significance: the aid that Athens and Eretria sent the rebels was a provocation which reawakened Persia's aggressive instincts, but it was not the real cause of her expansionism. Mardonius referred to the vengeance motive, but with a cynical twist: Persian imperialism had developed and progressed thus far without it, he said, for the various peoples whom the Persians conquered had done Persia no wrong; but now, when the Persians did possess a vengeance motive, it would be too bad if they failed to exploit it! Vengeance was a good reason for imperial expansion if there were grounds for it, but if there were not, the impulse that drove imperial aggression could make do without it.

As an *alleged* cause of action, the importance of vengeance in the *Histories* cannot be denied.[25] It could hardly be otherwise. Retribution was part of the moral and intellectual baggage that Herodotus had inherited from the epic and the whole tradition of Greek mythopoeia. "Famine and blight do not beset the just," wrote Hesiod. Zeus exacted great penalties from proud men who worked evil.[26] On the level of popular theology, Herodotus was not far removed from that view. He recorded that, in the general opinion of the Greeks, Cleomenes, king of Sparta, went mad as retribution for sacrilege (the Spartans were the exception: they attributed his madness to heavy drinking). But Herodotus himself thought his insanity was retribution for his unjust treatment of Demaratus. Talthybius exacted retribution for the Persian heralds whom the Spartans killed in 491 B.C., and the whole story of the Trojan War, reflected Herodotus,[27] as he compared the Egyp-

---

[22] Hippocrates, *Acute Diseases*, 18.

[23] 5.97.3.

[24] Herodotus may have intended his listeners to recall *Iliad* 5.62–63, where similar (but not the same) words are applied to the ships that brought Helen to Troy, but there are other examples at *Iliad* 11.604 and Thucydides 2.12. The Homeric echoes in the *Histories* are tabulated by Elisabeta Poghirc, "Homer şi opera sa în Istoriile lui Herodot," *Studi clasice* 19 (1980), 7–18.

[25] The most elaborate statement of vengeance as causation is by K.-A. Pagel, *Die Bedeutung des aitiologischen Momentes für Herodots Geschichtsschreibung* (Leipzig, 1927). See also A. Maddalena, *Interpretazione Erodotee* (Padova, 1942), 51–81; J. de Romilly, "La vengeance comme explication historique dans l'oeuvre d' Hérodote," *REG* 84 (1971), 314–37; H. R. Immerwahr, "Aspects of Historical Causation in Herodotus," *TAPA* 87 (1956), 241–80.

[26] *Works and Days*, 238–45.

[27] 7.134–37; 2.120.

tian account of it with Greek legend, was a revelation of how the gods exacted great penalties for great wrongdoing.

This theological mindset left its mark in the world of diplomacy as well. "You started this war," the Spartans told the Athenians in the spring of 479 B.C., when Mardonius tried to entice them into a separate peace, "and we had no wish for it. The struggle began as a war for your territory and now it involves all Greece."[28] In the Spartan view of things, the Athenian intervention in the Ionian Revolt began the war. It was a starting point, which led directly to Xerxes' invasion. But nowhere does Herodotus suggest that Persian aggression would never have taken place if the Athenian contingent of twenty ships had not set sail for Ionia in the first year of the revolt!

Alleged causes might serve very well as justifications, but they were not necessarily real causes. Darius remembered the Athenian part in the Ionian Revolt: he assigned a slave the task of reminding him of it, but Herodotus labels it a *prophasis*: a prior injury that can be put forward to justify revenge.[29] It was only his ostensible motive for the dispatch of Datis and Artaphrenes to Marathon; his real intention was to conquer all of Greece that had not surrendered to him by giving earth and water. And finally, Herodotus states his own view of the matter, which by implication rejects vengeance for the twenty ships as the cause of the war. The expedition of Xerxes, he says, was nominally against Athens, but in fact its objective was to subjugate all of Greece.[30] The Athenian intervention was never more than a provocation, and when such provocations were available, Persian imperialism might exploit them as pretexts, but when they were not, it continued on its course equally well without them. Herodotus does not display the cynicism about allegations of prior wrongs used to justify aggression that Thucydides[31] evinces, but he seems merely to have included them among the tactics of war.

Darius' Scythian expedition is a case in point, which illustrates how useful a tactic the *prophasis* of vengeance could be. Darius' motive for the expedition against Scythia was revenge for an ancient wrong, but in the same breath Herodotus[32] adds the economic argument for expansion: Asia was full of wealth and population: hence the time was ripe to put this casus belli to practical use. The Scyths, faced with the invasion, sent envoys to their neighbors to seek help. They argued that the Persian motive for aggression was not revenge but simple appetite for conquest: otherwise the attack

---

[28] Hdt. 8.142.2.

[29] Hdt. 6.94.1. Cf. R. Sealey, "Thucydides, Herodotus and the Causes of War," *CQ* 7 (1957), 1–12, esp. 4–5; L. Pearson, "*Prophasis* and *Aitia*," *TAPA*, 83 (1952), 205–23.

[30] 7.138.1; cf. 7.157.2.

[31] Cf. 5.89.

[32] 4.1.1. A similar economic cause is given for Spartan expansion at 1.66.1; cf. Aldo Corcella, *Erodoto e l'analogia* (Palermo, 1984), 196.

would have been directed against the Scyths alone, and Darius would have ignored the Getae and the Thracians whom he swept up along the way.[33] The reply was mixed: some agreed to help but more rejected the Scythian argument, replying that the Persians were really reacting to an unprovoked wrong, the Scythian conquest of Asia that had lasted twenty-eight years. A god had presided over the Scythian rule of Persia as long as he had ordained it, and now the same god presided over the interaction of vengeance and countervengeance. These neutrals felt confident that they would suffer no harm from Darius if they did him none. "However," they added, "if he enters our land and starts doing us wrong, we shall not put up with it."

This exchange is close to a parody of the diplomatic efforts that the Hellenic League made to find allies against Xerxes, and on one point it twists historical accuracy. It was the Medes, not the Persians, whom the Scyths had conquered. Herodotus pretends that the neutrals saw Darius' attack within the larger context of chronic strife between Europe and Asia, a premise that makes the parallel between the Scythian expedition and Xerxes' invasion all the closer.[34] And in the answer of the neutrals to the appeal of the Scyths for help, there is an echo of the debate in Greece over the responsibility for the Persian attack. Darius could allege vengeance, though he had to delve back into history and distort it a bit to find a wrong that merited retribution, but this vengeance motive served well enough to justify his attack that it partially aborted the Scythian effort to form an alliance against him.

But it is affluence that Herodotus puts forward as the premier cause. "For, as Asia was at its flower in numbers of men, and great wealth was coming in, Darius conceived the desire to take vengeance on the Scyths."[35] This is not Herodotus speaking as a modern economic historian, nor is it an example of a tragic pattern, where *koros* leads to blindness, and blindness to a fall. Darius returned safely from Scythia, having established Persian authority in the north Aegean area. Rather, Herodotus is stating simply that the possession of power, measured in population and revenue, is a stimulus to imperial expansion. The Scythian act of aggression that Darius decided to avenge was not pure fiction: alleged causes rarely are. Their purpose is to shift the blame away from the perpetrator of the aggressive

[33] Hdt. 4.118.1–5.

[34] The parallels have frequently been pointed out: see esp. Hans-Friedrich Bornitz, *Herodot-Studien. Beiträge zum Verständnis der Einheit des Geschichtswerkes* (Berlin, 1968), 125–30; Henry Wood, *The Histories of Herodotus. An Analysis of the Formal Structure* (The Hague and Paris, 1972), 94–100; Virginia Hunter, *Past and Present in Herodotus and Thucydides* (Princeton, 1982), 206–25; F. Hartog, *The Mirror of Herodotus*, trans. J. Lloyd (Berkeley and Los Angeles, 1988), 34–60.

[35] 4.1.1.

act, and they would serve it poorly if they were patently false. But they mask the true reason.

Miltiades, after the victory of Marathon, led an attack on Paros, and he had a well-founded *prophasis*: Paros had contributed a trireme to the fleet of Datis and Artaphrenes. But he also had a private motive, which Herodotus is careful to point out. Aryandes, satrap of Egypt, dispatched an expedition against Cyrene, and his pretext was vengeance for the murder of Arcesilaus. Yet Herodotus considered it merely an excuse to conquer Libya, for it was full of tribes and most of them paid Darius no attention.[36]

Vengeance, therefore, was a respectable justification for aggression, and Heaven deemed it satisfactory, as the neutral neighbors of the Scyths reminded them. It was equally acceptable in the Athenian law courts, where the strict relevance of what was being avenged was not required.[37] But ostensible causes were not to be confused with real ones. Xerxes might retort wrathfully to Artabanus that Persia must attack or be attacked, but he forgot the point once his anger had cooled. The dream that visited Xerxes did not tell him that he *had* to avenge wrongs inflicted by the Athenians on the Persians; it stressed instead the consequences if he did not. Xerxes' mission went beyond vengeance. As he told his magnates, he wanted to subdue both the *aitioi* and *anaitioi* to slavery.

This conclusion, that on the level of international politics, vengeance served more as an alleged cause than as a real one, is all the more remarkable because in two other spheres Herodotus did regard vengeance as a causal agent. On the divine level, he believed that the gods exacted retribution. The Persians under Artabazus' command who were drowned by an unusually high tide as they assaulted Potidaea, suffered retribution for desecrating Poseidon's temple. So the Potidaeans said, and Herodotus agreed. The Aeginetans who put down the uprising of Nicodromus and killed the rebels who sought asylum in the temple of Demeter, suffered vengeance before they could obtain divine mercy: they were driven from their homes in the first year of the Peloponnesian War. Divine vengeance fell also upon the Pelasgians for murdering and raping Athenian concubines.[38]

But this was popular theology that was generally accepted, and Herodotus did not dispute it, for it made sense out of what would otherwise be irrational.[39] In instances such as the madness of King Cleomenes of Sparta, there might be a difference of opinion about the particular sin for which the sinner suffered retribution, but Herodotus had no doubt that his mad-

[36] Hdt. 6.133.1; 4.167.

[37] Cf. R. Sealey, *CQ* 7 (1957), 4–8.

[38] Hdt. 8.129.3; 6.91.1; 6.138–40.

[39] Cf. C. Darbo-Peschanski, *Le discours du particulier. Essai sur l'enquête hérodotéene* (Paris, 1987), 97–98.

ness *was* retribution from the gods. But vengeance on this level fell within
the province of Heaven, and could be recognized clearly only after it had
taken place. Then men might look back and discern (or think they discern)
the offense for which the gods had meted out condign punishment. But
the reasons why men acted as they did, and the motives that impelled them,
belonged to the human space.

The other level, where Herodotus recognized the working of vengeance,
is what we may call the realm of natural science, which had engrossed the
Presocratics. The winged snakes of Arabia that guarded the frankincense
bushes would have overwhelmed mankind but for the design of divine
providence.[40] The female killed the male after he had impregnated her, and
suffered retribution for it, for her offspring avenged their sire by chewing
their way out of her womb, thus killing her. In this way, divine providence
prevented the snakes from growing too numerous and overwhelming their
enemy, mankind. This is vengeance operating as a natural force to maintain
balance within the sphere of biology, and to our eyes, it seems completely
amoral; but perhaps not to Herodotus or his contemporaries, for whom
the universe itself was a moral construct, and thus we cannot make a sharp
distinction between natural science and the divine. The vengeance that
controlled the population growth of the winged snakes seems to be the
same sort of retribution to which Heraclitus[41] referred when he said that
the sun would not overstep its measures, for if it did, the Furies would find
it out, and before Heraclitus, Anaximander of Miletus had seen the same
force as a law of nature.[42] The earliest, and perhaps the most lasting influence upon Herodotus was the thought-world of Ionia, and when Xerxes
crossed the Hellespont, the reader of the *Histories* must sense that the natural boundary between Europe and Asia that was defined by the *logioi* of
the proem has been overstepped. For Herodotus, even the geographical
space within which human action occurs is commensurate and balanced,[43]
evidently reflecting in some way the mandate of justice. But did some inexorable law of nature demand that Xerxes avenge the outrages that Persia
had suffered at Sardis and Marathon, thereby making him overstep the
natural limits of Asia and opening him in turn to retribution?

Herodotus avoided any such conclusion. The dream of Xerxes merely

[40] Hdt. 3.107–9; cf. Plato, *Protagoras*, 321b, where Protagoras imagines that Epimetheus
had the foresight to suit an animal's reproductive powers to its role in nature.

[41] Diels-Kranz, frg. 94.

[42] Cf. G.E.R. Lloyd, *Polarity and Analogy. Two Types of Argumentation in Early Greek
Thought* (Cambridge, 1966), 212–24; Tadeusz Sinko, "L'historiosophie dans le prologue et
épilogue de l'oeuvre d'Hérodote d'Halicarnasse," *Eos* 50 (1959–60), 3–20, esp. 7–8.

[43] For a recent discussion of order and symmetry in Herodotus' world, see Gian Granco
Gianotti, "Ordine e Simmetria nella rappresentazione del Mondo: Erodoto e il paradosso del
Nilo," *QS* 27 (1988), 51–92.

warned him of the consequences that he would suffer if he canceled his expedition. It was Artabanus who thought it promised success: he had imagined that Xerxes would have a happy reign if he remained inactive, but "since there is some divine impulse, and some destruction sent from Heaven has fallen upon the Greeks, I of myself change my mind and abandon my view."[44] But Artabanus assumed more than the dream told him. The divine message was simply that Xerxes could not turn aside from what had to be.

The restricted choice of Xerxes resembles the choices that Sophocles allows Oedipus, but is the force that restricts it an iron law that demanded vengeance upon the Greeks? The evidence seems to point in another direction: whatever the directing power of vengeance might be in the dark workings of fate and destiny, on the human level of everyday international affairs, it was neither a natural force nor a divine law. Rather, it was a debating point: a justification for a policy that recommended itself for other reasons.

This was the conclusion of a shrewd observer of his own times, who saw the contemporary world without illusions. Vengeance as justification for imperialism was a leitmotiv of the fifth century. Revenge on the Medes was the advertised purpose of the Delian League: for that we have Thucydides as witness, though Herodotus, following another tradition that fitted his detached cynicism better, attributed Athenian imperialism to an innate desire for hegemony that antedated Xerxes' invasion.[45] An outside observer might have seen a chain of vengeance and countervengeance continuing from the Ionian Revolt right down to the date of publication of the *Histories*, following a kind of Hegelian dialectic that saw the opposition between the Persian Empire and the Hellenic League replaced by one between the centers of power in Greece itself.[46] In public discussion retribution served as a respectable motive for aggression; thus, in the winter of 432–431, Sparta put together a list of grievances perpetrated by the Athenians to justify the Peloponnesian War. But it was not the guiding force of imperialism. When Cyrus undertook to extend his empire to annex the Massagetae, his motives did not include revenge.[47] Rather, Herodotus suggests two: first, his birth, which made him superhuman in men's eyes, and second, his success in war. The first had to do with the psychology of kings, and the second with the psychology of empire: the reputation of Persia as a successful imperialist power, which Cyrus had created and

---

[44] Hdt. 7.18.5.
[45] Thuc. 1.96; 6.76.3; cf. Hdt. 8.3.1–2.
[46] Cf. Hdt. 6.98.2.
[47] Hdt. 1.201–4.

which now drove him forward.[48] The satrap Oroetes killed Polycrates of Samos out of wounded pride: his fellow satrap Mitrobates had taunted him with failing to bring Samos into the Empire. Polycrates had done Oroetes no wrong, and Oroetes sought no vengeance. He slew Polycrates to prove himself a worthy expansionist of the empire in the Persian tradition.

It is instructive to make a comparison with Thucydides. The Athenian envoys in Sparta who addressed the assembly of the Peloponnesian League in 432 B.C. made an attempt to state the reasons for Athenian imperialism. "We did nothing surprising nor contrary to human custom," they said, "if we accepted the rule (*arche*) that was given to us, and do not let it go, for we are conquered by overwhelming motives: honor, fear and profit."[49] The persona of the Persian king did not admit fear, but what of profit? Thucydides assumed that imperial exploitation for gain was a fact of nature.[50] But Greece was poor, and in Greek eyes, Pausanias, the son of Cleombrotus, made the definitive judgment on the profit motive: Xerxes' passion to add what few possessions Greece had to the wealth of Persia was proof of his utter lack of sense. The Persians had well-developed acquisitive instincts. Atossa told Darius that she wanted to add women from the leading states of Greece to her attendants, and Mardonius extolled the fertility of Greece, and its variety of trees. But both really acted from personal motives.[51]

For the most part, Herodotus saw the economic causes of expansionism working in a different way. For him, the increasing resources of the imperialist power itself, resulting from growth of population, prompted it to look beyond its borders, and the wealth of the people it proposed to subjugate was unimportant, to the extent that Pausanias could make no sense out of it. Thus, power grew avid for more power, and in Herodotus' view, the profit motive seems to play only a small role in Persian expansionism. But the third motive—honor—was a different matter.

The king's pride and honor were constant factors, along with the requirement that he appear a restless and ambitious man of energy. This was the reputation of Cyrus and of the Medes before him.[52] They would not keep still. "It is not proper, my lord, for the Athenians, who have done the Persians many wrongs, not to pay retribution for their deeds," said Mardonius, urging his *logos timoros* upon the still-reluctant Xerxes. But he de-

---

[48] Cf. Charles W. Fornara, *Herodotus. An Interpretative Essay* (Oxford, 1971), 24–36. Fornara notes the absence of any "eternal laws prompting the expansion of states" in the first six books of the *Histories*.

[49] Thuc. 1.76.2.

[50] Cf. Peter R. Pouncey, *The Necessities of War. A Study of Thucydides' Pessimism* (New York, 1980), 48–49.

[51] Hdt. 9.82.3; 3.134.5; 7.5.2.

[52] Hdt. 1.185.1; 1.190.2.

veloped his argument with a point that deserves particular attention. "Invade Athens, so that you may have a good reputation among men, and anyone in the future will have a care before he makes war upon your land." The king had to maintain his reputation. "I formed the opinion," said Artabanus, admitting his error to the king, "that if you kept still, in the eyes of all men you would be happiest." But Xerxes could not be a lesser man than his predecessors, for he had to maintain the integrity of the Great King's persona as a competent ruler who could not be challenged with impunity. Contempt of a ruler led to rebellion, as Aristotle[53] was to point out: the dignity and reputation of Xerxes defended both his empire and his own position as king, and both might suffer if he allowed a wrong to go unavenged. To that extent, Xerxes was governed by the vengeance motive, but this was no iron law of retribution that directed his actions: rather, it was a simple axiom of statecraft. A king had to sustain his prestige if he was to maintain his status.

NOMOS AS EXPLANATION

Xerxes began his speech to the Persian magnates with a significant statement: "Men of Persia, this *nomos* I set before you is not one that I am the first to put forward; it is because it has been handed down to me that I make use of it." For Thucydides, imperialism was part of human nature; it was natural for the strong to exploit the weak. For Herodotus, expansionism was a *nomos*, and therefore, if we want to understand it, we should look at an empire's *nomoi*. Imperialism, therefore, fell within the field of ethnology, which was Herodotus' initial interest.[54]

Nomoi, which Havelock[55] once translated correctly, if somewhat awkwardly, as "custom-laws," bulk large in the *Histories*, and we should define what we mean by the word. First, what it is not: it is not the antithesis of *physis*. In one instance, Herodotus could couple the two concepts in one breath: those Greeks were ignorant, he states, who accepted the silly myth that told how Heracles, upon his arrival in Egypt, was led out to be sacrificed, and at the altar turned on his captors and slew them in vast numbers.[56] The purveyors of this tale knew nothing of the *physis* and *nomos* of

[53] *Pol.* 1312a–b.

[54] Cf. Charles W. Fornara, *The Nature of History in Ancient Greece and Rome* (Berkeley and Los Angeles, 1983), 226, 232.

[55] Eric Havelock, *The Liberal Temper in Greek Politics* (New Haven, 1957), 85; cf. Max Pohlenz, "Nomos," *Philologus* 97 (1948), 135. On the meanings of *nomos*, see Martin Ostwald, *Nomos and the Beginnings of Athenian Democracy* (Oxford, 1969), 20–54.

[56] 2.45.1–3. Cf. Marcello Gigante, *NOMOS BASILEUS* (Naples, 1956), 11, 116. The antithesis of *nomos-physis* appears first around 430 B.C. with the Hippocratean *On Airs, Waters, Places*. Gigante cites 2.45.1–3 as the sole instance in Herodotus where there is a suggestion of such an antithesis. However, the coupling of the two concepts in the context of the passage

the Egyptians, and anyway, it was contrary to nature (*physis*) for a single mortal to kill such great numbers. It was not that Herodotus thought of *physis* and *nomos* as synonyms; rather, the *nomoi* of a nation were the outgrowth of its *physis*. A report could not be authentic if it failed to conform to the *nomoi* of the people it purported to portray, for their *nomoi* were rooted in their nature, and thus possessed an integrity that could not be disregarded.

Physis was in no sense a technical word: it might refer to the appearance of the hippopotamus, the life cycle of the crocodile, or the physical stature of man—all qualities over which man (or the crocodile or hippopotamus, as the case might be) has no control. There is also such an entity as human *physis*: the "nature of man," which defined human competence, as Cambyses discovered to his cost. He slew his brother Smerdis because, in a dream, he saw a messenger come from Persia to tell him that Smerdis was on the throne, and then he learned of the revolt of the *magos* by the same name, and realized that he had acted with greater haste than wisdom, "for it is not in the *physis* of mankind to turn aside what is going to be."[57] The natural condition of mankind was constrained by limits that were beyond the power of even kings to change.

Yet those limits did not rule out choice. Before the battle of Salamis, Themistocles told his sailors that in the nature and constitution of men (*physis* and *katastasis*), there were some qualities that were better and some that were worse, and he urged them to choose the better.[58] What Themistocles wanted his men to choose was the quality that would drive them forward into battle, and that quality might be expressed as a *nomos*. At least we may conclude as much from the discourse of Xerxes with the exiled king of Sparta, Demaratus, who equated the *nomos* that required the Spartans to take up arms with the royal power that compelled the Persian troops to fight.[59]

Thus, though men might not alter their *physis*, within the limits it set, they could make choices, and their *nomoi* were based on a choice, or a series of choices that they, or their ancestors had made. Herodotus has broken almost completely with the ancient view that *nomoi* were ordained by Heaven.[60] To be sure, he reported the tradition that Lycurgus took the

---

seems rather to indicate a close connection. It is instructive to compare Protagoras' view that *nomos* is not an arbitrary convention but an outgrowth of man's true nature: see Adolfo Levi, "The Ethical and Social Thought of Protagoras," *Mind* 49 (1940), 284–302.

[57] Hdt. 2.71.1; 2.68.1; 8.38.1; 3.65.3; cf. Corcella, *Erodoto e l'analogia*, 84–92, who points out (p. 86) that for every *nomos* there is an implication of what one might reasonably expect.

[58] Hdt. 8.83.1–2; cf. Democritus, Diels-Kranz, frg. 278, for a similar use of *physis kai katastasis*.

[59] Hdt. 7.104.4.

[60] W.K.C. Guthrie, *A History of Greek Philosophy* (Cambridge, 1969), 56–59; cf. J.A.S. Evans, *Athenaeum* 43 (1965), 146. G. P. Shipp, *NOMOS* "Law" (Sydney, 1978), argues that

Spartan *nomoi* from Delphi, but the Spartans themselves said that he borrowed them from Crete, and there is the implication that the Spartans were the weightier authority.[61] Gyges explained the origin of *nomoi* to Candaules: mankind had found out in the past by trial and error what was lawful and unlawful.[62] In much the same way, Hippocrates explained how primitive man discovered by trial and error what was good to eat and what was not: he experimented with all sorts of foods, raw and cooked, and learned to avoid those that made him ill. In like manner, the Lydians had discovered that viewing another man's wife naked was not lawful, and Gyges begged Candaules not to insist that he do it. But Candaules was bound by an evil destiny. And when Cambyses in Egypt laughed at Egyptian *nomoi*, Herodotus saw it as a symptom of madness.

For *nomoi* possessed authority. Every people preferred its own, and if given a chance to choose, would not exchange them for those of another people. Yet it was a mark of wisdom to respect alien *nomoi*, and recognize their authority. Herodotus quotes a gobbet of Pindar which is later quoted more fully by Plato:[63] "*Nomos* is king of everything," but quite out of context. Pindar spoke of *nomos* as justification for the right of the powerful to use violence against those who were weaker. Callicles in the *Gorgias* used the quotation to support the argument that Xerxes acted in accordance with the *nomos* based on nature that allowed the strong to seize the possessions of the weak. But Herodotus wanted only to show that *nomoi* exercised quasi-despotic power. Xerxes, bedazzled by the sheer bulk of his host, summoned Demaratus and asked if the Greeks would dare resist. Demaratus would speak only for the Spartans whom he knew, but they at least would fight, even though they had no despot to force them. "For though they are free," he said, "they are not free in everything, for *nomos* is over them as master, which they fear in their hearts more than your people fear you." Xerxes, like Cambyses, laughed.[64]

There is a degree of irony to the failure of Xerxes to understand the import of what Demaratus had to say, for the Persian borrowed alien customs most readily of all men, and yet their kings failed to comprehend the authority of *nomoi*.[65] Cambyses' reaction was laughter, while Xerxes dis-

---

nomos differs from *themis*, *rhetra*, and *thesmos* as being secular and popular, and is written law as opposed to oral law; cf. Ostwald, *Nomos*, 58. Herodotus' sense of *nomoi*, however, includes unwritten laws.

[61] Hdt. 1.65.4.

[62] Hdt. 1.8.3–4; cf. Ostwald, *Nomos*, 75, 85.

[63] Hdt. 3.38.4; Plato, *Gorgias*, 483D-484C; cf. H. E. Stier, "*NOMOS BASILEUS*," *Philologus* 83 (1927–28), 225–58; Albin Lesky, "Grundzüge griechischen Rechtsdenkens. II *Nomos*" *WS*, n.s. 20 (1986), 5–26, esp. 22–23.

[64] Hdt. 7.101–4.

[65] Cf. Hdt. 1.134.3. D. Lateiner, "Polarità: Il Principio della Differenza Complementare," *QS* 22 (1985), 79–103, points out (pp. 91–92) that there are instances where Persian kings

missed Demaratus with tolerant amusement. At Marathon, the Persians thought the Greeks were mad when they charged them; at Thermopylae Xerxes was angered by their impudence and suicidal folly; and at Artemisium, the Persian captains considered the Greeks demented. Before Salamis, Xerxes had come to realize that his great host had failed to live up to his expectations, but he believed the reason was that he himself had not been present to inspire his men. This failure of the Persians to comprehend the *nomos* that commanded the Greeks to resist is a leitmotiv which continues as far as their defeat at Plataea, where Mardonius led his men in a disorderly pursuit of the Spartans, imagining that they were running away![66]

Yet the Persians themselves were actuated by a *nomos* too—one that forbade them to remain inactive. "Men of Persia," Xerxes said to the assembled Persian notables, "I am not myself setting up this *nomos* among you to follow, but it is one I have inherited, and I shall use it. I learn from our elders that we have never remained inactive since we took over this sovereign power from the Medes, when Cyrus dethroned Astyages. It is a god who leads us on." An imperial regime never remained still; it was always stirring with ambition. Nitocris had recognized this quality in the Medes, the Babylonians recognized it in Cyrus, and years later, on the eve of the Peloponnesian War, the Corinthians are to point it out as the disposition of imperial Athens.[67] An ancestral *nomos* directed the Persians always to push on and maintain the momentum of expansion. Xerxes thought that they were led by a god, but he was wrong: *nomoi* in the *Histories* evolve on the human, not the divine level, and the *nomos* that brought Persia her empire was based on deliberate choice quite as much as any other custom. Xerxes' conviction that the *nomos* of expansionism had divine sanction was myopic. It was a symptom of blindness.

There are two pertinent stories in the *Histories* that make clear how the Persians acquired and maintained their *nomos* of imperialism. The first tells how Cyrus persuaded the Persians to revolt from the Medes. He summoned an assembly of Persians and set them to work clearing a parcel of land overgrown with weeds. The next day, he gave them a sumptuous banquet. Then he asked which they preferred: the toil that was the lot of a subject, or the good life of a ruler. They chose the latter.[68]

---

do not obey their own *nomoi*, and cites particularly Hdt. 3.11, where Cambyses tried to reconcile what he wants to do with Persian *nomoi*, and the Persian judges oblige with a legal quibble. Perhaps the great power of the Persian kings that allowed them to disregard their own *nomoi* led them to disrespect or misunderstand alien *nomoi*.

[66] Hdt. 6.112.3; 7.210.1; 8.10.1; 8.69.2; 9.58–59.

[67] Hdt. 1.185.1; 1.190.2; cf. Thuc. 1.68–71. For the Persian sense of "manifest destiny," see Wood, *The Histories of Herodotus*, 54–57; V. Martin, "La politique des Achéménides. L'exploration prélude de la conquête," *MusHelv* 22 (1965), 38–48.

[68] Hdt. 1.125–26.

The second story concludes the *Histories*. The Persians have made their choice, and have acquired the *nomos* of imperialism and an empire to go along with it. A Persian noble named Artembares suggested to Cyrus that the Persians leave their own rocky and infertile native land, and choose another from among their dominions, where life would be easier. Cyrus allowed his Persians a choice. But first he taught them a precept borrowed from the Hippocratic school of medicine: soft lands breed soft men, better fitted to be subjects than rulers. The Persians chose to rule, and remained where they were. This *nomos* of imperialism was a harsh master, and the story of Cyrus that ends the *Histories* has palpably ironic overtones, for by the fifth century, the Persians had long since abandoned the hard life, but the *nomos* of imperialism still drove them forward.

After the defeat at Salamis, Mardonius, the war hawk at the meeting of the magnates, continued to remain faithful to this *nomos*. He carried on where Xerxes left off, all the more determined because he had urged the expedition upon a disinclined Xerxes in the first place, and hence would have to bear some responsibility for its failure, if it should come to that. He was by no means pessimistic: "his judgement actually inclined him to think that he would subdue Greece," to quote Grene's translation of Herodotus' cautious, ironic Greek.[69] At Plataea, he was still eager to push forward and start the fight: in the council before the battle, he was uncompromising, urging his commanders to pay no attention to the negative omens produced by their sacrifices made according to Greek rites, but instead to abide simply by the Persian *nomos* and attack.

His last words were charged with irony. He was full of overconfidence: the Spartans had seemingly fled and he would make them pay for the wrongs they had committed.[70] The Persian *nomos* of never keeping still but always pushing forward led him in the end to disaster. He was already a marked man; Xerxes had appointed him to make amends for Leonidas' death (which Delphi had demanded), and at Plataea the ironic purport of that appointment becomes clear: it was Mardonius, not the Spartans, who had to pay for the wrongs that had been done.[71]

Some two decades ago, I wrote an article which examined the connection between the role of *nomos* and causation in the *Histories*.[72] In his proem, Herodotus states a two-fold purpose: he had the praise-poets' concern to impart renown to the exploits of the warriors in both camps, and

[69] Hdt. 8.100.1; David Grene, trans., *The History of Herodotus* (Chicago, 1978), 592.
[70] Hdt. 9.41.4; 9.58.4; cf. J.A.S. Evans, "The Dream of Xerxes and the *Nomoi* of the Persians," *CJ* 57 (1961), 109–11.
[71] Hdt. 8.114.
[72] "*Despotes Nomos*," *Athenaeum* 43 (1968), 142–53. See also Sally Humphreys, "Law, Custom and Culture in Herodotus," *Arethusa* 20 (1987), 211–20, and in the same volume, James Redfield, p. 252, on Herodotus' use of *nomos* as an explanatory principle.

the philosopher's concern to find the reason for the conflict. I concluded that the reason (for which Herodotus uses the equivocal word *aitia*) could not be discovered among Persian *nomoi*, but that the *nomoi* of a people did explain their course of action, and consequently understanding *nomoi* was a mark of wisdom. In any given situation, one might expect a people to behave according to its *nomoi*. I have not abandoned that view, for *nomos* does serve as an explanatory principle, but I gave insufficient weight to *nomos* as a governing force. The *nomos* of ambition and restlessness that Xerxes inherited from his forebears exercised a directing influence over his policies which is akin to the "divine intention" in the *Oedipus Tyrannus*. It did, therefore, supply a reason why he had to attack Greece.

Perhaps Xerxes might have paid no attention to this *nomos* of expansionism, and adhered to the decision he had reached upon reconsideration. But the weight of tradition was against him: it was appropriate for a Persian king who was young and master of great wealth to achieve something worth notice, as Queen Atossa had told Darius in a bedroom conversation that led to Persia's first expedition to Europe.[73] The cost of refusing to invade Greece would have been great. The apparition that appeared to Xerxes threatened him with loss of this throne. It did not promise victory, although Xerxes and Artabanus inferred it. Rather, its message was that there was a high price to be paid if Xerxes failed to follow this *nomos* of imperialism which the Persians had chosen years before, when Cyrus had given them a choice—and *then* it had been a free choice. Herodotus did not treat imperialism itself as an expression of human nature, as Thucydides[74] did, but rather as a *nomos* that is elected freely, but once chosen, cannot be abandoned without cost. The Persians had followed their chosen *nomos* with good fortune thus far, and now Xerxes was governed by it.

The Greeks were equally directed by *nomos*. Wisdom and *nomos* were the basis of the courage with which they resisted both poverty and despotism.[75] Demaratus' attempt to explain this to Xerxes proved futile, and yet the *nomos* that directed the Greeks to fight possessed as much authority as the Great King himself. But Xerxes could not understand. The power and glory of Persia's monarchy had brought her kings to the point where they found the *nomoi* of other people at best amusing. This incomprehension was a kind of blindness, and, as the outcome of the Persian Wars was to prove, it was a dangerous state of mind.

[73] Hdt. 3.134; cf. Corcella, *Erodoto e l'analogia*, 141.

[74] Cf. Thuc. 5.105.

[75] Cf. Hdt. 7.102; cf. Albrecht Dihle, "Herodot und die Sophistik," *Philologus* 106 (1962), 207–20.

The Concept of Guilt

Any reader of the first sentence of Herodotus' proem must wonder what part he assigned to war guilt as a factor working its way through the strands of history, for he concludes with a statement that he was looking for the *aitia* of the conflict. The word *aitia*, or in the Ionian Greek of Herodotus, *aitie*, occurs fifty-one times in the *Histories*.[76] Twenty-two times, the meaning is fault, blame, or the sort of charge a plaintiff might launch in a court of law, and an equal number of times it can be translated simply as "cause," though the cause can imply a degree of blame. There are a few remaining instances, but they do not help to resolve the ambiguity. What, for instance, can we make of Herodotus' tale of the bond that existed between Cleomenes of Sparta and Cleisthenes' rival, Isagoras? "*Aitia* had Cleomenes going into (i.e., having sexual intercourse with) the wife of Isagoras." *Aitia* here is an accusatory morsel of gossip, not, to be sure, without moral connotations, which people suggested as the reason for the claim Isagoras had upon Cleomenes.

Or let us take another example: the *aitia* of Cambyses' attack on Egypt. "Cambyses, son of Cyrus, made an expedition against Amasis . . . for an *aitia* of such a kind as this."[77] *Aitia* here, Powell assures us, means "the reason why." Then follows the story of how Cambyses demanded Amasis' daughter as wife, which he did at the instance of an Egyptian eye doctor whom Cyrus had demanded from Egypt. The verb "to demand" is *aitein*, and there may be a play of words here between the *aitia* that means "the reason why," and the demands that brought about this reason: the *aitia* of the Persian invasion was the response of the pharaoh to Cambyses' demand, and hence by reciprocation this demand develops into a cause. Yet at the same time, the *aitia* was a charge that Cambyses brought against the pharaoh.

Finally, there is the use of the word in the proem. It carries the suggestion that someone was to blame for the war, and the debate of the *logioi* develops upon that assumption. Yet, at the same time, it looks forward to the common usage of *aitia* among the philosophers of the fourth century B.C., where it is the synonym of the Latin *causa*, meaning "reason," "motive," or "inducement."

Guilt is closely tied to vengeance, and it may be argued that the two concepts should not be separated. But in a Greek court, guilt had to be established before punishment could be applied, and, to quote Arthur Adkins, "In Greek there can be no *phonos* (violent death) without someone

---

[76] J. E. Powell, *A Lexicon to Herodotus*[2] (Hildesheim, 1960), 9; cf. Bornitz, *Herodot-Studien*, 139–63.

[77] Hdt. 3.1.1.

being *aitios phonou* (guilty of murder)."[78] The same should be true of the supreme act of violence, war. Some person or thing should be guilty of it, and ordinarily the guilty party should be the one that initiated the war. Thus, as I have argued, it was to shift guilt to the targets of aggression that invaders alleged retribution.

Given the opening sentence of the *Histories*, we might be excused for imagining that the concept of war guilt bulked large in his thought. But this was not so. Herodotus gives first a Persian story of how strife between Europe and Asia began, and this story is marked by a pronounced distinction between being "guilty" and "greatly guilty."[79] The Phoenicians incurred guilt first by kidnapping Io, but the Greeks were guilty to the second power by mounting a military expedition, the Trojan War. The Phoenicians have a gloss to add to the story, but that is all. Then Herodotus dismisses this speculation and the logic that went along with it, and chooses his own starting point: the imperialist action of the king of Lydia, Croesus.

His existence was solid enough: there were his dedications at Delphi to attest it. He was more than a mere aggressor. Earlier Mermnads had attacked the Greeks, but Croesus established a polity that exacted tribute from them, thus fitting the definition of empire. Upon succeeding his father to the throne, Croesus moved first against Ephesus, and then against the other Ionian and Aeolian cities one by one, putting forward various *aitiai*, the best he could find, though some of them were trivial indeed. Nevertheless, Herodotus imagined that Croesus sought to assign some guilt to the Greek cities to justify his aggression: "He brought different *aitiai* against various cities: important ones when he could find them, but against others he brought *aitiai* that were truly slight."[80] These *aitiai* were accusations: hardly more than stratagems to shift the burden of guilt, and they did nothing to explain the real motive of Lydian imperialism. Herodotus himself preferred to present Croesus within a tragic framework: he was a great king whose imperialism was the outgrowth of his wealth and prosperity: his consequent power and affluence resulted in blindness, which in turn allowed him to blunder into fatal error. He attacked a people toughened by a hard life, whose poverty could add little to his wealth even if he were victorious. Herodotus has sunk his teeth into a traditional tale

---

[78] *Merit and Responsibility* (Oxford, 1960), 103.

[79] There is a similar escalation of guilt in Aristophanes, *Acharn.* 515–40, which is usually taken as a parody of Herodotus' introduction. It might equally well be a parody of the popular traditions that were peddled by the *logioi* in their oral presentations. In any case, Herodotus appears to turn his back on such speculations, and instead begins with a clarification of what an act of imperialism is (the collection of tribute from a subject people) and the first king to perpetrate it, namely Croesus.

[80] Hdt. 1.26.

here, but it sets a pattern, and his aim in telling it is moral as much as it is historical.

The story of Croesus seems to present the rise and fall of empire *in parvo*: a sort of paradigm of imperial development that suggests comparison with the career of Xerxes. But it leaves us little wiser about the *aitia* of the Persian Wars. The reason for Croesus' fall, according to Delphi, was bound up with *moira*; Croesus was expiating Gyges' sin after five generations, which was the portion of time allotted to his dynasty. According to Herodotus, whose view does not quite tally with Delphi's, "great *nemesis* overtook Croesus, as one would guess, because he thought himself the most blessed of all men."[81] So Croesus had fallen for two reasons: *moira*, because he had reached the end of an allotted span established before he was born, and *nemesis*, for which he bore some guilt himself: he considered himself more fortunate than a mortal should.

These are two separate concepts that are uneasily coupled here. Just how uneasy the coupling is, becomes apparent in another instance: the men of Paros consulted Delphi on the proper punishment for the priestess Timo, who had attempted to betray them to Miltiades, and received the reply from the Pythia that she was blameless, for Miltiades was doomed to a bad end, and Timo was only the instrument of his fate.[82] Similarly, Apollo did not accept any blame for Croesus' fall. Indeed, he went so far as to argue that Croesus himself was blameworthy. The oracle had warned him that he would destroy a great empire if he attacked Cyrus, but he had failed to ask which empire was meant. Croesus had taken care to test the reliability of the oracles, but when it came to the central issue, his astuteness was clouded by his egocentrism and overconfidence. So much for Delphi's view of Croesus' guilt.

At whose feet, then, should the guilt for the Persian Wars be laid? I have already argued that the motive of revenge did not account for Persian imperialism. Their conquests took place equally well with or without it. Herodotus was as skeptical of Persia's *aitiai* as he was of those that Croesus put forward. But the conventional wisdom which no *logios* could ignore without provoking comment from his audience had it that Athens had incurred guilt by intervening in the Ionian Revolt, thus committing an unprovoked wrong. Given the Greek concept of guilt, followed (when proven) by retribution, it was arguable that Athenian guilt caused the Persian attack. Quite unfairly, punishment that should have fallen on Athens alone involved all Greece. That, at least, was how the Spartans viewed the matter: they were innocent bystanders, whereas Athens had stirred up the war.[83]

---

[81] Hdt. 1.34.1.
[82] Hdt. 6.135.
[83] Hdt. 142.2.

Herodotus thought that Darius, angry as he was with the Athenians for their part in burning Sardis, nonetheless used their intervention in the revolt only as a pretext, and the war hawk Mardonius refers almost cynically to the guilt of the Greeks[84] as he develops his case for Xerxes' invasion. Yet on the actual question of guilt, Herodotus seems to lean toward conventional wisdom. The twenty ships that Athens sent to help the Ionians were the beginning of evil in the sense that they started a fresh chain of events which led directly to Xerxes' invasion. Herodotus found it quite possible to accept that point of view, and at the same time, recognize that they were not the real reason for the onslaught. The Ionian Revolt deserved faint praise, and the Athenian decision to intervene showed how easily a democracy could be gulled by an adventurer like Aristagoras. But as Herodotus[85] saw it, the troubles (which began with Naxos and Miletus, and expanded into a revolt thanks to Aristagoras and Histiaeus) served to revive the restless expansionism of Persia, and the twenty ships that Athens sent to help the rebels channeled it in the direction of Greece. To that extent, Athens was *aitios*. She made Greece an immediate objective of Persia's imperialism. Thus, Herodotus did not altogether reject the Spartan view of the matter even though he was at pains to point out that Xerxes' expedition was only ostensibly directed against Athens; in fact, its object was all Greece.[86]

The search for who or what was to blame for the war, which Herodotus announced in his proem, runs to ground. To take him literally, the primal *aitia* for which he could vouch, belonged to Croesus, who was the first to wrong the Greeks by making them tributary, which was the mark of empire.[87] But Croesus' legacy was taken over by Persia, which followed its own imperative, and whatever interlinked chain of causes Croesus started, it mattered little as a reason why Xerxes invaded Greece. His aim was to subdue guilty and guiltless alike, and although Athens might be guilty in the limited sense that she attracted the attention of a king who had already expanded into Europe, the expedition of Xerxes was within the tradition of Persian expansionism.

There was, therefore, little purpose in asking who was to blame for the war. Blame might serve as a debating point or as a gambit in diplomacy, or as a satisfactory notion to give point to a story illustrating a historical pattern, but it did not explain the motive force behind Persian imperialism. A keeper of tradition might assign guilt for the war to this party or that, sometimes with a degree of justification, but guilt did nothing to explain the motive force behind Persian imperialism.

---

[84] Hdt. 6.94; 7.1; 7.9.1.

[85] Cf. 5.28; 5.30.1; 5.97; 6.1.

[86] 7.138.

[87] 1.5.3; cf. A. E. Wardman, "Herodotus on the Causes of the Greco-Persian Wars: Hdt. 1–5," *AJPh* 82 (1961), 133–50.

I suspect that this was a verdict which Herodotus reached not without hesitation, first because a good portion of Greece thought otherwise, and second because Herodotus shared the Greek attraction to tragic patterns in history. His story of Croesus is a case in point. The primal *aitia* was Candaules' wayward resolve to display his wife, naked, to Gyges, and from this *aitia* a chain of cause and effect led to Croesus' final expiation of an ancestor's forgotten wrong. Yet the causes and effects did not become apparent until *after* Croesus' fall, when the underlying pattern at last became clear. This was the sort of moral template that Herodotus' listeners expected him to use in his reconstruction of what happened when Persia expanded into Europe: an act of violence, in this case war, implied a guilty party that was to blame for it. The Greeks were familiar with the pattern, both in the theater and in the lawcourts. One feels that Herodotus would have been not unhappy if he had found some such design in Persian history. It would have provided easy explanations. But in fact, Herodotus made no consistent effort to discover who was guilty of causing the war, in spite of his announced intention in his proem, for it had no bearing upon the fundamental cause of Persian expansionism.

THE FATE OF THE PERSIAN EMPIRE

Finally, there is the question of fate. To what extent was Persian imperialism and its consequences governed by fate? It needs little imagination to discover tragic patterns in the *Histories* that compare with those we find in *Oedipus Tyrannus* or the *Antigone*, and cross-fertilization is more than possible: the friendship of the two men is documented well enough. Herodotus makes more than the occasional obeisance to the dark workings of necessity. Candaules commanded his bodyguard Gyges to view his wife naked, because it was necessary for things to turn out badly for him. Candaules was a foolish king; yet it was necessity that decreed his false step. It was not merely the consequence of his own lack of wisdom. At the end of the *Histories*, Herodotus said very much the same about a royal scion as unwise as Candaules, Xerxes' daughter-in-law, and niece, Artaynte. Things were bound to turn out badly for her and her house.[88] She acted foolishly, but her action conformed to a foreordained pattern.

There are other examples scattered throughout the *Histories*. The Naxian expedition that served as prologue to the Ionian Revolt was a failure because Naxos was not fated to fall to the Persians at that point in time. It fell later to Datis without a blow because the Naxians remembered the futility of their earlier resistance! Fate accomplished the dethronement of Demaratus, king of Sparta. Skylas, the Scythian king who was initiated

---

[88] Hdt. 1.8.2; 9.109.2.

into the Dionysiac rites, was fated to end badly. His adoption of Greek rites was a *prophasis* that served to explain why the Scyths revolted from him; but at a deeper level, fate directed events. The pharaoh Apries, whose subjects rebelled after his defeat in Cyrene, was also a casualty of fate: the disastrous attack which he launched against Cyrene, took place so that fate could work itself out. Miltiades, the victor at Marathon, was destined to come to a bad end. Finally, Herodotus appears to make an explicit acknowledgment of the omnipotence of fate. He related a story told by Thersander of Orchomenos, who attended a banquet given by the Theban medizer, Attaginus, for Mardonius and fifty Persian nobles before the battle of Plataea. The Persian who shared Thersander's couch told him in tears that few of the banqueters would survive. Men could not turn aside what God had decreed. Many of the Persians—so said Thersander's companion—knew what the outcome would be, but they were bound by necessity.[89] "Thus, out of the darkness, the hand of divine superiority guides the destinies of humanity, the will and behaviour of men, according to its own purposes."

The quotation comes from Erwin Rohde's *Psyche*,[90] and refers to the fates of Deianeira in the *Trachiniae* and Oedipus in *Oedipus Tyrannus*. Fate as inexorable as any that dogged Oedipus seems to close in upon Mardonius at the end of the *Histories*, so much so that Sir John Myres[91] once argued that it is he who should be seen as the tragic hero of the last three books. Herodotus, who professed trust in oracles, used them skillfully to show how Mardonius was trapped by necessity. He discovered an oracle which predicted that the Persians would plunder Delphi and then perish; therefore the Persians would not plunder Delphi, and nothing would prevent their victory. But Mardonius had misunderstood; the oracle did not refer to the Persians at all.[92] However, the oracles had not been silent, for there were prophecies of Bacis and Musaeus that Mardonius overlooked, which did foretell the Persian defeat. Mardonius, who more than any other Persian embodied Persia's imperialist impulse, could not for all his acumen escape his destiny.

Finally, we return to the dream of Xerxes. He assumed that he was free to launch an invasion of Greece or not, as he saw fit. Then, out of the dark, of night, he was told that he was not a free agent, and even Artabanus, after seeing the vision, withdrew his objection, imagining that some *daimonie horme* awaited the Greeks. Was there a "hand of divine superiority" behind the imperialist thrust of Persia?

[89] Hdt. 5.33.2; 6.96; 6.64.1; 4.79.1; 2.161.3; 6.134–35; 9.16.1–5.
[90] Translated from the eighth edition by W. B. Hillis (London, 1925, repr. New York, 1966), 428.
[91] *Herodotus, the Father of History* (Oxford, 1953), 78.
[92] Hdt. 9.42–43.

The question is fair to ask, and the answer cannot be an easy one. Herodotus, who disagreed with the creeping cynicism of his day about oracles that we find in Thucydides, held up a prophecy of Bacis as an example of oracular accuracy.[93] This oracle attributed the Persian defeat to "divine Dike" which quenches Koros, the son of Hybris. There is a close parallel in the second stasimon of the *Oedipus Tyrannus*: there Hybris begets Koros, and the result is disaster. Sophocles' chorus here portrays the traditional unrighteous man who is the victim of Hybris, Koros, and Ate. Guilt which is described in this Aeschylean fashion does not sound like the involuntary guilt of a man who has acted in ignorance.[94] The oracle of Bacis which Herodotus quotes does not suggest any such thing, and since Herodotus held up this oracle as an example of divine prescience, I do not think he saw it that way either. At some point, the Persians had made a choice.

In fact, what must impress the reader of the *Histories* is the number of times that individuals are presented with choices that they must make. The clearest of these are placed in the *Histories* before the battles of Marathon and Salamis, and they are introduced with the same words. "It lies in your hands, Callimachus, whether to enslave Athens or keep her free," said Miltiades before Marathon; and before Salamis, Themistocles put the choice equally sharply to Eurybiades: "It lies in your hands to save Greece."[95] In both instances, men who deserved the label "makers of history" approached relative nonentities and told them that the choice was theirs. They could decide whether or not Greece would be free. But these are only the most dramatic choices. The Ionians who guarded the Danube bridge for Darius on his Scythian expedition had a choice to make, and they could make it freely without incurring guilt, for they had done their duty and remained at their post for as long as they had pledged. Their leaders debated the question, first supporting Miltiades and then switching their support to Histiaeus, after he had pointed out to them where their own interests lay. Thus, the Ionians chose servitude.[96]

Once again, before the battle of Lade, the Ionians faced a similar choice. Dionysius of Phocaea put it to them with a flourish borrowed from Homer: "Our affairs are on the razor's edge."[97] The consequence of the choice was important: there could be no doubt of it, and the Ionians repeated the response they had made at the Danube bridge. They rallied at first to the cause of freedom and then they changed their minds.

[93] Hdt. 8.77.
[94] Cf. Hugh Lloyd-Jones, *The Justice of Zeus*[2] (Berkeley, 1983), 111.
[95] Hdt. 6.109; 8.60a; cf. F. Solmsen, "Two Crucial Decisions in Herodotus," Amsterdam, 1974, who notes the importance of *proairesis* in the *Histories*.
[96] Hdt. 4.136–42.
[97] Hdt. 6.11.2; cf. *Iliad*, 10.173.

Before Cyrus launched his Persians on the path to empire, he showed them the advantages both of servitude and imperial power, and let them choose. They chose imperialism. Even Gyges, who brought a curse upon the Mermnads that destroyed Croesus' empire after five generations, was given a choice. The queen summoned him and laid before him the alternatives. "There are two roads before you, Gyges, and I give you your choice which you will travel." It was a grim choice: Gyges might kill his king and usurp the throne, thereby incurring guilt, or die himself. But it was a choice nonetheless, and Gyges chose to survive and become king.[98]

These situations where men are faced with alternatives are analogous to the tragic choices of Aeschylus: Pelasgus in the *Suppliants* faced such a choice, and the plot of the *Agamemnon* hung upon a choice made by Agamemnon at Aulis ten years before the story represented by the play began. "In Aeschylus," writes Bruno Snell, "the hero's choice becomes a problem whose solution is contingent on nothing but his own insight, but which is nevertheless regarded as a matter of compelling necessity."[99] The choice once made might be hard to unmake, or it might not. Athens judged it natural enough that Sparta should fear that she might accede to the overtures which Mardonius made her in the spring of 479 B.C., but the Athenians themselves believed there was only one answer they could give.[100] Yet in all these cases, the act of decision seems to be entirely within the human sphere of action.

The situation in which Xerxes found himself when he chose to invade Greece appears to differ. He first announced his resolve to undertake the expedition, confident that he could choose to make it or not as he pleased, and Artabanus gave his counsel in the belief that Xerxes could countermand it. Then an apparition in a dream warned Xerxes that his choice was limited, and when the same apparition visited Artabanus, it threatened him with punishment for trying to turn aside "what had to be." Similarly, before the battle of Plataea, Mardonius appears to have a choice: he may have urged his officers to attack, following the Persian *nomos*, but he had the option of yielding to the counsel of Artabazus and the Thebans, and withdrawing to Thebes, a plan that seemed more sensible to Herodotus. Yet Mardonius too was moving toward a predestined end. He was to render *dike* for the murder of Leonidas, as the oracle had predicted.[101]

[98] Hdt. 1.125–26; 1.11.2.

[99] *The Discovery of the Mind*, trans. T. G. Rosenmeyer (Cambridge, Mass., 1953), 103; cf. Gerald F. Else, *The Origin and Early Form of Greek Tragedy* (Cambridge, Mass., 1965, repr. The Norton Library, New York, 1972), 85–102.

[100] Hdt. 8.139–44. I cannot agree with Solmsen (*Two Crucial Decisions*) that a choice such as Athens made would be inconceivable at a Persian court.

[101] Hdt. 9.41; 9.64.1.

We need not expect from Herodotus any solution to the dilemma of predestination and free will. They exist in uneasy partnership throughout the classical world and the problem passes into Christian theology unresolved. But here we are looking at the narrower question of why Xerxes' freedom to choose between an imperialist policy and a nonaggressive one was so restricted. If Dionysius of Phocaea, Miltiades, and Themistocles could all propose free choices, why should Xerxes have been deprived of one before he took the fateful step of invading Greece? For though he was not left *absolutely* without choice, the apparition made it clear that the penalty attached to countermanding the expedition was such that no Persian could endure it and survive.

We may find part of the answer in Sophocles. To what extent were Oedipus and Antigone free agents? They made free choices, but when the pattern of events was finally revealed, their choices appear to have directed them to an end that was determined before they were born. They were unwittingly working out the ancient curse of the Labdacids.[102] In the case of Xerxes, it was not an ancient curse that directed his decisions; instead, he was governed by a choice that Cyrus had put to the Persians before he was born. The Persians had elected the *nomos* of imperialism when they chose for themselves the life of masters rather than subjects, and the choice that they had made freely under Cyrus so restricted the options of Xerxes four generations later that, for practical purposes, he had to invade Greece. The alternative involved penalties that he could not contemplate.

Xerxes was not the only player in the *Histories* who was governed by an ancient choice. Lycurgus chose laws for the Spartans, and as Demaratus was to tell Xerxes, their law ruled them as firmly as the Persian king ruled his subjects. The Medes, gathered in an assembly, chose Deioces as king; thereafter they were constrained by their choice and lived under a monarchy with all its trappings. Gyges chose to kill Candaules, and Croesus' fate was governed by that ancient choice made five generations before his time.[103]

The Persians had chosen the *nomos* of imperialism under Cyrus, and by the time of Xerxes it had attained the status of ancestral law. Time had increased its insistence on obedience. Cyrus attacked the Massagetae because he set his heart on conquering them. Darius invaded Scythia because Asia was overflowing with population and wealth. Both kings conformed to policies that were in line with the *nomos* of imperialism, and hence no conflict arose. Yet there is no hint that they acted under compulsion. But Xerxes wavered between what Thucydides might have called *apragmosyne*

[102] Cf. Lloyd-Jones, *Justice*, 104–28; Robert Coleman, "The Role of the Chorus in Sophocles' *Antigone*," *PCPS* 198 (n.s. 18, 1972), 4–27.
[103] Hdt. 1.97–98; 1.13.

and *polypragmosyne*, and discovered that there was a penalty he must pay if he transgressed this *nomos*. He was in the grip of a dark, ambivalent force that was driving him on to overstep the natural boundaries of his empire, and that force obtained its power from a free choice which the Persians had made long before Xerxes was born: their decision to be rulers rather than subjects, and to possess the good things of an imperial people rather than the toil and sweat of servitude. It was a choice with consequences quite as much as the choice that Agamemnon made at the bay of Aulis, and they reach their consummation with Xerxes. Cyrus might have restrained his hunger for more subjects before he attacked the Massagetae, and Darius might perhaps have held back before he invaded Scythia, but under Xerxes the empire was at such a pitch of wealth and extent that obedience to the *nomos* of expansionism had to take him beyond the natural boundaries of Asia.

THE IMPERIALIST IMPULSE

During the years that Herodotus researched his *Histories*, the Persian Empire, grown soft and luxurious, was in decline and another empire, that of Athens (which, like Persia, exacted tribute), had come to dominate the Aegean world, and showed the same restless ambition that marked the Persians under Cyrus. It was a remarkable peripeteia, which seemed to corroborate Herodotus' dictum that in the course of time, great cities became small and small ones became great, and good fortune is forever inconstant. Persian expansionism seemed to have ceased. It was time to ask what had been the nature of the impulse behind it?

Joseph Schumpeter[104] once remarked that the Hellenic world found the reason for Xerxes' campaign utterly baffling. Schumpeter himself explained Persian expansionism as the manifestation of a warrior nation's essence: the Persians had acquired a warlike disposition, and the social organization that went along with it, before their energies could be absorbed by the peaceful exploitation of the land they had settled. They undertook conquest as a manifestation of their ethos, and they introduced imperialism into the Greek world, although Herodotus thought that Croesus had taken the first step. Before the Persian Wars, warfare had been a common state of affairs in Greece; but wars to acquire empires were not—not even the Trojan War, which was a constant comparison. Achaemenid Persia's effort to make Greece a tribute-paying province was the first attempt at empire in the Greek experience, and after Persia, Athens had taken up her legacy.

The conventional wisdom in the Greek world judged the causes of war

[104] *Imperialism and Social Classes*, trans. Heinz Norden (Blackwell, Oxford, 1951), 34–39.

in terms of provocation, guilt, and vengeance, and behind them all, the working of fate. Herodotus, who had an audience to consider (unlike Thucydides), chose not to ignore conventional wisdom. Thucydides may have been cranky and unjust to refer to the *Histories* as a prize essay designed for the taste of the immediate public—almost certainly he had Herodotus in mind—but nonetheless Herodotus knew the sort of reasoning with which his audience was familiar. He knew what they would expect. The search for who or what was to blame for the wars was the stock-in-trade of the *logioi*: the oral chroniclers whom Herodotus in his proem imagines in a debate on the cause of the Persian War. Aristophanes[105] ridicules their logic, but is nevertheless witness to the popularity of this sort of reasoning: retribution fell upon the *aitioi*, or at least it should in a just world.

Herodotus puts a modicum of distance between himself and all that sort of speculation; instead, he will proceed dealing equally with cities great and small, for the world was changing ceaselessly. For individual changes there might be individual causes, some of which could entail guilt, and in retrospect, the past might disclose tragic motifs, such as tales of divine jealousy following upon great success, and calamity falling upon the overconfident. Foretime was a vast deposit of tragic themes and motifs for poets to mine. But flux was the underlying condition of mankind. For Herodotus, human fortune was by nature inconstant. But the specific problem for which he sought an answer was: why did the Persians choose to attack Greece? For that, tragic story patterns did not supply an answer.

In the end, his explanation was not far removed from Schumpeter's. Imperialism was a *nomos*: the word embraces Schumpeter's "disposition," but it meant more than that. It was a law that required obedience. However, the Persians had chosen it freely. Cyrus allowed them to taste both the hardships that subjects endured and the good life of a ruling people, and though ancient imperial conquests were not generally motivated by economic concerns,[106] Herodotus imagined the Persians making their choice out of self-interest, but their decision was taken with deliberate intent and it was binding. It took a tough people of the sort which a hard land produced to acquire and maintain an empire, and yet the luxuries that an empire provided its rulers made them soft and eventually unfitted to rule. There was an internal dynamic to the rise and fall of empires that forced them to conform to the ebb and flow of history.

Under Xerxes, Persian expansion reached its zenith. He had inherited the *nomos* of imperialism. Chosen freely under Cyrus, it had become an expression of Persian nature by the time Xerxes reached the throne. Xerxes

---

[105] *Acharn.*, 514–34.

[106] Cf. M. I. Finley, *The Ancient Economy* (Berkeley, 1973), 157–76.

could not transgress it with letting go his power. The apparition that came
to him in his dream warned him rightly of the consequences of his refusal
to invade Greece: he would lose his throne. The abandonment of imperialism would have meant changing the nature of the Persian Empire, and
the king himself could not expect to survive so fundamental an innovation.

INDIVIDUALS IN HERODOTUS

SCHOLARS have not ranked Herodotus high as an artist of the portrait sketch. "The *History* of Herodotus is a very personal work," wrote Westlake,[1] contrasting our historian with Thucydides, "and he sometimes fails to provide his readers with a clear and coherent picture of a leading personality; apparently he has not formed such a picture in his mind." However, it is his portraits, coherent or not, that have come to dominate the historical tradition. The fact that Thucydides thought it necessary to add corrective touches to Herodotus' etchings of Themistocles and Pausanias demonstrates how powerful his influence was in molding the reputations of these men in his own day. Moreover, his characters must be taken as his own artistic creations. He may have spoken with informants who knew Themistocles, Pausanias, or Miltiades personally, or conceivably Mardonius and Xerxes; but what he learned from these sources would be treated as raw material that was shaped to fit the general pattern of his history. His artistic freedom, when it came to sketching character, was not a great deal less than that of Aeschylus, whose *Persians* is the one great imaginative recreation of Xerxes' invasion antedating the *Histories* that has come down to us. Herodotus knew the *Persians*,[2] and his Xerxes has traits in common with Aeschylus. But we cannot demonstrate significant borrowing, and the Darius of Aeschylus is quite simply a different character altogether.

But when Herodotus went back to earlier generations, he was dependant upon traditions that were often contradictory. These were the ancient stories that were the stock-in-trade of the *logioi*, or, as Thucydides called them, *logographoi*;[3] for by his time, prose chroniclers used writing, although reading aloud still remained the most common means of publishing a work of prose. Herodotus was not uncritical, but he was respectful; he would repeat variant versions when he found them,[4] and he was aware that the severity of Thucydides would be unattractive to his audience. For that matter, Thucydides knew it equally well, though he held up an alter-

---

[1] H. D. Westlake, *Individuals in Thucydides* (Cambridge, 1968), 16–17.

[2] W. W. How and J. Wells, *A Commentary on Herodotus* (Oxford, 1912, repr. with corrections, 1928), 1:21.

[3] See below for discussion.

[4] Hdt. 7.152.3. However, in spite of Herodotus' statement here that he must report "what is said," whether he believed it or not, he was far from being a mere reporter: cf. R. Bichler, *Chiron* 15 (1985), 125–47.

native ideal for a historian and claimed to be writing "a possession for all time." When Herodotus dealt with earlier generations, his task was not unlike that of the teller of folktales: he had to create credible personalities who acted with understandable motives and objectives, and failed or succeeded for reasons that touched human emotions.

The character with whom Herodotus chose to begin, Croesus of Lydia, was a remote figure for whom Herodotus had only relative dates, though his *erga*, particularly his dedications at Delphi, lent some solidity to the traditions about him. Yet essentially, he was no more substantial than the great figures of the epic tradition. The Lydians of Herodotus' day had become docile subjects of Persia; the fall of Sardis was a myth, and Croesus himself had been dispatched to the land of the Hyperboreans by Bacchylides in his third *epinikion*.[5] It was Herodotus' task to extract Croesus from legend and remake him as a character who was historically credible and artistically valid.

At the same time, the new genre of history that Herodotus was pioneering made demands too. Aristotle was to put it well when he drew the contrast between poet and historian. "The poet and the historian differ not by writing in verse or in prose. The work of Herodotus might be put into verse, and it would still be a species of history, with metre no less than without it. The true difference is that one relates what has happened, the other what may happen."[6] The historian's mission was to write the truth: the words eventually became hackneyed, but when Herodotus wrote, the genre was still in the process of development, and it was this feeling for truth that was to divide history from storytelling. Every new production of the myth of the Labdacids that appeared in the tragic theater might become a new reality in the realm of literature, but the historian did not possess the freedom of a poet to adapt and change his plot. He was restricted by the facts, or as Aristotle called them, "what actually happened."

However, the "facts" were less secure when Herodotus dealt with faraway places and oriental despots than when he described figures from Greek history who belonged to the home turf of his audience. Yet the Greeks had an imaginative concept of what an oriental despot was like, and of the life of his court, and this perception was derived not merely from the theater and art, but from regular communication between Greece and Persia. The fact that Aramaic documents could be translated in Athens (and apparently

[5] Cf. J.A.S. Evans, "What Happened to Croesus," *CJ* 74 (1978), 43–60; Vincenzo La Bua, "Sulla Fine di Creso," *Studi di Stroia Antica offerti degli allievi a Eugenio Manni* (Rome, 1976), 177–92. Charles Segal, "Croesus on the Pyre: Herodotus and Bacchylides," *WS* 5 (1971), 39–51, points out (p. 38) that some verbal parallels suggest that Herodotus knew Bacchylides' ode, and is deliberately "correcting it."

[6] S. H. Butcher, trans., *Aristotle's Theory of Poetry and Fine Art*[4] (London, 1907, repr. New York, 1951), 1451b, p.35.

in Sparta too) without undue difficulty is some indication of the level of diplomatic activity.[7] And though it would be hazardous to guess what reports got back to Greece from Greek artisans working at Persepolis or Susa, or from the *Yauna* in Persian service, we cannot discount their contribution to the general level of knowledge. There was no doubt a thin but steady stream of reportage about the exotic kingdoms of Egypt and the Orient which made its way to Greece, and though much of it may have been garbled, it meant that Herodotus was not publishing his *logoi* in a vacuum.

Finally, though biography had not yet developed into the definitive literary type that it was later to become,[8] there were lives of famous personages antedating Herodotus, or contemporary with him. Herodotus knew Scylax of Caryanda, the author of a life of Heracleides, the tyrant of Mylasa, who led an ambush against the Persians in the Ionian Revolt,[9] and though the pseudo-Herodotean *Life of Homer* that we have today cannot be earlier than the Roman imperial period, its antecedents could date to Herodotus' century.[10] He certainly knew something of the archaic *Life of Aesop*, for he refers to it,[11] and stories of Hesiod, Archilochus, and the Seven Sages circulated in his world. These were biographical folktales, but they mark a beginning and Herodotus' "lives" share features with them, such as the structural importance given to oracles. But in his portrayals of Oriental monarchs, he develops the model further, for his treatment of figures such as Croesus and particularly Cyrus have parallels with the kind of life that Plutarch wrote: a chronological narration of the deeds and events that shaped the subject's life, leading to his fall. It goes without saying that the sketches of individuals in the *Histories* owe a debt to the folktale, which cannot always be separated from the equally great debt they owe to the epic. As a result, the portraits which Herodotus drew of his Oriental kings, to be credible, had to approach an archetype that was lodged in the Greek consciousness.

---

[7] Cf. Thuc. 4.50.2.

[8] Cf. H. Homeyer, "Zu den Anfängen der griechischen Biographie," *Philologus* 106 (1962), 75–85; Friedrich Leo, *Die Griechisch-Römische Biographie nach ihrer Literarischen Form* (Leipzig, 1901), 147–48, 179–85; A. Momigliano, *The Development of Greek Biography* (Cambridge, Mass., 1971), 23–42; F. Lasserre, "L'historiographie grecque archaïque," *QS* 4 (1976), 113–42, esp. 127–33; B. Gentili and G. Cerri, *History and Biography in Ancient Thought* (Amsterdam, 1988), 61–66.

[9] Hdt. 5.121. Robert Drews, *The Greek Accounts of Eastern History* (Cambridge, Mass., 1973), dates Scylax's *Life* not long after 480 B.C. The same Scylax explored the Indus River for Darius, and wrote an account of his voyage.

[10] Wolfgang Schadewaldt, *Legende von Homer dem fahrenden Sänger* (Zurich and Stuttgart, 1954), 42–43, 71–73.

[11] 2.134.4.

CROESUS

Herodotus begins with Croesus, king of Lydia.[12] The choice calls for comment. The introductory words of Thucydides' *History* states his subject directly: "Thucydides the Athenian wrote the history of the war fought between Athens and Sparta." Herodotus begins with a sentence which announces that he is publishing his research. He does not state that the topic was to be the invasion of Xerxes, or even the war with Persia from start to finish, but rather, he will tell about the deeds and achievements of both Greeks and Persians, and the *aitia* of the war. Croesus was the first man whom he knew that had begun unrighteous acts against the Greeks.

Herodotus reached Croesus by a one-sided antilogy. He imagined Persian memorialists putting the case for Asia. The Phoenicians were responsible in the first instance, for they kidnapped Io, but then the Greeks took Europa and Medea. Paris, who came from a city in Asia, then took Helen; the Greeks retaliated with war, which was a disproportionate riposte, and therefore the burden of guilt belonged to the Greeks. The capture of Troy began the enmity, for the Persians considered Asia theirs, but Europe they thought was separate.

This gives us half the argument, and we might expect a Greek rebuttal to follow. But not yet: Herodotus inserts a Phoenician gloss on the Io legend, which placed the blame for her rape squarely upon her own head, and then he dismisses the argument and begins with Croesus. We cannot fail to notice that if the Persian claim to Asia was valid, then Croesus committed no wrong when he subjugated Greek cities which belonged quite as much to Asia as Troy, for he was taking only what was rightfully his. He did not fit the premise that lay behind the arguments of the Persian *logioi*.

However, Croesus was the first oriental empire-builder to impinge upon the Greek world that could be defined by shared language and blood, common religious rites and gods,[13] and with the confidence of the critical spirit of his age, Herodotus pronounced him the first of the barbarians "whom we know" to subject Greeks to payment of tribute, albeit Greeks whose cities were in Asia.[14] Yet he was also answerable for the first contact between an imperial power of Asia and mainland Greece, for he made friend-

---

[12] On the Croesus-*logos*, see esp. G. de Sanctis, "Il *logos* di Creso," *RFIC, ser. 2, 15 (1936)*, 1–14; Henry R. Immerwahr, *Form and Thought in Herodotus* (Cleveland, 1966) pp. 154–61; Ann Cornell Sheffield, *Herodotus' Portrayal of Croesus: A Study in Historical Artistry*, diss. Stanford, 1973; T. Krischer, "Solon und Kroisos," *WS* 77 (1964), 174–77.

[13] Cf. Hdt. 8.144.4.

[14] G. de Sanctis, *RFIC*, ser. 2, 15 (1936), 2–3, points out an apparent contradiction here: at 1.6.3, *all* the Greeks before Croesus are said to have been free, whereas at 1.14.4, we learn that Gyges conquered the *asty* of Colophon. Herodotus clearly saw a difference: Croesus was an imperialist, whereas Gyges was simply an aggressor.

ships there, specifically with the Lacedaemonians.[15] Croesus was an attractive, likeable king with good qualities, and he was affluent and undeniably preeminent: the sort of man who fitted Aristotle's desiderata for a tragic hero.

There were other reasons too why Croesus was a satisfactory starting-point. His dedications at Delphi had survived the burning of the temple there in 548 B.C., and they provided a solid basis for the traditions about him.[16] Then, too, there were the cross-references between the tale of Croesus and the historical traditions of Sparta and Athens, which gave the *logos* a dimension in time. But chiefly, Croesus served to stake out Herodotus' subject. This was not to be a tale of kidnappings and combats; rather, he would deal with the rise and maturation of oriental imperialism until it reached its tidewater mark and began its ebb. Croesus was the first Asiatic despot whose empire stretched into the Greek world.

Thus, his story was to establish a pattern for an imperial dynast. Wealthy, powerful, generous, and without vindictiveness, he was ultimately vulnerable, for all his might and glory. What brought him down? Mischance? The jealousy of the divine, which Herodotus calls *to theion*, and its propensity for disorder? A moment of unwisdom? The resentment of the gods against a mortal who thought himself blissfully happy? Herodotus refrained from stating a verdict of his own; he was not a philosopher,[17] but a historian, and the history of a king was the sum of his deeds, which a historian should relate. Yet the history of Croesus seems to show that somewhere there existed forces working against the stability of empires, negating the best efforts at planning. The glory and the fall of the last king of Lydia is a parable of imperial power.

The Logos of Croesus

The general consensus of scholars is that the Croesus-logos is dramatic, tragic and theatrical, and perhaps even derived, in its outlines, from the Athenian stage.[18] The prologue explained the ancient curse of the Merm-

---

[15] Hdt. 1.6.2.

[16] Cf. Henry Wood, *The Histories of Herodotus. An Analysis of the Formal Structure* (The Hague, 1972), 36–37; H. W. Parke, "Croesus and Delphi," *GRBS* 25 (1984), 209–32.

[17] Cf. Walter Potscher, "Götter und Gottheit bei Herodot," *WS* 71 (1958), 5–29, esp. 28–29.

[18] D. L. Page, "An Early Tragedy on the Fall of Croesus," *PCPS* 188 (1962), 47–49; H. R. Immerwahr, *Form and Thought in Herodotus*, 97–101; J. L. Myres, "Herodotus the Tragedian," *A Miscellany Presented to J. M. MacKay* (Liverpool, 1914), 88–96; David Grene, "Herodotus: The Historian as Dramatist," *Journal of Philology* 58 (1961), 477–88; cf. R. Meiggs, *The Athenian Empire* (Oxford, 1972), 387; cf. also Lionel Pearson, "Personalities in Greek History," *JHI* 15 (1954), 136–45, who regards Croesus, Cyrus, Cambyses, and

nads. The last king of the preceding dynasty, Candaules, whom the Greeks knew as Myrsilos (a tidbit of information that suggests Herodotus knew a Greek version of the tale which we do not have),[19] contravened Lydian customs by showing off his wife naked to his bodyguard, Gyges. The queen spotted Gyges in her bedroom, guessed immediately who was responsible for the outrage, and next morning gave Gyges the choice of avenging her, and winning Candaules' kingdom, or dying himself. Gyges chose to live. Then, by a bit of annular geography, the queen concealed Gyges armed with a dagger in the same place where he had hidden to see her naked. But the Lydians rose in arms when they learned of Candaules' murder and Gyges' usurpation, and the quarrel was referred to Delphi. The Pythia supported Gyges. But it foretold vengeance for Candaules' line in five generations, though at the time no one heeded the warning.

The dramatic importance of all this is to show the Mermnads as a house under a curse, quite as much as the Labdacids and the Atreidae in Greek mythology. At the end of the story, we are to return to Delphi's forgotten prophecy. The tale of Candaules, who had to come to a bad end, provided the check-points for Croesus, who became king at thirty-five and forthwith embarked on a policy of aggressive imperialism, first attacking Ephesus and then various other Greek cities. His empire grew until he possessed a respectable list of tribute-paying subjects, comparable in its way to Darius' roster of satrapies. Then, at the height of his power, he was visited by Solon.

There are chronological objections to this story, which perhaps Herodotus knew, for Plutarch[20] mentioned them as common knowledge. But this is a case where Aristotle's distinction between poetry and history breaks down. It is not always the case, as Aristotle[21] wrote, that poetry is concerned with universal truths, and history with what actually happened, for it is universal truth that Herodotus meant the meeting of Solon and Croesus to convey. Solon was a suitable spokesman. He was one of the Seven Sages and a poet, and one line of his surviving poetry seems particularly germane to the story of Croesus: surfeit (*koros*) of wealth, he sang, gives birth to *hybris*, in men that lack a proper mental outlook.[22] His long speech to Croesus was pure folk-wisdom, and he spoke with the language of conversation, not philosophy. He pointed out the moral that the life of Croesus was to illustrate.

Xerxes all as conventional tragic characters who draw the vengeance of the gods upon themselves.

[19] See J.A.S. Evans, "Candaules Whom the Greeks Call Myrsilos," *GRBS* 26 (1985), 229–33.

[20] *Solon*, 27.

[21] *Poetics*, 9.

[22] Fr. 5.9f. D.

Croesus, the most successful prince of his dynasty, secure in his prosperity, was hungry for approval and praise, and he wanted Solon to admit to the awe which his affluence should have produced.[23] He had Solon shown his treasuries rich with the tribute of empire. We have the impression of an imperial monarch who delights in the glitter and magnificence of power. But he was quite without the premonition that Xerxes had years later, when he viewed the armed might of his empire at Abydos first with joy and satisfaction as great as any Croesus felt, and then with sorrow as he reflected upon the brevity of life.[24] Croesus asked Solon to name the happiest man he knew. But to his chagrin, Solon did not choose him, nor did he count him even the second most happy, and when Croesus expressed annoyance, Solon's reply was that mankind was all chance. "To me, you seem very wealthy, and you are king of many men. But the question you ask me I cannot answer until I know that you have completed your life span well." And further on: "We must look at the end of everything to see how it turns out. For many to whom God has given blessedness he utterly destroys." The burden of Solon's wisdom is that the great should remember the mutability of fortune and the unreliable temper of the gods. Croesus failed to comprehend. But that is as far as his sin extends. He committed no act of *hybris*; what overtook him was the indignation of God.[25]

Only here in the *Histories* does the word "*nemesis*" occur, and the meaning assigned to it in Powell's *Lexicon*, "divine vengeance," is surely too strong. I have translated it as "indignation." It is rather the exasperation that the gods felt for a man who thought his great good fortune exempted him from the regular order of things, and its mastery was recognized only when it had done its work. After Croesus had dismissed Solon's advice and Solon along with it, *nemesis* took hold of him. First, he lost his son and only heir, Atys, for though he had a second son, he was mute and could not succeed to the throne. Then, on hearing that Cyrus had overthrown Astyages, his brother-in-law, he resolved to attack him, paying no heed to the wise counsel of Sandanis,[26] who warned him that the Persians were poor but hard men: they wore leather garments, lived in a stony land, and drank only water. What might Croesus hope to gain by making them sub-

[23] Sheffield, *Herodotus' Portrayal*, 51–52, points out that the word *himeros* (1.30.5), which Croesus uses to express his desire to question Solon, is commonly used to denote the excessive desires of tyrants.

[24] Hdt. 7.44–46.

[25] Hdt. 1.32. D. Lateiner, "A Note on the Perils of Prosperity in Herodotus," *RhMus* 125 (1982), 97–101, argues that excessive prosperity is the moral equivalent of *hybris*, but *hybris* usually implies some degree of violence; mere insolence is a much rarer meaning, and in any case, Croesus' "insolence," if it existed, was a very mild variety. On this, see R. Lattimore, *Story Patterns in Greek Tragedy* (Ann Arbor, 1965), 22–23.

[26] Cf. Hdt. 1.27, where Croesus earlier in his career does accept advice not to invade the Ionian island cities.

jects? But if he suffered defeat, the Persians would sample Lydian luxury, and learn quickly to like it, and Lydia would never be rid of them. Croesus was unconvinced. He crossed the Halys River, which marked the frontier between the empires of Lydia and Media, and by so doing, transgressed a boundary that had served in the past to delimit two empires.

Herodotus[27] assigned Croesus three motives: he wanted to increase the size of his empire, avenge Astyages, and he trusted his interpretation of a Delphic oracle that foretold the fall of a great empire. After his defeat, as he sat on the funeral pyre with flames licking at its base, he thought of Solon's advice and called out his name. Cyrus, curious, wanted to know the meaning of the cry; and when he learned it, he realized that he shared a common humanity with Croesus and ordered him saved. But saving him was beyond his power, and Apollo had to intervene to preserve Croesus from the flames.

Croesus was a changed man. He held the Delphic oracle responsible for inciting him against Cyrus, but Delphi would accept no blame. Croesus' time was up, and the ancient curse of the Mermnad house demanded its due. Apollo had delayed the doom of Sardis for three years, and if the oracle had misled Croesus, it was Croesus' own fault. Croesus, reported Herodotus, was satisfied. There is, after all, if not a happy ending, at least due acceptance.

Such is the Croesus-*logos*: a story of how appetite for empire brought a king great prosperity and the pride that accompanied it; and when his appetite pushed him toward a blunder, his magnificence clouded his understanding so that he could not foresee it. There is a tragic pattern here—not a very common one in the dramas that have survived, but a variant of it does occur in Herodotus' treatment of Polycrates, tyrant of Samos. Yet the fall of Croesus is a qualified one. He has achieved understanding, and though he may have ceased to exist as a historical figure, Herodotus let him live on as a literary archetype. He became a wise adviser, dispensing counsel of the sort that he himself had received from Solon and Sandanis, and had disregarded. Suffering had brought him wisdom.

How should we interpret the tragedy of Croesus? He is, on the one hand, a decent man, an imperial master for some Greeks but a friendly ally for others, who was brought down by *nemesis*. The gods were affronted by his prosperity. In this view of the story, his tragic error is illustrated, if not expressed, by the question he put to Solon, and the answer he expected. The reception he gave Solon's advice demonstrated how far his greatness had removed him from reality.

But there is another interpretation that is equally valid. The prime mover in Croesus' tragedy turned out to be the curse of the Mermnads, for which the choice of Gyges, taken five generations before, was responsible. Gyges had placed the preservation of his own life before loyalty to his master, and his choice had brought him the oracle's warning that Candaules' royal house would eventually have its revenge. But Gyges' choice had also brought his descendants imperial power: Croesus was his last and most successful heir, and it was he in turn who made the choice that activated the curse of the Mermnads. He chose to attack Cyrus, and he made the tragic error of failing to recognize the good sense of the advice given him by Sandanis, who pointed out that conquest of the Persians could bring no profit to Lydians, whereas defeat by them would bring on them a penalty from which they could never rid themselves.[28] Within a few years, the tables would be turned: it would be the Persians who assumed the role of the affluent Lydians, and Greece would be the conquest that could bring no profit to Persia.

It seems that Croesus, for all his apparent good sense and diligence in testing the oracles, ultimately succumbed to an irrational desire to expand his boundaries and increase his power. He had no heir to succeed to this expanded empire of his, though by a twist of irony, Herodotus had his son, who was mute, find his voice during the sack of Sardis[29] and hence Croesus acquired an heir just as he lost his throne. But we should also note that the *logos*, for all the tragic patterning we may find in it, is quite as much folktale as tragedy. Croesus is a type of despot that has counterparts among the kings and caliphs of *The Thousand and One Nights*, and the story of his son Atys follows the myth-motif of the Attis legend. The Croesus-*logos* is a fable intended to make a point. Its function, aside from providing entertainment (which was never an unimportant consideration for Herodotus), was to foreshadow the course of empire that was to follow.

Successful imperialism brought Croesus great wealth and even (he thought) the friendship and approval of the gods. But it also established a certain momentum that eventually drove him, as it did Xerxes later, to attack a people who possessed no wealth and whose conquest could bring him no gain.[30] Yet the actions of Croesus were rational: he waged a preventive war not only to avenge Astyages but to secure his own kingdom. He investigated the oracles and tested them for accuracy, and he took care to win over Apollo with generous gifts. None of this saved him from defeat.

[28] Cf. Kurt von Fritz, *Die Griechische Geschichtsschreibung*, I (Berlin, 1967), 239–43. The comments of R. D. Dawe, "Some Reflections on *Ate* and *Hamartia*," HSCP 72 (1967), 89–123, on tragic error have a bearing on the fall of Croesus.

[29] Cf. Thomas A. Sebeok and Erika Brady, "The Two Sons of Croesus: A Myth about Communication in Herodotus," QUCC n.s. 1 (1979), 7–22.

[30] For other examples of this recurrent theme: Hdt. 1.206–7; 3.21; 4.83. Cf. F. Hellmann, *Herodots Kroisos-Logos* (Berlin, 1934), 77–90.

Yet in the end—though only in retrospect did the truth become clear—Croesus was trapped in a web of history for which the choice of Gyges, the founder of the Mermnad dynasty, was responsible. Apollo's oracle, whose reliability he had proved, lured him on to destruction with an ambiguous prophecy. A king less confident of success might have asked what was the realm to which the oracle referred, when it foretold that a great empire would fall, but in the *Histories*, successful imperialism goes hand in hand with failure of insight.

Croesus yielded to Cyrus, who took over his kingdom and inherited his ambitions. He inherited as well some seeds of destruction: before the Persians conquered Croesus, they had known no luxury, but they quickly learned it from the Lydians. The Lydians themselves were transformed from rulers into docile subjects by a dose of epicureanism legislated with intent by the Persians. The Lydians rose in revolt, and to keep them tractable in the future, Cyrus, on the advice of Croesus, ordered them to wear soft clothes, play the flute, and bring up their children as shopkeepers. Thus, the Lydians forgot their imperial status and became the unwarlike people that they were in Herodotus' own day. A soft, unheroic life made soft men, who were uninterested in building empires. Herodotus was to conclude the *Histories* with a story that pressed home the same theme.

The leap from Croesus to Cyrus takes us from the end of one dynasty to the inception of another that was to take up Lydia's imperial burden and eclipse it. However, Croesus did not die with his empire. Suffering had brought him enlightenment. On the funeral pyre, he had been converted to the wisdom of Solon, and now he was to offer counsel to the new conquerors, Cyrus and Cambyses, who were to receive it in the same spirit as he had himself, when his own empire was at its height. From the precursor of Xerxes, he becomes the precursor of Artabanus, who was to counsel both Darius and Xerxes.

The advice Croesus offered was familiar: fortune was mutable; human affairs are a wheel that turns and never allows prosperity to remain constant for any man. This was the warning he gave Cyrus on his last campaign, as a preamble to his advice to try to defeat the Massagetae with a trick.[31] He survived Cyrus, and lived on to weep at the fate of Egypt and to warn Cambyses to curb his madness or face revolt.[32] From being an Oriental despot himself, he became a commentator on despotism, though at the same time he could be a courtier not above adroit flattery. "Son of Cyrus," he told Cambyses, "you do not seem to me to be your father's equal. For you have as yet no son the like of him whom he left behind."[33]

[31] Hdt. 1.207.
[32] Hdt. 3.36.1–3.
[33] Hdt. 3.34.5.

But though Cyrus valued Croesus' wisdom, and recognized that he was a good man and a favorite of the gods, he continued on his career as an empire-builder, following Croesus' example rather than his advice. The enlightenment of Croesus on the funeral pyre did nothing to change the course of events.

The story of Croesus is intended to illustrate many things: the vainglory of imperial power, the futility of trying to read the future with only human intelligence, the inconstancy of fortune, and the inevitability of fate. But in particular, it is a parable intended to demonstrate an imperial pattern. Croesus is the precursor of the Achaemenid kings. Cyrus recognized a common bond with him in defeat, and yet he and his descendants would find the imperatives of empire equally demanding. They would, in one way or another, follow Croesus' pattern.

CYRUS

Now that the conquest of Lydia was finished, the plan which Herodotus followed took him next to Cyrus. "The course of my story hereafter," he wrote, "demands that I say who this Cyrus was who destroyed the empire of Croesus,"[34] and thus he launched into a genuine "life," which like the *Life of Homer* mentioned earlier, took his hero from nativity to death. The story of Cyrus' birth took Herodotus back into Persian legends and sagas, which had penetrated Ionia by the early fifth century.[35] How deeply he tapped the Iranian epic tradition, even at second hand, is hard to judge, but he claimed that he found four versions of the hero-myth of Cyrus, and chose the one that sought least to glorify him, which shows a nice awareness that the traditions about Cyrus were tinged with hagiography. Yet his claim may be only partly true. One of the discarded versions he knew, which told how Cyrus was suckled by a bitch, is preserved in Justin's abridgment of Pompeius Trogus, who may have had it in turn from the *Persika* of the fourth-century historian, Dinon. Ctesias got another tale, which may have been one that Herodotus rejected. But neither of these seems to have glorified Cyrus a great deal more than Herodotus' own ver-

---

[34] Hdt. 1.95.1. Here Herodotus makes clear the theme of his *Histories*; cf. Fornara, *Herodotus*, 25–26.

[35] Cf. Immerwahr, *Form and Thought*, 161–62. See in general, J. M. Cook, *The Persian Empire* (London, 1983), 25–27, who suggests that Herodotus may have rejected one story as glorifying Cyrus that was historical fact: that Cyrus belonged to the royal line of Persis and inherited its throne legitimately. Ragnar Hoistad, *Cynic Hero and Cynic King. Studies in the Cynic Conception of Man* (Lund, 1948), 73–94, argues that Herodotus tapped Ionian "Cyrus-traditions" that already presented him as a type of ideal king. In fact, the evidence fails to support the view that Cyrus' methods differed significantly from those of the Medes or the Assyrians before him: Josef Wiesehofer, "Kyros und die Unterworfenen Völker. Ein Beitrag zur Entstehung von Geschichtsbewusstsein," *QS* 26 (1987), 107–26.

sion, which he probably chose because it shared in mythopoeic archetypes with which the Greeks were familiar.

Laius, father of Oedipus, was warned by an oracle that his son would kill him, and Hecuba dreamed, before she gave birth to Paris, that her offspring would bring destruction upon Troy. Astyages, king of the Medes, is likewise a man touched by fate. He had two dreams: the first warned him that the unborn son of his daughter Mandane would menace his rule, and so he wedded her to a Persian, imagining that her son would take the status of his father; and since the Persians were vassals of the Medes, the boy could be no threat to him. In fact, what Astyages had done was to set the stage in all ignorance for the loss of Median hegemony. The second, more insistent dream, led him to order the death of his infant grandson, for it portended that Mandane's offspring would be king.

The motif of the Oedipus legend now asserts itself. Astyages gave the infant Cyrus, dressed for his funeral, to Harpagus to kill. But Harpagus would not slay the child himself, for Astyages was old and had no son, and if Mandane succeeded to the throne, what vengeance might she take? The final irony of this hero-myth was that Cyrus was, in any case, Astyages' natural heir through his mother, and if he was a Persian, that was the result of a marriage alliance which Astyages had himself devised. Harpagus gave the child to the herdsman Mitradates to kill. The clothes which the child wore, and the mourning in the palace, told Mitradates that this was no ordinary infant, and he got the whole story from the attendant who escorted him out of the city: this was the son of Mandane and Cambyses the Persian, whom Astyages had ordered slain.

But now the wife of Mitradates intervened. Herodotus named her "Spako," meaning "dog" in the language of the Medes, and this allows him to rationalize the version of the hero-myth that had Cyrus suckled by a bitch: Cyrus' parents, at a later date, exploited the equivoque of Spako's name, and spread the story that Cyrus had been suckled by a bitch when he was exposed to die, for they wanted it believed that some divine power had saved their son. Spako had just given birth to a boy, stillborn, and his corpse was substituted for Cyrus. Thus, the retainers were gulled whom Harpagus sent to examine the body and see that it was properly buried. Harpagus himself was careful to remain at arm's length. Coincidence, Harpagus' caution, and the royal funeral dress that was available to disguise the stillborn infant all combined to save Cyrus' life.

By the age of ten, Cyrus had shown his royal nature by playing king, with the boys of his village as his subjects. This brought him to the notice of Astyages, who rapidly realized that this was no herdsman's son. When he uncovered the truth, he directed his anger, not at the herdsman nor at Cyrus (for since he had become a play king, the Magi agreed that the prophecy of the dream had been fulfilled),[36] but at Harpagus, who had disobeyed orders. That he could not tolerate, for it was a challenge to his autocracy. Thus, he meted out to Harpagus a punishment borrowed from the myth of the Atreida: at the banquet which he gave to celebrate the return of Cyrus, he served him the flesh of his only son. But the borrowed motif heightens the contrast between Greek society with its freedom of expression, and the world of oriental despotism. Upon realizing that he had eaten his child, Harpagus suppressed any protest; instead, his only comment was that all the king's acts were acceptable to him, and he went home to bide his time.

Astyages was old and apparently still without male heir, but he did not count on dying. His harsh despotism continued while Cyrus grew up in his father's house, until Harpagus thought the time was right. He then smuggled a message to Cyrus sewn in a hare's belly, urging him to raise the Persians in revolt. But first Cyrus allowed his Persians a choice: he staged a bit of theater to illustrate the advantages of being imperial overlords, and the disadvantages of being subjects. The Persians chose to be overlords.

Astyages, "blinded, as it were, by a god,"[37] placed Harpagus in command of the army sent to suppress the revolt. He had forgotten about the Thyestean banquet. Harpagus went over to Cyrus. Astyages raised a second army of youths and old men, and with these he fought Cyrus again and was defeated. Thus, the Medes became subjects of the Persians, but Astyages himself was spared and lived on in Cyrus' entourage. The public image of Cyrus, which probably went back to Cyrus' own propaganda, was of a king who was merciful to conquered princes.[38] It was to have a long life in the Greek sources.

Croesus had been a decent man, and his fall aroused pity; whereas with Astyages it was otherwise: he was a ruthless monarch, and his fall was well deserved. Yet the story of his fall incorporates myth-motifs which, if not borrowed directly from Athenian tragedy, at least have a cousinly relationship. Astyages was a man attempting to escape fate. He was a combination of Laius and Atreus, and his effort to thwart the destiny of Cyrus resulted directly in his own fall. It was a peculiarly irrational effort, for Astyages was an old man without a son, and Mandane, the mother of Cyrus, was his heir. A couple of features are to reappear. Astyages' punishment of Harpagus for disobeying an order that no longer mattered, parallels the story

---

[36] Cf. Immerwahr, *Form and Thought*, p. 165: the magi agree that Cyrus showed his royal nature "without anyone's foresight," i.e., by accident (1.120.3).

[37] Hdt. 1.127.2.

[38]. Cf. Sidney Smith, *Babylonian Historical Texts Relating to the Capture and Downfall of Babylon* (London, 1924), 34–35. The idealized portrayal has lasted up to the present: cf. Max Mallowan, "Cyrus the Great (538–529 B.C.)" *Iran* 10 (1972), 1–17.

of how another unbalanced autocrat, Cambyses, punished his attendants who had disobeyed his command to kill Croesus, even though he himself had already repented of the order.[39] Both are examples of despotism carried beyond reason. Harpagus' message to Cyrus sewn into the belly of a hare has a counterpart in the story of how Histiaeus sent Aristagoras a message to revolt, tattooed on the scalp of the messenger.[40] Yet there was one aspect of Cyrus' ascent that was unique: both Deioces (who became the first king of the Medes) and Darius (king of Persia) acquired the throne by trickery. Cyrus, by contrast, was destined to rule; he was by nature kingly, and he had established his first royal court by the age of ten. The effort of Astyages to subvert Cyrus' destiny had the result of giving Harpagus a motive for helping to bring it about.

Astyages was singularly purblind and foolish; yet Herodotus allowed him a last speech that had a degree of wisdom. He told Harpagus, who mocked him after his capture, that he had been both stupid and unjust: stupid for making Cyrus king when he might have been king himself, and unjust because he made his fellow Medes vassals of Persia in order to get vengeance for himself. The Medes did eventually repent of having yielded to the Persians and rebelled against Darius,[41] but Cyrus' takeover was smooth, helped along by Harpagus' lack of ambition and his willingness to betray his countrymen to get revenge for himself.

Thus, Cyrus became king, and his first act was to conquer Croesus. The Ionians and Aeolians he left for his generals to defeat, but not before he made Persia's initial contact with the world of the Greeks, and expressed his scorn for the Greek way of life. Never yet, he said, had he feared men who set up market-places in the middle of their cities where they might cheat one another![42] The *agora* was the center of the free political and economic life of the city-state. There was no equivalent in Persia, and Cyrus felt only contempt for what it represented. This is no longer quite the same Cyrus that saved Croesus from the pyre, recognizing that he was a man like himself. He was developing an oriental despot's persona and it was antithetical to things Hellenic.[43]

There are only two more episodes to the life of Cyrus. The first was the capture of Babylon. The city fell easily, but on the march there, Cyrus dis-

[39] Hdt. 3.36.

[40] Hdt. 5.35.3.

[41] Hdt. 1.130.2. Perhaps there is another reference to this rebellion at 3.126.1. Cf. R. A. McNeal, ed., *Herodotus, Book I* (Lanham, Md. 1986), 161.

[42] Hdt. 1.153.1–2.

[43] Cf. H. C. Avery, "Herodotus' Picture of Cyrus," *AJPh* 93 (1972), 529–46, notes the conflict in Cyrus' persona, and suggests that conquest of Babylon marks the transition between the Cyrus who was the founder of Persian freedom and the despot Cyrus. The indications of change are even earlier.

played a flash of imperial anger that foreshadows Xerxes' supreme act of arrogance later, when he had the Hellespont flogged for destroying the floating bridges that were to take him into Europe. Cyrus lost one of his sacred white horses in the river Gyndes, and he punished the insolent stream by dividing it into three hundred and sixty channels.[44]

The Persian army entered Babylon without a battle. The Nabonidus Chronicle[45] names Gobryas as its leader; Cyrus himself entered the city about two weeks later, and peace was imposed. Of that, Herodotus says nothing. But he was careful to weave the fall of Babylon into the great symmetries of history: Cyrus took Babylon for the first time,[46] he noted, looking forward to its second fall to Darius.

The last episode in the life of Cyrus was his campaign against the Massagetae, and it illustrates the final development of his persona. The casus belli was the simplest expression of imperialism: he wanted to make the Massagetae his subjects. First, he offered to marry their queen, Tomyris, and when she rejected his overtures, he advanced to the river Araxes that marked the boundary of Massagetic territory, and bridged it. Then Tomyris made a proposal. Let the Persians advance three days' journey into her lands, and fight there; or alternatively, let the Massagetae advance the same distance into Persian territory and do likewise.

Cyrus' Persian counselors advised the latter course. They preferred to allow Tomyris to commit the symbolic act of aggression by crossing the river that marked the boundary between the two realms. But Croesus urged Cyrus not to retreat before the Massagetae, and his reasons were sound, although he added a courtier's appeal to royal pride: Cyrus, son of Cambyses, should not yield ground to a woman! Instead, he advised Cyrus to advance into the queen's realm and attempt to overreach his enemies with a trick. The Persians, he suggested, should try to soften up the Massagetae with wine and fine food and then launch an attack, for the Massagetae were savages in the root sense of the word, and once they were corrupted by the delights of civilization, they would be easy victims.

Cyrus took the advice of Croesus and the immediate result was a victorious engagement: he destroyed a third of the Massagetic army and captured the queen's son. Tomyris then sent Cyrus an ultimatum: let him restore her son and depart unscathed, or she would give him his fill of blood. But the choice was no longer open: the queen's son had killed himself with his own hands. In the final, bitter battle with the Massagetae, Cyrus and most of his army were destroyed, and Tomyris gave him what she had

[44] Hdt. 1.189–90; 1.202.3.
[45] *ANET*[2], 306.
[46] Hdt. 1.191.6.

promised: she filled a skin with human blood and lowered his cadaver, headfirst, into it.

Cyrus had come full circle. Saved from death at the order of a cruel despot as an infant, he died in the end, a man of blood. Destiny had marked him as a boy to be king, but once he became lord of Asia, his expansionism acquired a momentum of its own. He fought Croesus in self-defense, for Croesus was the aggressor. But Babylon he attacked simply because it was next on his agenda, and he launched his campaign against the Massagetae because he wanted to.[47] He let the Persians choose to be an imperial people, but once they had chosen, imperialism became the *nomos* that ruled not merely the Persians themselves but their king as well. There were many accounts of Cyrus' death, as there were of his birth, but Herodotus claimed he followed the one that he considered most convincing: Cyrus died in bloody battle, in an assault upon a people who knew no luxuries, and lived beyond the Persian frontier. The river that had to be bridged before the Persian army could advance into Massagetic territory looks backward and forward: back to the Halys that Croesus crossed to attack Cyrus, and forward to the Hellespont that Xerxes would yoke.

Cyrus appears once more, at the conclusion of the *Histories*. He has become again the ideal wise king, as he was when he rescued Croesus from death, recognizing, like Odysseus in Sophocles' *Ajax*,[48] the common humanity that he shared with his former enemy, and the insecurity of human greatness. In both the Croesus-*logos* and this final story, where Cyrus points out the moral that soft living breeds subjects, not rulers, we see him as a type of perfect prince. Herodotus has returned to the idealizing traditions about Cyrus which made him into a model king—moderate, a peacemaker among his friends, and free from divine wrath in all his doings—as Aeschylus[49] portrayed him. Antisthenes and Xenophon were to develop this tradition into a *speculum principum*, but the Cyrus of the "biography," as opposed to the Cyrus of the Croesus-*logos* and the concluding fable, did not follow traditions that idealized or sought to glorify. Herodotus deliberately turned his back on them. Rather, his aim was to portray the sort of king who started the Persian Empire on its way.

DARIUS

The life and condign death of Cambyses need not detain us long. Herodotus chose to portray him as a sinner and a madman, citing as evidence of his insanity his sacrilegious acts while he was at Memphis: he opened cof-

[47] Hdt. 1.177–78; 1.201.

[48] Karl Reinhardt, *Sophocles*, trans. Hazel Harvey and David Harvey (Oxford, 1979), 15; cf. Segal, *WS* 5 (1971), 49–51.

[49] *Pers.* 768 ff; cf. Hoistad, *Cynic Hero*, 92–94.

fins and examined the mummies inside, and he mocked the image in the temple of Hephaestus.[50] No one but a madman would ridicule holy places and religious customs, Herodotus opined, and went on to demonstrate that every people held to its own *nomoi*. Darius, Cambyses' successor, conducted an experiment that proved the point, and that consummate politician was anything but mad. The revolt of Smerdis was to follow immediately after Cambyses' madness became manifest, and it would bring about the fulfillment of a dream which Cyrus had on his last campaign, that showed the eldest son of Hystaspes with wings on his shoulders, one outspread over Asia and the other over Europe.[51] Cyrus suspected Darius of plotting revolt, but the revolt that fulfilled Darius' destiny was unlike anything Cyrus had imagined.

Darius himself makes his entry into the *Histories* just after the six conspirators led by Otanes had confirmed their suspicion that the magus Smerdis was an imposter, but had not yet decided what action to take. We learn later[52] that Darius had been one of Cambyses' bodyguards in Egypt, but he had returned to Fars where his father was satrap, and from there came to Susa to tell the conspirators that he already knew what they had just discovered. He also warned them not to move cautiously, as Otanes advised, but to enter the palace boldly and kill the usurper. Darius had a pretext that would gain them free entry: he would say that he brought a message for the king from his father. It was a lie, and learning to tell the truth was part of a young Persian's education,[53] but Darius had a sophistry ready to justify it: lying and telling the truth had the same purpose—to gain advantage.[54] What was right for Darius was whatever was effective, and there is a double irony to his casuistry, for after he secured the throne, he set up at Bisitun on the road from Hamadan to Kermanshah a great trilingual inscription describing how he overthrew the magus, whom he named Gaumata, and presenting himself as the representative of truth at war with falsehood.[55] This was the style that Darius proclaimed for him-

[50] Hdt. 2.37–38; cf W. H. Friedrich, "Der Tod des Tyrannen," *Antike und Abendland* 18 (1973), 97–129, esp. 116–19.

[51] Hdt. 1.209–10.

[52] Hdt. 3.139.

[53] Hdt. 1.136.2.

[54] Hdt. 3.72.4; cf. Eric A. Havelock, *The Liberal Temper in Greek Politics* (New Haven, 1957), 264–67, where this type of utilitarian argument is associated with the sophist Antiphon.

[55] R. G. Kent, *Old Persian Grammar, Texts, Lexicon*[2] (New Haven, 1953), 116–34; E. von Voigtlander, *The Bisitun Inscription of Darius the Great, Babylonian Version* (Corpus Inscriptionum Iranicarum, part 1, vol. 2, London, 1978); J. C. Greenfield and P. Porten, *The Bisitun Inscription of Darius the Great, Aramaic Version* (CII, part 1, vol. 5, London, 1982); Jack Martin Balcer, *Herodotus and Bisitun. Problems in Ancient Persian Historiography. Historia Einzelschrift* 49 (1987).

self. He was the righteous king, defending the truth, and yet Herodotus has given him here a persona that is the direct antithesis of this ideal. Moreover, Darius forced the pace of the conspiracy by an expedient that bordered on treachery. He told his fellow conspirators that if they failed to act swiftly, he would betray them.

The process by which Darius made himself king was similar. He employed swift, shrewd, and intelligent planning, not overburdened with scruples. After the overthrow of the magus, the Persian magnates held a debate on the merits of the three types of constitution that the Greeks recognized, and Darius spoke for monarchy. His final, clinching argument was that Persia had benefited from monarchy in the past, and she should not desert her ancestral customs now. However, it was by a trick which his groom contrived for him that he won the throne, and once he was king, he showed no great reverence for the ways of the past. He gave the empire a new organization, establishing satrapies and assessing tribute.[56] The Persians called him a huckster,[57] which was an epithet that might have aroused the scorn of Cyrus, who had expressed his contempt for the commerce of the marketplace.

Friends who had done him favors were rewarded: witness the brother of Polycrates, Syloson, who had given him his red cloak while they were both in Egypt, and got Samos in return.[58] Men like Oroetes, the satrap of Sardis who gave Darius no aid when the Medes revolted, were punished.[59] He continued the imperialism of Persia, but there is a perceptible change. Cyrus had attacked the Massagetae because he wanted to, and Cambyses invaded Egypt because he decided to do it. Their appetite for conquest had built the empire, but now it was mature, and grown wealthy with tribute. Darius' first foreign invasion was motivated by an excess of resources and an inclination to avenge an ancient wrong. Babylon was secure, Asia rich and well populated, and Darius considered the time ripe to retaliate for the Scythian invasion that had taken place years before, while the Persian Empire was still unborn. There is another change as well. Darius crossed the boundary that separated Asia from Europe.

Herodotus imagined that the subject came up in bed. The wife of Darius, Atossa, upbraided him because he had added nothing to the realm. The Persians expected a ruler to increase their empire, and in addition, Atossa suggested, if Darius kept his subjects occupied with war, they would have no time to plot against him. Atossa had an ulterior motive, but her reproach was put in terms that Darius understood. He pointed out that

[56] On the debate of the magnates, see J.A.S. Evans, "Notes on the Debate of the Persian Grandees in Herodotus 3.80–82," *QUCC* 7 (1981), 79–84.

[57] Hdt. 3.89.3.

[58] Hdt. 3.139.2–3.

[59] Hdt. 3.126–27.

he intended to cross into Europe and invade Scythia. Atossa replied that he should invade Greece instead: she wanted Greek girls to add to her bevy of servants! This seemed reasonable enough to Darius, and he dispatched a reconnaissance party to Greece led by the Crotoniate doctor Democedes, who had instigated Atossa to arouse Darius to his imperial duties in the first place simply because he wanted to return home. The prospect of invading Greece did not divert Darius from Scythia, but the dialogue in bed portrays vividly both the imperatives of Persian imperialism and, within the context of these imperatives, the happenstances that could set a fresh wave of expansion in motion.

Darius' Scythian campaign presents both parallels and contrasts with the later expedition of Xerxes. A Persian who had three sons serving in the army asked Darius to allow one to remain behind, and Darius, with treacherous generosity, granted him all three, and thereupon gave orders that their throats be cut. Pythius the Lydian, who had five sons in Xerxes' army, asked exemption for one, and Xerxes, who had none of his father's affable treachery, burst out in anger, and sacrificed the eldest son in a purification ritual.[60] Darius spanned the Bosporus with a pontoon bridge; Xerxes built two floating bridges across the Hellespont. Artabanus pointed out the difficulties that an attack on the Scyths would encounter, and years later he would also counsel Xerxes against invading Greece.[61] The attempt of the Scyths to form an alliance with their neighbors against Darius begs comparison with the effort of the Greeks to form a league against Xerxes. Darius returned home with his army largely intact, but only because Histiaeus of Miletus persuaded his fellow vassal-tyrants that they had a selfish interest in preserving Persian hegemony. Xerxes would return safely himself, but the flower of the Persian army would perish in Greece.

Herodotus' attention shifts somewhat from Darius in his last years, but he remains a coherent character, with some traits of a tyrant. But at the same time, he possesses all the attributes of a Great King of Persia who maintained the traditions of the Achaemenids. He was grateful to his friends, and swift to seek revenge for any wrongs done to him. Histiaeus of Miletus did not have Darius' implicit trust, but he did get rewarded for his loyalty at the Danube bridge, and when he was later crucified at Sardis and his embalmed head sent to Darius, the king reproached the men who had done the deed and had what was left of Histiaeus given a proper burial. When news that Athens had intervened in the Ionian Revolt came to Darius, he vowed vengeance,[62] and when he learned of the defeat at Marathon, he began at once to raise a great force to invade Greece. But he died

---

[60] Hdt. 4.84.1.2; 7.39–40. Cf. J.A.S. Evans, "The Story of Pythius," *LCM* 13/9 (1988), 139.

[61] Hdt. 4.87–88; 7.33–36; 4.83.12; 7.10; 7.46.1.

[62] Hdt. 6.30.2; 5.105.1–2.

with Greece unpunished, and consequently Xerxes was to enter upon a drama for which his father had already produced the prologue.

Yet Herodotus has also painted the character of Darius with some of the colors of a tyrant. The circumstances surrounding Darius' accession already belonged to folktale by the time Herodotus learned of them,[63] but traditions which he found were based, second-hand, upon the official version that appears in the Bisitun inscription. However, Herodotus differed in one significant detail: Darius was not the righteous man who suppressed falsehood and evil as he presented himself at Bisitun—he was instead a shrewd politician who lied to gain advantage, and he won the throne by a trick. Once he was king, and one of the seven confederates who overthrew Smerdis, Intaphernes, entered the palace unannounced,[64] Darius immediately suspected a plot. The parallel is close with the persona of Zeus that Aeschylus draws in the *Prometheus Bound*: a tyrant figure who defeated the Titans with guile, and distrusted his friends[65] once he had secured the throne. Atossa's bedroom advice to Darius—that he should keep his subjects occupied with war—was in the same vein. Tyrants, Aristotle was to point out,[66] imposed taxes and waged wars to give their subjects no time to conspire against them. These are brush strokes that are superimposed upon a picture of a Persian monarch which is otherwise not unconventional.

However, this Darius of Herodotus has practically nothing in common with the elder statesman that Aeschylus depicts in his *Persians*. He may impress the reader as a shrewder wielder of imperial power than his son, but there is no effort to draw the contrast that Aeschylus made. On the contrary, Darius is the precursor of Xerxes, who sets Xerxes on the course he must follow. His career was foretold to Cyrus in a dream that showed him with wings outspread over both Asia and Europe, and he was the first to move Persian imperialism across the frontier that divided the two continents. He left the invasion of Greece to his son as unfinished business.

XERXES

The popular concept of Xerxes that took hold of the Greek imagination in the fifth century, and which is reflected in the *Persians* of Aeschylus pro-

---

[63] Cf. E. J. Bickerman and H. Tadmor, "Darius I, Pseudo-Smerdis and the Magi," *Athenaeum* 56 (1978), 239–61. On Darius' accession, see esp. M. A. Dandamaev, *Persien unter den ersten Achämeniden (6. Jahrhundert v. Chr.)* (Wiesbaden, 1976), 108–58. R. N. Frye, *The History of Ancient Iran* (Munich, 1984), 96–106 gives a balanced account of the controversy over Darius' accession.

[64] Hdt. 3.118–19.

[65] Aeschylus, *PV*, 200–228; cf. Brian Vickers, *Towards Greek Tragedy* (London, 1973), 307–9.

[66] *Pol.* 1313b; V, 9–10.

duced in 472 B.C., was that he was young, rash, and arrogant, and led astray by bad advisers who reproached him for failing to add to the empire. The king who lashed and fettered the Hellespont became a symbol of vainglory in the rhetorical tradition. With Xerxes, Herodotus did not start with a clean canvas. The Xerxes to whom readers of the *Histories* are introduced as he announced the expedition he intended to make against Greece, has more in common with the young king of Aeschylus than otherwise.

His pride and quick anger we might expect. They are conventional attributes of an oriental despot. His youth was also part of the tradition. His headstrong temper led to his flash of rage against Artabanus, who dared to oppose him. The facts, however, do not fit this picture, as Herodotus may have known: Xerxes was in his mid-thirties when he succeeded his father, and he had already been viceroy of Babylon for a dozen years.[67] He was an older man when he came to the throne than his father had been, and yet there is an ambience of immaturity about him that contrasts with Darius.

But there are additional touches that seem to be Herodotus' own. First, he had a degree of magnanimity. He burst out in hot anger against Artabanus, but the next day, apologized handsomely before the Persian magnates. Other instances were to follow of his willingness to accept adverse comment, and their cumulative effect is to endow Xerxes with a certain grace and charm. He is by no means an unappealing figure. Second, he was the product of a tradition that accepted an aggressive stance as a necessary attribute of a king. "I am no son of Darius, son of Hystaspes son of Arsames son of Ariamnes son of Teispes son of Cyrus son of Cambyses son of Teispes son of Achaemenes if I take no vengeance on the Athenians," he told Artabanus, and with Greece there could be no half measures. Persia had to defeat the Greeks or be defeated by them. Finally, there was in his character a degree of insecurity that fitted strangely with the royal persona of a conqueror whose worth must be judged by the growth of his empire. Even his quick temper masked some uncertainty and irresolution. Once his wrath against Artabanus had cooled, he decided that his advice was right: he would not expose himself to the jealousy of the gods but would heed Artabanus' warning. It took a menacing dream, which convinced even Artabanus, to firm his resolve.

Yet Xerxes' insecurity and irresolution is at first only a nagging undertone. An eclipse of the sun that Herodotus dated to the time when the army left its winter quarters at Sardis, brought it momentarily to the surface, but the magi soothed his apprehensions.[68] He was all confidence as he reviewed his forces at Abydos.[69] Once again, he listened to the forebod-

---

[67] H. S. Nyberg, *Historia Mundi* 3 (Munich, 1954), 98–99; A. T. Olmstead, *History of the Persian Empire* (Chicago, 1948), 230; cf. Immerwahr, *Form and Thought*, 179.

[68] Hdt. 7.37.2–3.

[69] Hdt. 7.44–52.

ings of Artabanus, but this time he dismissed them cheerfully: no man should shrink from risks, he said, for it was by taking risks that the kings of Persia had built a great empire. Xerxes could not take the dangers that lay ahead seriously. He was the legatee of an imperial tradition, and in any case, his confidence was swollen by the size and brilliance of his armament. When the Persians captured three spies whom the Greeks had sent to Sardis, Xerxes saved them from execution and freed them, saying that it was better that the Greeks should know how vast his army was: they would then surrender the more speedily.[70] Size and appearance were what mattered to him; they were the yardsticks by which he measured his forces, and he could not believe that he would encounter resistance from an enemy as small and weak as he imagined the Greeks to be.

But his insecurity emerged more strongly after the defeat at Salamis. He reflected immediately that he was in personal danger and decided to retreat, though he was at pains to conceal his intention. Artemisia gave him the advice he wanted to hear: he should himself return to Persia and keep the dynasty safe, and leave behind Mardonius, who had, in any case, decided that it was better to remain than become a scapegoat for the king's defeat. It would be no great matter, said Artemisia with a hard-boiled appreciation of dynastic politics, if something should happen to Mardonius.[71]

Thus far there is a discernible tragic pattern to the career of Xerxes that invites comparison with the Croesus-*logos*. Led astray by bad advice from Mardonius, which was seconded by a dream-figure, Xerxes embarked, overconfident, upon an ill-fated expedition. He put pontoon bridges across the Hellespont, and when a storm destroyed his first pair, he ordered that the strait be given three hundred lashes and manacles be let down into it. In the *Persians* of Aeschylus, this was Xerxes' supreme act of *hybris*. It was a gesture that signified a mad belief that he could master Poseidon himself.[72] It made clear, for all the world to see, Xerxes' lack of restraint and self-knowledge.[73] As Herodotus told the story, a man of the Hellespontine area who witnessed the crossing of Xerxes' army into Europe likened Xerxes to Zeus.[74] Like Croesus, only more so, Xerxes is the victim of

[70] Hdt. 7.146–47.

[71] Hdt. 8.97–103.

[72] Cf. S. M. Adams, "Salamis Symphony: The *Persae* of Aeschylus," *Studies in Honour of Gilbert Norwood. Phoenix, Suppl. Vol. I* (Toronto, 1952), 46–54; cf. Donald Lateiner, "Nonverbal Communication in the *Histories* of Herodotus," *Arethusa* 20 (1987), 83–107, esp. 92–93.

[73] Cf. Helen North, *Sophrosyne. Self-Knowledge and Self-Restraint in Greek Literature* (Ithaca, N.Y., 1966), 33.

[74] Hdt. 7.56.2.

self-delusion which is aided and abetted by supernatural power, and his *hybris* is more conspicuous than that of the Lydian king.

Yet we should look carefully at how Herodotus tells the story. Xerxes' *hybris* at the Hellespont was done in a flash of royal anger: he acted much as Cyrus did when he punished the river Gyndes for drowning one of his sacred horses. In both instances, Persian kings violated Persian *nomoi*, for the Persians customarily treated rivers with exaggerated respect.[75] Yet it was not a calculated insult, and Herodotus thought it possible that Xerxes offered recompense once his anger had cooled. Before his army crossed into Europe, he threw an offering of a cup, a golden bowl, and a sword into the waters of the strait. Herodotus was not sure whether this was atonement for the flogging, or a sacrifice to the rising sun.[76] If it was the former, then Xerxes had had a change of heart, for the "barbarous and impious words" that Xerxes had ordered intoned over the Hellespont as it was flogged had concluded thus: "Justly do men not sacrifice to you, for you are a turbid and salty river."[77] Herodotus was not certain that Xerxes had repented of his *hybris*. But he thought it possible.

There is a similar ambiguity to the remark of the Hellespontine who saw the Persian army cross into Europe and drew the analogy between Xerxes and Zeus. Why, he wondered, had Zeus taken the likeness of Xerxes and come to destroy Greece with a great host when he could have done it all by himself? The ostensible meaning was that Xerxes was like Zeus, and the remark seems a tribute to his power. But the alternative meaning was that everything Xerxes was attempting—with a vast army that took seven days and nights to cross the Hellespont—could have been done by a real god acting on his own. The message is that Xerxes in his pride was magnificent and godlike, but in reality his power fell far short of a god's: he was merely a man. Was this Herodotus' own editorial comment? Or was it, like the suggestion that Xerxes offered atonement for flogging the Hellespont, an effort to reduce the impact of his *hybris*?

Just how far Herodotus has amended the tragic pattern is clear when we compare his Xerxes with the protagonists of two tragedies that we can safely believe Herodotus knew: the *Persians* and the *Ajax*. I have already referred to Aeschylus' play. There *moira* drove the Persians on in pursuit of war, but *ate* and divine deceit led them into a snare: the yoking of the Hellespont was an attempt by a mortal to control the gods.[78] Xerxes complained that an incomprehensible *daimon* had assaulted the Persians, and

---

[75] Hdt. 1.138.

[76] Hdt. 7.54.3.

[77] Hdt. 7.35.2.

[78] ll.93–114; 745–50. Cf. Hans-Joachim Newiger, "Colpa e responsibilità nella tragedia Greca," *Belfagor* 41 (1986), 485–99, esp. 488–89; cf. R. P. Winnington-Ingram, *Sophocles. An Interpretation* (Cambridge, 1980), 155–56.

his father recognized the action of Zeus. So far there is a parallel of sorts with the *Histories*, though with changed emphasis. Aeschylus was not constrained by the canon of historical accuracy. His Xerxes left the stage a tragic figure, sadder but wiser, and bewailing the calamity that had befallen him and his empire. In the *Histories*, the Persians at Susa rejoiced to hear that Xerxes had taken Athens, and lamented the defeat at Salamis,[79] but Xerxes himself remained untouched and curiously remote from the tragic consequences of the debacle.

In the *Ajax*, the messenger reports Calchas' words on the fallen hero who has gone off to kill himself, speaking in terms that might apply equally well to Xerxes' vast army.

> For those oversized and insensate bulks of men
> go down heavily in disaster the gods contrive.
> So spoke the prophet; such a one, grown great in man's
> stature, then thinks of himself as something more than man.[80]

Xerxes' entry into Europe was the occasion for putting his vast armament on display and for showing his pleasure in it. The trappings of power delighted Xerxes. He seemed to be something more than a mortal man. The exaggerated size of the Persian host was part of the Greek tradition, but Herodotus has used these swollen numbers with effect: the army that gladdened Xerxes qualified well as an "insensate bulk" that "went down heavily." Its great size flouted the human condition. It did not know how to be flexible, a flaw that contributed to its own downfall. But Xerxes himself met no such misfortune. Having led to destruction these forces that he had reviewed with such delight at Abydos, he returned to Sardis, safe and sound, and there he attempted to seduce his brother's wife.

In all this, the final scene is important: as Solon had reminded Croesus, one must look to the end before passing judgment. What was Xerxes' final scene? A historian did not have the same freedom to manipulate his plot that the tragic poet had; yet Herodotus knew where to place his emphasis. Xerxes was assassinated in his bedchamber in 465 B.C.,[81] and Herodotus might have transmuted this historical datum into a satisfactorily tragic end if he had wished. Xerxes' murder might have served as an example of divine retribution, if Herodotus had been interested in pursuing that theme. But he chose instead as the final episode in Xerxes' career a sordid little story of how his uncontrolled passions brought destruction upon his brother's family. Xerxes lusted first after the wife of his brother Masistes, and then, switching his affections to his brother's daughter, who had married his son

[79] Hdt. 8.99. Cf. H.D.F. Kitto, "Political Thought in Aeschylus," *Dioniso* 43 (1969), 159–67, on Aeschylus' use of historical inaccuracy.
[80] ll.758–61, trans. R. Lattimore. See Lattimore's *Story Patterns*, 18–35.
[81] Frye, *History of Ancient Iran*, 127.

Darius, proceeded to seduce her. Xerxes' queen, Amestris, took terrible revenge. The story motif parallels thus far the myth of Zeus and Semele, but the sequel differs. Masistes and his sons rode for Bactria to raise a revolt, but Xerxes' guards overtook them and cut them down. "So much for the lusts of Xerxes and the death of Masistes," concluded Herodotus,[82] wasting no words on reflections about Xerxes' character, but rather letting his story make the point.

On that note, Xerxes makes his exit from the *Histories*. He was not an unappealing man, nor by nature intolerant or cruel, but he was without self-control and self-knowledge: the qualities that can be summed up in the Greek word *sophrosyne*. Croesus had acquired wisdom from his vicissitude, and even Astyages and Cambyses achieved a clear grasp of reality in their final scenes. But suffering taught Xerxes nothing; for that matter, he himself suffered little—it was the men around him who were destroyed. Success had made the Persian Empire wealthy and self-indulgent, and yet the weight of her imperial tradition still drove her king onward to match the reputations of his predecessors as conquerors. To that extent, Herodotus appears to have seen Xerxes as the victim of an illness that attacked mature empires, but he treats the constraint that governed him like the curse which manipulated the fates of Oedipus and Agamemnon. After the battle of Plataea, Pausanias voiced the appropriate judgment on Xerxes: it was senseless for a wealthy king like him to covet the possessions of a poor people, for there could be no profit in it. The sheer greatness of the position that Xerxes occupied had isolated him from that sort of realism. But Herodotus does not leave us with an impression of a tragic king. On the contrary, Xerxes at the end of the *Histories* seems almost immune from tragedy.

This is not to deny that there are tragic elements in his persona. It would be remarkable if there were not, for tragic patterns were deeply rooted in the Greek weltanschauung in the fifth century, and the Persian invasion was the one subject from recent history that accorded the tragic poets a theme as acceptable as the myths and legends of the distant past.[83] Xerxes was the Great King par excellence, who had suffered a notable reverse of fortune. The rash, headstrong young king of Aeschylus, led on by bad advice, is to be found in the persona of Xerxes that Herodotus etches in the *Histories*, but there are other elements as well. The headstrong king of the *Histories* is also quick to repent, and willing to consult advisers and accept criticism, though he might not change his course of action as a result. He could not understand the *nomos* that impelled the Greeks to resist him, but after the terrible struggle at Thermopylae, he was willing to accept its existence.

[82] 9.113.2.

[83] Cf. John Herington, *Poetry into Drama. Early Tragedy and the Greek Poetic Tradition* (Berkeley and Los Angeles, 1985), 253n91.

Herodotus put no great emphasis on his *hybris*, except for the brief episode of flogging the Hellespont, and it was already a *topos* by the time Herodotus told the story. His quickness to anger was a royal characteristic that he shared with Cyrus and Darius, and the latter had yoked Europe and Asia with a bridge long before Xerxes. Yet the reader of the *Histories* senses that this king is an unworthy successor to the throne of his ancestors,[84] and that under his rule the cycle of Persia's fortunes has started its downward curve. This sense that there is something rotten at Xerxes' core comes out sharply in two stories that Herodotus relates: both are digressions intended as commentary.

The first is the admonitory tale with which Herodotus concludes the *Histories*. I have already referred to it in another connection, but it bears repeating. In the reign of Cyrus, the courtier Artembares advised the Persians to move from their rugged land to a more fertile part of Asia, now that they were masters of an empire. Cyrus was not surprised at the suggestion, but he warned that soft lands bred soft men. Good warriors did not come from rich soil, and if the Persians took the advice of Artembares, they must expect to be subjects rather than rulers.[85] The Persians decided to remain in their hard land. The moral was that luxury is the enemy of an imperial people.

The second story shows how far Xerxes had become a paradigm of the luxurious life that Cyrus had warned the Persians to avoid. The tableau that Pausanias staged after his victory at Plataea consisted of two meals set side by side: one was a Persian banquet prepared by Mardonius' cooks, with tables and couches of gold and silver, and the other was a Spartan meal prepared by his own servants. Pausanias drew the moral that Xerxes was mad to want to add the small possessions of poverty-stricken Greece to his wealth which was already so great.[86] But the luxury that amazed the Greeks illustrated another point as well. It was the iron law of imperialism as Herodotus understood it: hard men from hard lands are needed to build an empire, the empire in turn brings them wealth and soft living, and the soft living destroys the toughness of the conquerors and eventually makes them unfit to rule. Successful empires bear the seeds of their own destruction.

[84] Xerxes' surviving inscriptions show a man who appears to have been very much in the shadow of his father: cf. M. Mayrhofer, "Xerxes, König der Könige," *Almanach der Österreichischen Akademie der Wissenschaften* 119 (1969) 158–70.

[85] Hdt. 9.122. As part of his coronation ceremony, a king ate a peasant meal of fig-cake, turpentine wood, and sour milk, perhaps as a reminder of Persian fare before they won an empire. The demoralizing effects of luxury may also have been part of Persian tradition. Cf. Cook, *The Persian Empire*, 137.

[86] Cf. Hanna Roisman, "*Ate* and its Meaning in the Elegies of Solon," *Grazer Beiträge* 11 (1984), 21–27, where it is argued that *ate* in Solon's usage is manifested by a "lack of proper measure in acquiring possessions," and the result of *ate* is violence (*hybris*).

Yet Herodotus avoided a tragic fall for Xerxes. The last story the *Histories* tells of him is a sordid tale, which relates how his lechery brought destruction on his brother's family. Xerxes himself lived on, untouched by the consequences of his deeds. Herodotus might have referred forward to his death, and told how retribution eventually befell him; in fact, the story of Masistes' wife must have suggested it, for it involved peripherally the crown prince Darius, who had married Masistes' daughter and whose ill will for his father led to suspicion that he was involved in Xerxes' assassination. Or Herodotus might have shown Xerxes, as Aeschylus did, returning to his mourning subjects at Susa, and stressed the tragic results of the defeat. It will not do to argue that these endings would have taken Herodotus beyond his stopping point. He made a deliberate choice when he had Xerxes exit from the *Histories* as he does. We have no feelings of pity or fear for this king, but merely the sense that he is, somehow, unsound.

MARDONIUS

Mardonius is the last great Persian who deserves notice. He was the war hawk of the story, and Myres'[87] choice as the tragic hero of the last three books. Herodotus pitted him against Artabanus in the debate that followed the announcement of Xerxes to the Persian magnates that he would invade Greece, and most readers of the *Histories* must feel that Mardonius came off poorly. Both men spoke like Greeks, but Artabanus must have warmed the hearts of a Greek audience, for he uttered Hellenophile sentiments and eternal verities mingled with cautionary advice, whereas Mardonius spoke like a self-seeking politician. But Artabanus proposed a wager that, to anyone who knew the outcome of Xerxes' expedition, was charged with cruel irony. Let Mardonius lead the army himself, he said, and both men would pledge the lives of their sons on it: if the Persians won, then the sons of Artabanus would die, and if they lost, Mardonius would lose his. One, at least, of Mardonius' sons did survive to concern himself about his father's burial.[88] But his body vanished from the battlefield of Plataea, and Artabanus' grim prophecy that the Persians would hear that it had been devoured by dogs and carrion birds was close to the truth.

But Artabanus had to recant. The apparition that came to both Xerxes and himself in a dream convinced him that a divine impulse drove the Persians on, and that the gods had defeat in store for the Greeks. Aeschylus[89] called it a *daimon* that drove the Persians on, and more than any other Persian, Mardonius embodied it.

Yet Mardonius already had a past and there is more flesh and blood to

---

[87] *Herodotus*, 78; *con.*, Immerwahr, *Form and Thought*, 183n.105.
[88] Hdt. 7.10.1; 9.84.
[89] *Persians*, 472–73, 725.

him than to Artabanus. He appeared first in the *Histories* at the end of the Ionian Revolt, a young man recently married to Darius' daughter. He established democracies in the Ionian cities. He took command of a great army and fleet that purposed to advance through Europe and attack Athens and Eretria; but off Mt. Athos a storm wrecked his navy, and Mardonius returned to Europe, "having waged war disgracefully."[90]

In fact, none of this can have taken place quite as Herodotus describes it. The marriage to Darius' daughter was not recent, and the hint that he owed his prominence to it is a little unfair. What became of his political reforms in Ionia is not clear, but the story of how Mardonius set up "democracies" was probably intended as a comment on the imperial policies of Periclean Athens in the Aegean world.[91] And the expedition that encountered the storm off Mt. Athos probably achieved its objective, which was to reestablish Persian rule in the northern Aegean area. Athens and Eretria came later on the Persian timetable. There is a light odor of denigration about the introduction that Herodotus accords Mardonius, reminiscent of the similar odor that later surrounds his introduction of Themistocles. Mardonius does not deserve it.

Mardonius reemerged after the death of Darius to promote the expedition that Darius had left as unfinished business. He argued for the need to punish Greece, but to this he added another point that, to Greek ears, was patently untrue: Europe was a fertile land, with orchards of every variety, and worthy only of a king. The Xerxes of Aeschylus' *Persians* was an impetuous man led on by *kakoi andres*: evil men.[92] Mardonius in the *Histories* of Herodotus took the role of the leading *kakos aner*.

Once the expedition was under way and acquired its own momentum, Mardonius was temporarily eclipsed: he was only one of six commanders in charge of the Persian infantry. He played no role at Thermopylae, and at Salamis his only contribution was to act as majordomo at Xerxes' council before the battle, where Artemisia emerged as the voice warning against the policy of impetuous offensive. At the council itself, she merely asked Mardonius to give the king her advice to avoid an engagement; but after the defeat, she spoke with the hard-edged wisdom of realpolitik. Mardonius, fearful that the king might blame him for the failure of the expedition, had offered to remain in Greece to complete the conquest. Artemisia advised Xerxes to accept the offer, for if Mardonius succeeded, the success would be the king's; but if he failed, Xerxes would only lose a mere subject. Xerxes himself might return home and claim that his objective was accomplished: he had burned Athens. The position of the individual subject

---

[90] Hdt. 6.45.2.
[91] Cf. J.A.S. Evans, "The Settlement of Artaphrenes," *CP* 71 (1976), 344–49.
[92] ll. 753–56.

within the splendor of Persian imperial might could hardly have been put with greater realism or brutality. Xerxes was pleased with Artemisia's advice: he had intended to accept Mardonius' offer in any case.

Ten months after Xerxes took Athens, Mardonius occupied it again.[93] His Theban allies had advised against the move; instead, they argued, he should remain in Boeotia, avoid battle with the Greek alliance, and use judicious bribery to break it up. But Mardonius was driven on by a terrible longing, in part due to simple folly (*agnomosyne*), in part to a desire to signal the king, who was still in Sardis, that Athens was in Persian hands again. But there was some strategic rationale behind his move, though Herodotus does not say so, for he hoped that he might still detach Athens from the Hellenic alliance. So he reoccupied Athens, which the Athenians evacuated again, and there he waited, but in vain. Finally, when he received word from the Argives that Pausanias was marching north, he laid waste the city a second time, and beat a retreat to Thebes. His strategy to divide and conquer lay in ruins.

There was foreboding before the battle of Plataea, but not on the part of Mardonius. He sought out oracles diligently and attached the Greek seer Hegesistratus to his army; yet nothing dampened his ardor, not even the death of Masistius, which foreshadowed his own. When he met Artabazus and Gobryas in council after they had faced the Greeks for ten days along the river Asopus, his mindset was still *ischyrotere te kai agnomostere kai oudamos sygginoskomene*.[94] This was Mardonius' moment of choice, and he made it in the spirit of heedless obstinacy. Artabazus advised retreat to Thebes, but Mardonius urged his fellow commanders to ignore the evil omens that Hegesistratus' sacrifices had produced, and follow the Persian *nomos*, and join battle. He was the last spokesman for Persian expansionism and its most important victim.[95]

His final speech is full of overconfidence and incomprehension. He saw the Spartans withdrawing from their position and, thinking that they were fleeing, he crowed to the Aleuadai, "You who are their neighbours said that the Lacedaemonians did not flee from battle, but were the first men in war . . . and now we all see that they have run away last night!"[96] But he had no time for argument. The Lacedaemonians had to be caught and made to pay the penalty for everything they had done to the Persians. Without pausing to reconnoiter or draw up his forces in order, he set off on the chase, and died, fighting bravely on his white horse, surrounded by a thousand of the best Persian warriors. Mardonius, not the Lacedaemo-

[93] Hdt. 9.3.2.

[94] Hdt. 9.41.4.

[95] Cf. J.A.S. Evans, "Despotes Nomos," *Athenaeum* 43 (1965), 142–53; Immerwahr, *Form and Thought*, 321–22.

[96] Hdt. 9.58.2.

nians, paid the penalty. Xerxes had already designated him, with Sopho-
clean irony, as the man to give retribution for the killing of Leonidas at
Thermopylae.[97]

Mardonius was the supreme imperialist, who drove at the goal of conquest without hesitation or qualms. If the Persians were driven on by a
daimon to increase their empire, then Mardonius was possessed with it
more than any of his compatriots. He was also opportunistic, for he
wanted to be satrap of Greece, and was not notably honest, for he misrep-
resented its wealth. But he never wavered from his course, and on the battlefield of Plataea he was the bravest of the barbarians.[98] Herodotus portrayed many "wise advisers" in his *Histories*, such as Solon, Croesus, and
Artabanus, but Mardonius was a special breed: an "unwise adviser," who
gave the king faulty advice, which did, nonetheless, conform to the
traditions of the empire.

He had no time to learn from his suffering: a feature he shares with
characters from the theater such as Agamemnon and Clytemnestra.[99] But
nevertheless he is only a qualified tragic figure. In the first place, he is a
surrogate of Xerxes: when Xerxes went home, Mardonius took over his
mission as well as his tent and its luxurious furnishings that were to amaze
the Greeks. He suffered the penalty that Xerxes escaped. Second, he was
the moving spirit that accelerated the progress of Xerxes toward the final
debacle, though it may have been the *nomos* of Persian imperialism that
guided his way. He accepted the retribution that Xerxes escaped, and Artabanus' prediction to the assembly of Persian magnates was fulfilled, if not
to the letter, at least accurately enough. Yet Artemisia's judgment was to
the point: if great misfortune fell upon Mardonius, it would be no great
matter, for he was merely a *doulos* of the king. His fall was the fall of an
ambitious functionary, not of a great man.

In the ebb and flow of history, the battle of Plataea straddled a tidewater
mark. Mardonius, who reminded his fellow commanders before the battle
that it was the Persian custom to be aggressive, led his army to defeat, and
Persia's encroachment on Europe came to an end.

The lives of all these great despots of Asia, from Croesus to Mardonius
(who was Xerxes' surrogate), are enclosed within a great annular structure
that begins with Croesus' aggression against the Greeks and concludes
where it started, with the retreat of Persian imperialism. The year 479 B.C.
ends with Greece and Persia, or to use a larger background, Europe and
Asia, in the state of balance that existed before Croesus committed the
initial offense. Since change was a continuum, the balance was presumably

[97] Hdt. 8.114.2.
[98] Hdt. 9.71.1.
[99] Cf. Vickers, *Towards Greek Tragedy*, 64–66.

momentary: the events of the years following 479 B.C. would alter it once again, but that was beyond the scope of Herodotus' *Histories*. These men we have examined were the chief dramatis personae on the Asiatic side within the cycle of imperialism that the *Histories* covers, and it is fair to look for common characteristics.

All these individuals but Darius have some tragic elements in their characters. Given the fact that tragedy was the major literary achievement of the fifth century, it would be odd if that were not the case. What is surprising is that the tragic note is not more dominant than it is. Among the Greeks who held Herodotus' attention, the tyrant of Samos, Polycrates, had a life that followed a truly tragic pattern: he was an exceptionally lucky man who could not evade his good fortune, which roused the envy of the gods, but he fell in the end as a result of human error. His life presented a tragic pattern more complete than that of any Asiatic despot. Croesus, who is often taken as a typical tragic king, had a fall that provided him with a new persona; his former one he passed on to the king who overthrew him, and the consequences of his fall were tempered by his conqueror's well-cultivated reputation for clemency. Cyrus, who founded Persian imperialism, was in the end driven by it to his death, and the treatment that the queen of the Massagetae accorded his corpse is a wry comment on his life. But there is no great sense of tragedy. Nor is there anything tragic to Darius' life,[100] and Xerxes left a subject behind him in Greece to act as a surrogate for his fall.

Mardonius has the best claim to be a tragic figure, but he is so much the personification of the *daimon* that spurred the Persians on to conquest that we feel some satisfaction at his death. It marks the final failure of this cycle of imperialist aggression against Greece. To be sure, Herodotus was a historian, not a tragic poet, and he could not portray fictive characters in order to make the tragic patterns fit: the evidence of history showed that Xerxes did return home safely, and Mardonius did perish in defeat. But if we pose the question thus: Is the *Histories* more influenced by tragedy than it is by epic?—the answer must be no. Both Herodotus and the tragic poets abstracted elements from the same matrix of mythopoeic thought, but if we look for direct borrowings that Herodotus took from tragedy, they amount to this: he explained the relationship between gods and men, and

---

[100] I would not deny that there are incidents that can be given a tragic construal: for instance, I. N. Perisinakis (*I Ennoia tou Ploutou stin Istorie tou Irodotou*, Ioannina, 1987, 107–55) in an excellent discussion of the tragic interpretation of the *Histories*, points out that Darius invaded Scythia as a result of a surfeit of wealth, and that his bridging of the Bosporus and the Danube were examples of *hybris* (pp. 134–35). But Darius suffers no tragedy as a result, unless his hurried (but safe) retreat from Scythia can be made to qualify. His bridging of the Bosporus and Danube tempers the *hybris* of the yoking of the Hellespont by Xerxes, for he was following the paradigm of his father.

between human destiny and the human adventure in ways that could be found on the Athenian stage, particularly in the plays of Aeschylus and Sophocles.

However, all these individuals that we have examined represent various faces of imperialism. Croesus sets the pattern *in parvo*: that is his purpose, second only to getting the cycle of Asiatic expansionism started. Cyrus, introduced with the birth-myth of a founding hero, took over Croesus' kingdom and his imperial persona, and died fighting beyond the frontiers of his empire, having become a man of blood. Cambyses showed the ugly side of imperialism, but he was mad. Darius was more shrewd politician than hero: a king who organized and consolidated, but there could be no doubt of his importance in the evolution of Persian imperial power. Xerxes obeyed the *nomos* of expansionism that he had inherited, and Mardonius completed Xerxes' destiny. The career of Xerxes harks back to Croesus: Croesus listening to the cautionary advice of Sandanis against attacking the Persians foreshadows the conversations of Xerxes with Artabanus. These great imperialists repeat each other's patterns of behavior, particularly their mistakes. But these, as Herodotus conceived them, were the personas of the men who directed the rise of Asia and brought its expansion to the tidewater mark.

Finally, these leaders are not unappealing. Compare Xerxes with the tyrant Periander, and the Greek does not have the advantage. Individual characters on the Greek side, such as King Cleomenes or Themistocles, betray the denigration of special interest groups that have warped the historical tradition, but this process has left these oriental despots more or less unscathed. The exception was Cambyses, for the brutality of his conquest of Egypt was part of a tradition that the Egyptian priesthood promoted. But for the most part, in his sketches of these characters, Herodotus seems to have relied upon his own imagination. His aim was to show the sort of individuals who founded an empire in Asia, organized it, and once Asia was replete with wealth and population, crossed the natural boundary of the continent and invaded Europe. When he reached Xerxes and Mardonius, he portrayed them as the sort of men who presided over the turning point in Persia's expansion. Finally, at the end of the *Histories*, the imperialist impulse from Asia has retreated to the point where it started, when Croesus undertook to subjugate the Ionian cities.

If we turn to the Greeks and look among them for similar individuals, we face disappointment. Perhaps the reason is that biography is a genre that fitted great kings better than it did Greek politicians, but for whatever reason, until we reach Themistocles and Pausanias, we find no attempt to present a coherent picture of a man who is the product of the genius and the failings of his society. Instead, we have a series of vignettes. Polycrates of Samos enjoyed such good fortune that he roused the jealousy of the gods. His friend, the pharaoh Amasis, recognized the danger of his situation, and urged him to inflict some ill fortune on himself. Polycrates accepted the advice, and had an emerald ring which he valued thrown into the sea; but five or six days later, a fisherman presented a great fish that he had caught to Polycrates, and in its belly was the ring. Polycrates recognized the divine hand, and Amasis realized that no man can save another from his destiny. Polycrates eventually made a misstep: the satrap of Lydia offered him treasure in return for a safe haven from Cambyses. But Polycrates' greed blinded him to danger, although his seers warned him, and his daughter dreamed an ominous dream. Polycrates went to meet the satrap, who slew him and crucified his body.[101] His career illustrated two maxims that Herodotus accepted: that human experience is always changeable and the gods begrudge great good fortune to men.[102] The story of Polycrates is a tragic folktale, and its motif is familiar: it follows an inexorable human pattern that great prosperity and wealth leads to craving for greater wealth, which in turn blinds man to danger, causing his ultimate ruin.

The career of Miltiades illustrates the shifts of human fortune that affect the course of human events. He made his entry into the *Histories* on the bank of the Danube, where the Ionians posted there by Darius to guard his pontoon bridge deliberated whether or not to break it down. "On the one hand, it was the opinion of Miltiades the Athenian, who was commander and tyrant of the people of the Chersonese on the Hellespont, to obey the Scyths and free Ionia, but the opinion of Histiaeus was the opposite of this."[103] Histiaeus prevailed, and Miltiades dropped out of sight until after the Ionian Revolt was crushed and a Phoenician fleet sailed north against the cities of the Chersonese. When word reached Miltiades that it had reached Tenedos, he fled with five triremes and got away with four of them; the fifth, commanded by Miltiades' eldest son, fell into Persian hands.[104] This was one narrow escape, and it was followed by a second: when Miltiades reached Athens, his enemies brought him to trial on a charge of tyranny. But his luck held; he escaped this danger too, and was one of the ten elected generals of Athens in the year of Marathon.

At Marathon (490 B.C.), Miltiades is the center of a scene that would be repeated with only changes of detail before the battle of Salamis. The ten Athenian generals were evenly divided, and Miltiades turned to the polemarch Callimachus to break the deadlock. "It lies with you, Callimachus, to enslave Athens or make her free." Callimachus was persuaded: Miltiades, who had been unable to convince at the Danube, reversed his earlier failure, and the Athenians resolved to fight. Thereupon Miltiades waited

[101] Hdt. 3.40–43; 3.122–25.
[102] Cf. Hdt. 1.5.4; 7.10d.
[103] Hdt. 4.137.1.
[104] Hdt. 6.41.1–4.

for his own day of command to come round, even though the generals who supported him transferred their own days of command to him. Was his motive punctilio, or a wish to share not even a small part of the glory? The question did not matter to Herodotus. It made a better story if Miltiades won the battle on his own allotted day.

Probably the truth is that Marathon was a battle of desperation.[105] The Persians managed to force the Athenians to fight before the Spartans could arrive to help them. But that is not how Herodotus chose to present it. First, chance had to bring Miltiades to Marathon. He survived two narrow escapes; then fortune smiled again, and he was elected one of the ten generals. Second, the polemarch had to make the right choice. But that done, Miltiades took command of the situation: he waited until his own day in order to be completely in charge, then drew up his battle line and attacked. Fortune was favorable, the right man was in command, and the right choice taken, but Herodotus has also made his readers aware of the human will and courage behind the victory. Miltiades and the Athenians whom he led were the first Greeks to face, unafraid, men in Persian dress. But Miltiades had exhausted his good fortune.

Now at the height of his career, Miltiades asked the Athenians for seventy triremes, telling them only that he wanted to make an expedition that would bring them wealth, and with this fleet he attacked Paros. He had a private motive that we do not understand: a Parian had denounced him at one time to the Persian Hydarnes. The expedition failed, and the verdict of Delphi was that Miltiades was destined to a bad end. He was prosecuted in Athens, condemned to an enormous fine and died, with it unpaid, from a wound received at Paros. Fortune had saved him for a great moment in history; his resolve was responsible for the victory of Marathon, but then, after three instances of favorable luck, the wheel turned, and Miltiades' fall from glory to ignominy was remarkable for its speed and thoroughness. Nonetheless, we must admit that Miltiades accelerated his own downfall, for he used the great prestige that Marathon had brought him to settle a private score.

Leonidas is a different case: a hero who does not quite emerge as an individual. Herodotus[106] introduces him with his pedigree, which was a proper introit for a Spartan king; Leotychidas is given a similar introduction when he takes command of the Greek fleet in 479 B.C.[107] There was a council before the battle of Thermopylae, as there was at Marathon and at Salamis, and Leonidas chose to stay and hold the pass, but there is no theater. Leonidas is never given a speech. Herodotus accepted the tradi-

---

[105] I have argued this case in my "Herodotus and Marathon," *Florilegium* 6 (1984), 1–27.
[106] 7.204.
[107] Hdt. 8.131.2.

tion—though he admitted differing views and the consequent ambiguity—
that Leonidas sent his allies home but remained behind in the pass himself
with his Lacedaemonians to preserve the greatness of Sparta and to fulfill
a prophecy which said that Sparta would lose either her freedom or a king.
He is a truly laconic hero. He says nothing, and dies loyal to the *nomoi* of
Lacedaemon.

Leonidas was an irreproachable hero, just as Aristides the Athenian was
preeminently just,[108] but, to appropriate a dictum from Aristotle, it is not
men who are preeminently virtuous or villainous that make the most satisfactory dramatic characters. But when we come to Themistocles and Pausanias, the son of Cleombrotus, we encounter individuals who are both
entire and complex. Herodotus, because of his self-imposed limits, did not
tell the whole story about them, but he performed before audiences that
had strong opinions concerning these two men, whether well-founded or
not. Both were to fall after Xerxes' invasion was over, as totally as Miltiades. Herodotus refers briefly to Themistocles' exile in Persia, and suggests
that as early as 480 B.C., he foresaw that it might happen, and prepared for
it; but the character of Pausanias, as he portrayed it, must have been a
standing reproach to the great Spartan's later critics. Herodotus[109] makes
one reference to the later darkening of his record; nevertheless, with Pausanias he came close to fleshing out the character of a genuine hero.

THEMISTOCLES

Themistocles enters the *Histories* with a verbal echo of Homer. "There was
a man among the Athenians who had but lately come to the forefront."[110]
Subtle comparisons with the epic were part of the stock-in-trade of the
logios: not for nothing does the author of *On the Sublime* call Herodotus
"very Homeric." Xenophon in his *Anabasis*[111] was to follow his example
and use the same tag to introduce himself. Yet had Themistocles "but lately
come to the forefront"? He was, it seems, archon in 493–492 B.C.[112] But
"recently" for Herodotus was an elastic term: to cite a parallel that I have
already noted, Mardonius' marriage to Darius' daughter, which Herodotus
calls "recent" in 492 B.C., was of at least seven years standing. It suited
Herodotus to present Themistocles as the man of the hour, competent and

[108] Hdt. 8.79.1; 8.95.

[109] 8.109.5; 8.3.2. Herodotus never explicitly denies the *hybris* of Pausanias, it should be
noted: cf. Fornara, *Herodotus*, 62–66, who sees Herodotus' portrayal as a "magnificently
ironic and tragic picture."

[110] Hdt. 7.143.1; cf. *Iliad*, 10.314; Ps-Longinus, *De Subl.* 13; cf. also Fornara, *Herodotus*,
68–69.

[111] 3.1.4.

[112] Dion. Hal. 6.34.1. The date is generally accepted: see A. Podlecki, *The Life of Themistocles* (Montreal, 1975), 196.

ready to rise to the occasion. Fearful oracles had come from Delphi; yet Athens stood her ground.[113] The second of these oracles made an enigmatic reference to a wooden wall, which some Athenians thought referred to a palisade around the Acropolis, but the *kresmologoi*, who made oracle interpretation their specialty, thought it was the fleet, but whether the one or the other, the purport seemed to be defeat. Themistocles had already given the Athenians a recommendation that was "best for the season."[114] He had convinced them to use the revenues from the silver mines at Laurion to build a fleet of two hundred triremes for their war against Aegina. "For the outbreak of this war saved Greece," wrote Herodotus, emphasizing the fortuity of events quite as much as Themistocles' foresight.

Yet there emerges a portrayal of the man which is not dissimilar to that drawn later by Thucydides,[115] of one who, by the power of his intellect, could take advantage of happenstance openings and do precisely the right thing at the right time, and who knew how to reach correct conclusions on matters that had to be settled swiftly. The admiration of Thucydides is more unreserved, but Herodotus seems to accept a similar criterion for a prudent and effective statesman. Thucydides saw Themistocles as a prototype of Pericles,[116] and perhaps Herodotus did too, but with the difference that Herodotus' admiration for Pericles was less unalloyed.

The narrative moves on. Themistocles accompanied the force that the Greeks sent to hold Tempe, but after a few days it abandoned its position. The immediate result was the loss of Thessaly with its fine cavalry to the Persian side. The Greeks next decided to make a stand at Thermopylae and Artemisium, and now Themistocles, in command of the Athenian naval contingent, began to emerge as the proponent of vigorous resistance. His role was to be a counterpart of that of Mardonius, so far as historical facts allowed. Mardonius was not without self-interest, and his devotion to truth was imperfect, but his policy was unswerving: it was to press on with the attack. Themistocles too had private motives, and Herodotus notes them with such care that most scholars have inferred that he had a lively prejudice against him.[117] But Herodotus' portrait is a complex one.

[113] Hdt. 7.139.6.

[114] Hdt. 7.144.1.

[115] 1.138.3.

[116] Cf. J. de Romilly, *Thucydides and Athenian Imperialism*, trans. P. Thody (Oxford, 1963), 119.

[117] Cf. Podlecki, *Themistocles*, 71; R. J. Lenardon, *The Saga of Themistocles* (London, 1978), 82–86; K. H. Waters, *Herodotus the Historian* (Norman, Okla., 1985), 142–43; John Hart, *Herodotus and Greek History* (London, 1982), 150–52. Hart and Lenardon think that the hostility has been exaggerated, but Lenardon calls Herodotus' picture 'shockingly candid.' The standard explanation is the bias of Herodotus' sources, generally believed to be Athenian, aristocratic, and probably Alkmaeonid. However, what Herodotus wrote about Themistocles represents a deliberate choice on his part, and we should not assume that he was unable to

Themistocles was a political opportunist who used his opportunism and political skill to save Greece. He had a forthright policy, which was one of vigorous resistance. Before the battle of Salamis, he put the choice whether to fight or not to the admiral Eurybiades as clearly as Miltiades put it to Callimachus at Marathon, and after the victory he urged the Greeks to press home the attack by sailing to the Hellespont and destroying the pontoon bridges there. But he failed to convince. Eurybiades, who is as faceless as Callimachus was at Marathon, supported Themistocles at Salamis, though, to be sure, his freedom of choice was restricted, for Themistocles threatened that the Athenians would sail off to southern Italy if Eurybiades would not fight. But when the Greek commanders debated at Andros whether or not to pursue the Persian fleet, Eurybiades opposed Themistocles, and the proposal failed.[118] Thereupon Themistocles accommodated to his own advantage the policy that was forced upon him, and persuaded the Athenians to accept the unadventuresome tactics that the other Greeks wanted. The strategy which he had not wanted, had become the "best for the season," and he adopted it forthwith, for Athens could not yet act alone.

Themistocles was every commander's second choice for the prize of valor, and this was an honor of sorts, for every commander's first choice was himself.

Yet this picture of a vigorous, foresighted but flexible commander had a darker side. At Artemisium, Themistocles took thirty talents from the Euboeans who had tried without success to persuade Eurybiades to stay and fight. He used five to bribe Eurybiades and three to bribe the Corinthian admiral, Adeimantus, and the rest he pocketed for himself.[119] He schemed to persuade the Ionians and Carians in the Persian fleet to rebel, or failing that, to rouse suspicions about their loyalty; thus, whatever the result, the Greeks would gain advantage. In the event, however, most of the Ionians fought well for their Persian masters. When Themistocles accommodated himself to the Greek refusal to pursue the Persian fleet after the victory at Salamis, he contrived to put Xerxes in his debt by claiming credit for the decision, so that if his fortune changed, he might have a place of refuge.[120] And so it turned out, Herodotus added. His audience understood the allusion.

exercise judgment in his use of sources. He has opted for stories that show Themistocles crafty and self-seeking. See in general, W. den Boer, "Themistocles in Fifth Century Historiography," *Mnemosyne*, ser. 4, 15 (1962), 225–37.

[118] Hdt. 8.108.2.

[119] Hdt. 8.4–5. The Euboean payment may have been no more than the normal process of financing within the Hellenic League: M. B. Wallace, "Herodotus and Euboia," *Phoenix* 28 (1974), 22–44.

[120] Hdt. 8.85.1; 8.109.5.

Here was a man marvelously adaptable to circumstances, and wise enough not to trust fortune. Yet Herodotus diligently notes the examples of his deceit. He owed his recognition that Salamis was the right place to engage the Persian fleet to the shrewd counsel of Mnesiphilus, which need not have diminished his own astuteness, for Mnesiphilus was an archetype of political sagacity. But Herodotus hints at a degree of plagiarism: Themistocles took the advice of Mnesiphilus as his own, and gave its author no credit.[121]

Then again, once he had reconciled Athens to the cautious strategy of her allies after the victory at Salamis, he undertook to extort money from the islands that were now free of Persian domination. Andros refused his demand and stood siege, but Karystos and Paros paid. So, it seems, did other islands that Herodotus left unnamed. Themistocles used as his agents men whom he could trust to reveal nothing, even under torture, foremost among them Sicinnus, the *paidagogos* of his children whom he had already used twice as a messenger to Xerxes. He made a handsome profit for himself. The other commanders knew nothing of these activities, which must stretch the reader's credulity to a degree, for if the extortions of Themistocles were secret at the time, it is fair to ask how and why they were revealed later. Herodotus does not say.

Themistocles was a complex character: a man not only aware of the mutability of fortune but prepared for it, and hence, judged by the standard of Solon's advice to Croesus, he should be accounted wise. He accepted the truth of Herodotus' own pronouncement in his proem, that human fortune never stays at the same level of prosperity, and thus, even at the height of his success, he looked forward to the possibility of exile. Herodotus recognized that his shrewdness and intelligence saved Greece, but unlike Thucydides, who describes him as a man of unmistakable natural genius who deserves our admiration, Herodotus withheld admiration while he recorded the genius. There are parallel examples of sharp behavior: Deioces used a trick to found the empire of the Medes, Darius won the throne of Persia by a ruse that he memorialized with a monument, and Artemisia saved herself from destruction at Salamis with a deft, treacherous tactic that had the byproduct of winning her favor with Xerxes.[122] Deceit and shrewd maneuver could govern turning points of history quite as much as heroism, and Herodotus records them with a sagacious understanding of his audience's tastes. But if Themistocles redirected the thrust

[121] Hdt. 8.56–57. On Mnesiphilus, see Plut. Them. 2.4; cf. J. S. Morrison, "Introductory Chapter to Greek Education," *Durham University Journal* 10 (1948–49), 55–63, esp. 59–60.

[122] Hdt. 3.86–87; 1.96–100; 8.87–88. For the effectiveness of trickster-figures, see Carolyn Dewald, "Practical Knowledge and the Historian's Role in Herodotus and Thucydides," Raubitschek *Studies*, 47–63, esp. 53–55. See also Marcel Detienne and Jean-Pierre Vernant, trans. Janet Lloyd, *Cunning Intelligence in Greek Culture and Society* (Hassocks, Sussex, 1978).

of imperialism in the Aegean world, was that necessarily reason for esteem more than the old-fashioned virtues of honor and valor?

His natural foil was Aristides, the son of Lysimachus. Twice Herodotus[123] drew attention to his reputation for justice and virtue, quite as explicitly as he drew attention to Themistocles' deceit. No reader of the *Histories* can be blamed for concluding that Herodotus was a partisan of Aristides and biased against Themistocles. But that will not do. Herodotus never made Aristides into a fully effective figure, and if anything, he minimized his importance while praising his virtue. Aristides found the commanders of the Greek fleet quarreling bitterly when he joined them before Salamis, and he called Themistocles aside to tell him that further debate was futile: the Persians were already blocking the straits. Themistocles replied that this was a maneuver that he had wanted Xerxes to make, but would Aristides report it to the Greek commanders himself? For Themistocles was aware that if he brought them the report, it would not be credited. But neither did the Greek commanders believe Aristides, for all his integrity!

During the battle itself, Aristides led a force to the island of Psyttaleia and massacred the Persians stationed there. Herodotus' brief mention of this action contrasts sharply with the treatment it receives in the *Persians*[124] of Aeschylus, where it is a major disaster, equal in importance to the defeat on sea. At Plataea, Aristides commanded the eight thousand Athenian hoplites on the left wing; admittedly he is the only general of a *polis*-contingent mentioned by name, but even so, Herodotus is restrained. By contrast, Herodotus leaves little doubt that Themistocles was the architect of victory at Salamis quite as much as Miltiades was at Marathon. It was not the virtuous Aristides but the guileful Themistocles who turned back Xerxes. His ability to apprehend the reality of a situation and manipulate it to the advantage of the Greeks, and to himself served the cause of freedom well.

What Herodotus has drawn is a hard-edged portrait of a model, prudent politician, who was a mixture of virtues and vices. His shrewd ability to recognize an opportunity and grasp it at the right time brought him personal profit, but it also brought advantage to his *polis*. His astute intelligence saved Greece and ushered in a new development in her history. If Themistocles was guileful, that was also a characteristic of Athens, for she

---

[123] 8.79.1; 8.95.1. Donald W. Knight, *Some Studies in Athenian Politics in the Fifth Century B.C., Historia Einzelschrift* 13 (1970), 43–44, notes the paucity of information about Aristides in fifth-century sources. His reputation seems to have flourished particularly after the fifth century.

[124] ll.447–71; cf. Richmond Lattimore, "Aeschylus on the Defeat of Xerxes," in *Classical Studies in Honor of William Abbott Oldfather* (Urbana, Ill., 1943), 82–93, esp. 88–89; C. W. Fornara, "The Hoplite Achievement at Psyttaleia," *JHS* 86 (1966), 51–54.

concealed her ambition for the hegemony of Greece until after the immediate danger from Persia was past, and then pursued it with single-minded
determination. Themistocles, more than any other Athenian, typified to
Herodotus the restless, energetic spirit of Athens that led her to develop
an empire. His moves, which were always well-fitted to the occasion, had
not only immediate results but subsidiary advantages as well. He knew
how to recognize opportunities and seize them, while at the same time he
remained ready for a change of fortune.

Before we leave Themistocles, we should note that it is into his mouth
that Herodotus[125] put the cosmic interpretation of the Persian War. It is
an instance where he assumes a role familiar in folktale, of a trickster who
mediates between opposing blocs. Upon failing to convince his Greek allies to pursue the Persians, he changed tack, and mollified the Athenians,
"for it was they who were most annoyed at the escape of the barbarians,
and were eager to sail to the Hellespont." It was not the Athenian fleet that
had defeated Xerxes, he told them, but the gods and heroes, who be-
grudged dominion of both Europe and Asia to one man, and an impious
one at that, who had sacked their temples and flogged and fettered the sea.
It was Themistocles who attempted to fit the victory at Salamis into a pattern of *hybris* followed by *nemesis*. He spoke as a supple politician, and yet
his words were those of a wise man. His awareness of the place of man in
the cosmos was one that Croesus attained only after his downfall.

Sophocles provides a distant parallel that is nonetheless worth noting.
Odysseus in the *Ajax* entered the quarrel between Teucer and Agamemnon
over the body of Ajax and urged forebearance.[126] He had hated Ajax when
it was proper for him to do so, but he saw no virtue in a rigid lust for
vengeance once his old enemy was in the dust. Like Odysseus, Themistocles was neither entirely admirable nor virtuous, but he could respond with
intelligence rather than passion to a given situation, and he was capable of
a reasoned response to the vicissitudes of the human condition.

PAUSANIAS

The other individual among the Greeks with a striking and well-developed
persona is the controversial figure of Pausanias, the son of Cleombrotus.
Pausanias was the central figure in a tradition that Sparta's arrogance and
incapacity for leadership caused the Greek alliance to split apart within two
years of the victory at Plataea: the Peloponnesian allies withdrew from the
war and the rest continued to fight, leagued together in a new confederacy
led by Athens. Pausanias was eventually found guilty of medism and killed,

[125] 8.109.2–4.
[126] ll.1318–69.

and at some later date, Delphi was consulted, and judged that his death was sacrilege. Themistocles also medized, but in his case there was no ground for doubt: he became a vassal of the Persian king and there was a story that he killed himself when he realized that he was unable to keep his promise to make Greece subject to Persia. Thucydides[127] preferred to believe that he died naturally of illness, but Aristophanes[128] accepted the story and so it must have been popular. But Pausanias was not without sympathizers: at the time of his arrest, one ephor at least was considered a secret supporter,[129] and it seems that his medism was patently clear only to the apologists for Athenian imperialism.

Thucydides included lives of both Pausanias and Themistocles in his history, though they were not strictly pertinent to his topic, but he had ulterior motives: in Themistocles he found a statesman with the qualities of Pericles, whom he admired, and in Pausanias he saw a leader who exemplified peculiarly Spartan shortcomings: he was arrogant, ambitious, and without principles. But Thucydides tried too hard to demonstrate his perfidy.[130] He quotes verbatim two letters that passed between Pausanias and Xerxes to clinch his case, but he fails to reveal when or where they were found. Herodotus gave no hint that he knew them, though if he did not, that would heighten their mystery, for he visited Sparta and had good Spartan sources. Yet one passage[131] in the *Histories* makes it clear that if he did know these letters, he disregarded them. Pausanias as Herodotus portrayed him was not quite "the epitome of the knight *sans peur and sans reproche*" as Fornara[132] puts it. He was a flesh-and-blood individual capable of fear in the face of the enemy, but taken altogether, he was a genuinely admirable warrior who embodied Greek virtue.

Pausanias belonged to the Agiad royal house of Sparta, and was the nephew of Leonidas and regent for his son. He won at Plataea what Herodotus called "the most glorious victory known to us," and his conduct in its aftermath was impeccable. He had a sense of what was appropriate: witness his refusal to mutilate the body of Mardonius in revenge for Leonidas, when the suggestion was made to him.[133] He treated chivalrously a concubine from Cos who deserted to the Greeks after the defeat.[134] There may be an intended incongruity with Pausanias' later reputation in the fact that it is he whom Herodotus made the spokesman for moderation and good

---

[127] 1.138.4.
[128] *Equites*, 82–84.
[129] Thuc. 1.134.1.
[130] J.A.S. Evans, "The Medism of Pausanias: Two Versions," *Antichthon* 22 (1988), 1–11.
[131] Hdt. 5.32.
[132] *Herodotus*, p. 62.
[133] Hdt. 9.78–79.
[134] Hdt. 9.76.1–3.

sense, for the Pausanias who pointed out the contrast between the frugal Spartan meal and a Persian banquet on the field of Plataea was the man who himself succumbed to the attractions of Persian luxury a year later.

There is one discordant note: before the battle of Plataea, Pausanias succumbed to a moment of fright when he heard from the Athenians (who in turn had heard it from Alexander of Macedon) that the Persians were about to attack.[135] He asked the Athenians to exchange their posting on the left wing with the Spartans on the right, where they would face the Persians, for the Athenians had fought at Marathon and thus had combat experience with the Persians, which the Spartans lacked, whereas they were familiar with the Boeotians and Thessalians whom the Athenians faced on the left.

This is a strange story, for one year earlier the Spartans had fought the best troops that Persia had at Thermopylae, without the benefit of any more experience than Pausanias' men had at Plataea. The implication must be that only the Athenians had actually defeated the Persians on land, whereas the memory of Thermopylae inspired the Spartans as much with dismay as with confidence. The Athenians thought that Pausanias' request was sensible and cooperated. But Mardonius noticed the exchange, and moved his Persians to face the Spartans in their new position, whereupon Pausanias returned to his former place on the right wing.

The tale sounds like an Athenian fabrication, for the right wing was the post of highest honor, traditionally held by the commander. But Herodotus did not suppress the report, and seemed quite unaware that he was casting a shadow upon Pausanias. His aim was not to make Pausanias a fearless hero, but rather a good soldier who felt a natural apprehension on the eve of battle, and thought that the honor of the right wing was less important than the effective posting of his troops in the battle line.

Yet Herodotus was aware of the comparison with Marathon. In that conflict, hoplites had charged a Persian force without fear, and won. At Plataea, the Spartans paid generous tribute to Marathon. Athens and Tegea quarreled on the battlefield over the honor of the left wing, which was second in prestige to the right, and Tegea based her claim on ancient tradition that went back to Heracles and the world of mythology. But the Athenians did not rely for their claim only upon heroes from myth, for time could change the worth of a city with a valiant past. At Marathon, they said, they alone had fought the Persians and defeated forty-six nations![136] The Lacedaemonians concurred with the Athenians with a great shout.

[135] Hdt. 9.46–48.

[136] Hdt. 9.27.5; cf. Liselotte Solmsen, "Speeches in Herodotus' Account of the Battle of Plataea," *CP 39* (1944), 241–53.

Here we have an explicit claim for the superiority of recent history over the mythical "facts" of the distant past. The verdict of myth could not withstand comparison with the present. The victory at Marathon was a historical reality that had already become both status symbol and justification; a half-century later, the Athenians still invoked its memory in debate with the Peloponnesians. "For it is our claim that at Marathon, we by ourselves stood against the barbarians and faced them down."[137] Thermopylae by contrast had been a defeat, where only one Spartiate survived, and the Spartans did him no honor. Marathon provided the standard of comparison against which the achievement of Pausanias had to be measured, and it is clear that Herodotus thought he more than matched it: Pausanias won a victory that was the most glorious "of those we know."

It is a retouched portrait of Pausanias that Herodotus has sketched, and if we compare it with the tradition we find elsewhere, mainly in Thucydides, there are five significant omissions or modifications.[138] First, Herodotus[139] twice mentions the golden tripod on a bronze serpent column which the Greeks dedicated at Delphi after the victory at Plataea, but passes over the information that Thucydides[140] relates: Pausanias had inscribed on the tripod a couplet so offensive that the Spartans removed it. Herodotus[141] makes a casual mention of a bronze mixing-bowl that Pausanias erected at the entrance to the Black Sea, but says nothing about the couplets that Pausanias had inscribed on them. Yet, according to the third century B.C. historian, Nymphis of Heraclea,[142] they were still to be seen in his day. These are not serious omissions, and taken by themselves they should not arouse our suspicions. But there is more.

Herodotus[143] refers en passant to a betrothal between Pausanias and the daughter of Megabates, the satrap at Dascyleum, "for" (to translate literally) "he possessed the desire to become tyrant of Greece." This is Herodotus' only reference to the medism that Thucydides[144] reports. But Thucydides tells nothing about a betrothal to Megabates' daughter. Instead, he quotes two letters: one of Pausanias, addressed to Xerxes, wherein he offered to marry Xerxes' daughter, and the other Xerxes' reply. The two traditions cannot be reconciled, and Herodotus did nothing to lessen the mystery by adding, after his reference to the betrothal, "if, indeed, the story be true." The offhand reference indicates that Herodotus' story was famil-

---

[137] Thuc. 1.73.4.
[138] I have outlined these in *Antichthon* 22 (1988), 1–11.
[139] 8.82.1; 9.81.1.
[140] 1.132.1.
[141] 4.81.3.
[142] *FGrHist* 432.9, ap. Athenaeus 12, p. 535 ab.
[143] 5.32.
[144] 1.128.7.

iar, and the skeptical addendum shows that it was unproved. He either knew, or chose to say nothing of the quite different tale that Thucydides tells about Pausanias' medism, with its documentary evidence that, not a year after Plataea, he was attempting to betray Greece to Persia! To add to the mystery, the descendants of Artabazus, who replaced Megabates as satrap,[145] and acted as Pausanias' contact in the Thucydidean tale, are sometimes conjectured to be among Herodotus' sources. Herodotus preferred traditions about Pausanias that differed sharply from those which Thucydides accepted.

There are two other instances where Herodotus reveals his mindset. One[146] is his famous comment about the Greek naval command: the Athenians accepted Eurybiades as admiral because the allies would have abandoned the league rather than accept an Athenian, but later, when the immediate danger was past, they wrested the hegemony that they had always wanted from the Lacedaemonians, using Pausanias' *hybris* as a *prophasis*. It was the reason, true or not, that served to justify their behavior. The implication is clear: the Athenians exploited the *hybris* of Pausanias in order to establish the Delian League with themselves at its head. Their ambition antedated Xerxes' invasion: if pressed, Herodotus might have said that the first substantial evidence of it was the naval program for which Themistocles was responsible. However, Herodotus dated the beginnings of Athenian superiority back to the expulsion of her tyrant in 510 B.C., and the establishment of free government.[147]

The second instance takes us back to the battlefield of Plataea, where Herodotus made Pausanias the spokesman for moderation. It was he who showed the Greeks a Spartan meal juxtaposed with a Persian banquet and underscored the folly of Xerxes' covetousness and luxury.[148] This tableau contradicts the Thucydidean portrayal of Pausanias as a typical Spartiate who degenerated once he was away from home and free of the discipline of Spartan *nomoi*, embracing the same luxury and greed that Herodotus has him contemn. If the character of Pausanias that we find in Thucydides was based on his reputation in Athenian circles, then his portrayal by Herodotus as chivalrous, moderate, and scrupulously fair appears to be a deliberate challenge to it. It was based on an assessment of Pausanias that was not popular in Periclean Athens.

Nowhere in his *Histories* does Herodotus draw an explicit comparison between Pausanias and Themistocles. Yet, among his contemporaries, the

---

[145] I have argued in *Antichthon* 22 (1988), 1–11, that Megabates could not have been replaced quite as quickly as Thucydides implies. However, Artabazus must have taken up his satrapy before Pausanias returned to Byzantium in 477 B.C.

[146] Hdt. 8.2–3.

[147] Hdt. 5.78.

[148] Hdt. 9.82.3.

comparison was a natural one. That much we may safely infer from Thucydides, who placed the lives of these two men side by side, and considered them important enough to include in his account of the Peloponnesian War, where they were relevant only as background. We are left with the feeling that Herodotus was aware of the comparison too, and that his portraits of these men were comments on the contemporary world, which they helped to usher in.

What Herodotus thought of that world is clear enough. "For in the days of Darius, son of Hystaspes, and Xerxes, son of Darius, and Artaxerxes, son of Xerxes," he wrote, "these three consecutive generations, more ills befell Greece than in the twenty generations before Darius, some falling upon it from the Persians and some from her own chief states warring over supreme power." And elsewhere, "Internecine strife is as much worse than a united war effort as war is worse than peace." Or witness the wisdom that Croesus had learned by suffering, "No one is so senseless as to choose war over peace. For in peace, sons bury their fathers; in war, fathers their sons." Into the mouth of the war hawk Mardonius, Herodotus puts his harshest comment on the Greek way of settling their quarrels by pitched battles instead of negotiation, and we may take it as an observation on the Peloponnesian War.[149] Herodotus realized that Athens started on her road to power not with her naval program, but with the expulsion of the tyrants, and thus Themistocles was not accountable for it. But it was the policy and intelligence of Themistocles that was responsible for Athenian sea power. Without it, Greece must have fallen to Xerxes, but it also supplied Athens with a vaulting ambition for hegemony that she barely suppressed until the immediate danger was over.

Themistocles had a sharp intelligence that served the requirements of Athens superbly. The hard-edged portrayal of him in the *Histories* is a comment upon the perception of the wise statesman by the political sophists in Athens who looked back to Mnesiphilus and Solon as their precursors.[150] Themistocles was prudent (*phronimos*) but he was also deceitful and alert for his own advantage. Herodotus does not condemn deception per se; in fact, the reader senses some admiration for the ruse that Artemisia used to save herself at the battle of Salamis and the lucky way it turned out.[151] He liked a good trick, provided that it succeeded. But he withheld admiration from the sort of cunning that brought Athens the leadership of the Delian League which they then transformed into their empire, all the while claim-

[149] Hdt. 6.98.2; 8.3.1; 1.87.4; 7.9.

[150] Morrison, *Durham University Journal* 10 (1948–49), 59; Detienne and Vernant, *Cunning Intelligence*, 312–14.

[151] Hdt. 8.87–88. Ph.-E. Legrand, *Hérodote I. Introduction* (Paris, 1955), 124–25, remarks that Herodotus' admiration for the "*bon tour*" was not unique. The practiced master of subterfuge was a favorite figure of Greek myth and literature.

ing that the hegemony was thrust upon them, and justifying their imperialism by alleging that they had saved Greece.

Herodotus granted the Athenian claim that the steadfastness of Athens had saved Greece,[152] and he recognized the strategic importance of the Athenian navy. But his representation of Pausanias was a challenge to Athenian imperial propaganda. It was he who won the most glorious victory known to man. So much for the claims of Marathon and Salamis. The sympathies of Herodotus were with the hoplite soldier, with the Spartans who produced the best hoplites,[153] and with Pausanias who led them. As for the report that Pausanias made a pact with the Persians in order to become tyrant of Greece, Herodotus was skeptical.

What then are we to make of Thucydides' well-crafted tale of Pausanias' medism, where he quoted two incriminating letters to prove his guilt? It will not do to dismiss Herodotus on the grounds that Thucydides could not get his facts wrong, for the tenet that Thucydides was an early Leopold von Ranke writing *sine ira et studio* has been tattered by recent scholarship, quite as much as the equally cherished view that Herodotus was a partisan of Pericles and an Athenian citizen at heart, though never in fact. The necessary conclusion is that the two historians were on different sides of the fence. The Thucydidean portraits of Pausanias and Themistocles on the whole support the Athenian doctrine on how she acquired her empire— that the allies, alienated by Pausanias' arrogance and medism, turned of their own accord to her and thrust the hegemony upon her. Their portrayal in the *Histories* does not.

I have attempted to argue that Herodotus sketched his chief characters to fit a cycle of history, as he interpreted it, that stretched from Croesus' conquest of the Greeks on the Aegean coast down to the end of 479 B.C., when the thrust of Xerxes' invasion was broken and the Greek cities that Croesus had subjugated regained their freedom. The great oriental despots were all animated by imperialism, and their lives were illustrations of it. Herodotus used tragic patterns and motifs taken from folktales, but these were part of his literary inheritance and they cannot prove that he saw history either as tragedy or as an extended folktale. We should take Herodotus at his word. He saw history as a continuum of change within time— large cities became small and small ones became large, within a world where there was constant flux, and by the same law, empires grew and diminished.

Croesus began the cycle of imperialist aggression against the Greeks. He fulfilled the destiny of the Mermnads that was determined by the choice of

---

[152] J.A.S. Evans, "Herodotus and Athens: the evidence of the encomium," *Antiquité classique* 48 (1979), 112–18.

[153] The contrast with *Aeschylus, Persians*, is well pointed out by Lattimore, *Oldfather Studies* (at n.123), 91–93.

Gyges five generations earlier, but he also, in his person, provided a paradigm for future imperialists. Cyrus took over not merely Croesus' initiative, but a part of Croesus' persona as well. Yet his imperialism had started with a free choice: the Persians chose to be rulers rather than subjects and Cyrus died in pursuit of the imperial mission they had chosen. Darius, who shared a capacity for deceit with Themistocles, consolidated the empire and made the first move into Europe. Xerxes was a complex and not unattractive character, though a failure if judged by the standards of his predecessors. But he was driven by the *nomos* of imperialism no less than they.

Years before, when the Persian Empire was still young, Croesus had told Cyrus, "First realize this: there is a wheel (*kyklos*) in the affairs of men, and it goes round and does not allow the same men always to enjoy good fortune."[154] Fortuity in its revolution brought Persia to the height of her power with the expedition that Xerxes launched against Greece, but the wheel continued to revolve. By the end of 479 B.C., it had returned to the point where it stood when Croesus initiated the aggression of Asia, and presumably a new revolution began.

Xerxes, whom the imperialist *nomos* of Persia would not let keep still, marked the apogee of Persian power and the start of her downward journey. He was a king whose greatness clouded his perception, and who saw the pomp and circumstance of empire but could not comprehend the *nomoi* that would make the Greeks resist him, much less give them due respect. He was not a bad man, but Herodotus leaves us with the impression of a king of immoderate passions and greed.

Among the Greeks, there is an array of characters that flash vividly through the *Histories* and are gone. Herodotus, who deliberately chose an excursive style, built many of his digressions around the personas of these men, and the purposes of the digressions differed: sometimes philosophic, occasionally didactic, but often they are merely reflective of the human condition. In general, he allowed his Greek protagonists no ideals—Aristagoras was a gutless leader who stirred up the Ionian Revolt for personal motives, and Cleisthenes became a democrat against his own inclinations in order to gain political advantage for himself. He was interested in how

---

[154] Hdt. 1.207.2. Here Herodotus must owe something to the thought-world of Ionia, to which he was also indebted for some of his method of *historie*. In particular, there are points of similarity with Heracleitus: see Jonathan Barnes, *The PreSocratic Philosophers*, I (London, 1979), 57–81; W.K.C. Guthrie, *A History of Greek Philosophy*, vol. I (Cambridge, 1962), 403–92. In particular, cf. Hdt. 7.11.3, on the necessity of strife between Persia and Greece, in which one side must prevail, and Diels-Kranz 22B80 on the universality of war; Hdt. 1.5.3–4 on the eternal rise and fall of cities with Diels-Kranz 22A6 and 22B12; cf. Barnes, *Pre-Socratic Philosophers*, 71–75, 445–46. Herodotus' particular interest in *nomoi* that were the antithesis of those of the Greeks may owe something to this philosophic outlook. However, the Presocratic thought-world was only one of several influences upon the thinking of Herodotus.

great men fell: Cleomenes of Sparta died insane, Miltiades condemned and in debt, and Polycrates treacherously slain and crucified by the satrap of Sardis. He speculated about patterns of destiny and retribution in their careers, but wasted little time on moral judgments.

But with his portrayals of Pausanias and Themistocles, Herodotus did more than merely sketch vivid characters. He has chosen to make both these men, whose service to Greek freedom was undeniable, typical of the states to which they belonged. It is no coincidence that in the years when Herodotus was composing his *Histories*, there developed the type of classical portrait sculpture that portrayed the likeness of an individual, while at the same time, assimilating him to an ideal.[155] These two men are paradigms. Each represented the *polis* where he was born and reared: Pausanias was moderate, chivalrous, and admirable, while Themistocles was intelligent, shrewd, self-seeking, and deceitful.

The underlying sympathies of Herodotus seem to belong to Sparta and its Dorian way of life rather than to Athens, and yet between the two states, he is careful to give credit where he thought it due. One feels that, in the opening years of the Peloponnesian War, neither Athens nor Sparta would have been altogether happy with Herodotus' portrayals of these two great men who both had a right to claim they had saved Greece.

[155] Gentili and Cerri, *History and Biography*, 70–72.

ORAL TRADITION IN HERODOTUS

It is a fair question to ask if a history such as that which Herodotus wrote can be really finished, and there is no incontrovertible answer to it. He wrote only one work, and as far as we can guess, it occupied his lifetime, or at least that part of his life that he devoted to research. We assume that he died shortly after the *Histories* were published, although I know of nothing to prove it. So we may legitimately ask if the *Histories* are as complete as Herodotus intended, or as they would have been if he had lived longer. There are oversights that may be due to lack of revision. Herodotus twice referred to Assyrian *logoi* that he intended to write,[1] but unless they have dropped out of his narrative at some time, he failed to carry out his intention. Ephialtes, the traitor at Thermopylae, was killed by a Trachinian, and Herodotus[2] promised he would reveal why. But he never did. Possibly these are lapses that Herodotus might have corrected, had he lived longer. But the evidence is good that he reached what he considered a proper stopping point. The whole of the *Histories* is a ring composition, starting with the first reduction of Ionia by Croesus and ending with its liberation after the battle of Mycale. Within this cycle, there is a certain symmetry of events: Ionia was subjugated twice and revolted twice.[3] The circumstantial evidence is strong that Herodotus intended to extend his *Histories* no further: he had reached a point where he had finished an integral segment of historical space,[4] and his intention was to confine his researches to it.

The actual year of publication is not crucial, for the *Histories* of Herodotus must have been known while they were still a "work in progress." The

[1] Hdt. 1.106.2; 1.184; cf. F. Jacoby, *RE*, Suppl. 2 (1913), cols. 372–73; cf. J. G. MacQueen, "The Assyrian *Logoi* of Herodotus and Their Position in the *Histories*," *CQ* 28 (1978), 284–91, who suggests that the *logoi* followed 1.200 and later dropped out; R. Drews, "Herodotus' Other *Logoi*," *AJPh* 91 (1970), 181–91, who thinks Herodotus inserted his promises after he finished his second book but before final publication; Stefan Zawadzki, "Herodotus' Assyrian History," *Eos* 72 (1984) 253–67, who suggests that Herodotus intended to write a separate work and made *two* marginal notes to that effect which were mistakenly incorporated later into his text.

[2] 7.213.3.

[3] 1.169.1; 6.32; 9.105.

[4] The evidence is collected in Meyer, *Forschungen* 1, 189–92. Hdt. 8.3.4 makes it clear that a new phase of the struggle against Persia started in 478 B.C., which did not belong to *ta Medika*; i.e., the Persian Wars. Meyer points out that Thucydides uses *ta Medika* with the same connotation.

allusions to it in Aristophanes' *Acharnians* show that by 425 B.C., when the play was produced, the *Histories* already belonged to "the domain of the well known,"[5] at least in Athens, and this was not a phenomenon that could have come about overnight, given the circumstances of "publication" in a world without modern media and the instant fame which it makes possible. In any case, it is not reasonable to suppose that Herodotus, any more than a modern scholar, toiled away in isolation,[6] awaiting final completion of his work before releasing any part of it to the public. On the contrary, it is sensible to believe that parts of the *Histories* may have been in the public domain before the work was finished as a whole. Modern discussions of publication dates tend to conjure up anachronistic considerations that do not fit the conditions of the ancient book trade. The question that is pertinent is this: when did the prepublication life of the *Histories* end, and how early might a Greek with the necessary means have acquired a complete copy, perhaps not yet divided into nine books, but otherwise more or less what we have today.

Jacoby[7] argued for a date between 430 and 424 B.C.; the *terminus ante quem* rests on an argument from silence, and like most such arguments, it can be challenged. Herodotus makes one reference to the Spartan invasions of Attica between 431 and 425 B.C., in terms that he could have used only after they had ceased.[8] However, Jacoby is probably right to this extent. The *Histories, as we have them,* are a creation of the early years of the Peloponnesian War, though the research on which they were based engaged Herodotus' energies over a span of time stretching back a half century.

It is well to keep the context in mind. By the time the *Histories* were published, Pericles was probably dead. Sophocles' tragedy, *Oedipus Tyrannus*, had been produced only a few years before. Athens had already fallen victim to the plague, which proved the truth of Solon's maxim, "Man is all chance."[9] Athens and Sparta were both soliciting help from Persia: embassies went back and forth and it appears that in both states, there were individuals competent in Aramaic.[10] If Thucydides had not already gone into exile, he was soon to go; probably the complete *Histories* were not available for him to read before he left Athens. Themistocles had died in the service of Persia, but he was still remembered: a scholium on Aristoph-

[5] The phrase comes from Hartog, *Mirror of Herodotus*, 275.

[6] L. Canfora, "Il 'Ciclo Storico,' " *Belfagor* 26 (1971), 653–70, esp. 660, and n.23.

[7] *RE*, Suppl. 2, col. 233; cf. David Sansone, "The Date of Herodotus' Publication," *ICS* 10 (1985), 1–9; J.A.S. Evans, "Herodotus 9.73.3 and the Publication Date of the *Histories*," *CP* 82 (1987), 226–28. The chief proponent of a later date is C. W. Fornara, *JHS* 91 (1971), 25–34; *Hermes* 109 (1981), 149–56.

[8] Grene's note here is pertinent: D. Grene (trans.) *The History of Herodotus* (Chicago, 1987), 645n.30.

[9] Hdt. 1.32.4; cf. Thuc. 2.53.1.

[10] Thuc. 4.50.

anes reports that during the plague, the Delphic oracle told the Athenians to bring home his bones.[11] Pausanias, accused of medism, had perished at the hands of the ephors, and his death brought a curse on Sparta that Athens chose to recall on the eve of the Peloponnesian War.[12] Recollections of both men were still lively, but not any more accurate for that reason.

The Persian War itself—*ta Medika*[13]—had become a symbol of panhellenism, and the remembrance of it was charged with political meaning: it could be embarrassing as well as glorious. The Athenians claimed that the victories of Marathon and Salamis saved Greece; at Marathon they had stood alone, and at Salamis by far the largest contingent in the fleet was theirs. Thucydides had their claim voiced by their envoys who took part in the debate at Sparta in 432 B.C., and it was meant as a deliberate challenge to the reputation of Sparta as champion of Greek freedom, which she had maintained for more than a hundred years, from the sixth century until the Peloponnesian War.[14] Herodotus attested that most Greeks found the Athenian claim offensive, but he himself went so far as to agree that, had Athens failed to remain steadfast, the result of the *Medika* would have been the conquest of Greece.[15] For a perspective less complimentary to Athens we need only listen to the Corinthians at the same debate in Sparta: they said that the Persians were simply victims of their own errors.[16]

The Plataeans, under siege in 429 B.C., underscored panhellenic memories, and tried to move King Archidamus with an appeal to the remembrance of Pausanias, who had sacrificed to Zeus the Liberator in their marketplace, and pledged the freedom of Plataea. But the king turned their argument against them.[17] Thebes was sensitive: her medism was a reproach that she tried to explain away.[18] The contemporary pseudo-Xenophontic pamphlet called the *Old Oligarch* (for want of a better title), written during the early years of the Peloponnesian War, drew the connection between democracy and naval power: the *demos* manned the fleet, which was the basis of its prestige, whereas the "good, well-born men," the decent element least prone to indiscipline, made up the hoplite army.[19] Thus even

---

[11] Fr. Dübner, ed., *Scholia Graeca in Aristophanem* (Paris, 1877, repr. Hildesheim, 1969), 37 (l.84).

[12] Thuc. 1.128.1.

[13] The term was used first by Herodotus (9.64.2) to refer specifically to Xerxes' invasion, and Thucydides borrows the usage: cf. L. Canfora, *Belfagor* 26 (1971), 667, 42.

[14] Thuc. 1.73.2–5. William C. West III, "Saviours of Greece," *GRBS* 11 (1970), 271–82.

[15] Hdt. 7.139.1.

[16] Thuc. 1.69.5.

[17] Thuc. 2.71–72.

[18] Thuc. 3.56.1–4; 3.62.1–3. For the persistence of her sensitivity into the fourth century: Aesch., 3.116.

[19] Edmund Levy, *Athènes devant la défaite de 404*, Bibliothèque des Écoles Françaises d'Athènes et de Rome, Fasc. 225 (Paris, 1976), 273–75, gives a compelling argument for a

within Athens itself, a citizen's political views might color his assessment of the *Medika*. In the fourth century, the Athenian stranger in Plato's *Laws* was to praise the battles of Marathon and Plataea, for they were victories on land, whereas Salamis was a triumph at sea. Hoplite successes increased the status of the propertied class, whereas naval victories helped the *demos*, and thus contributed to degeneration.

Placed in this context, the *Histories* of Herodotus are an undiplomatic document. He did nothing to palliate the medism of Thebes: rather, the opposite.[20] He related a story of Corinthian cowardice at the battle of Salamis, which, he cheerfully admitted, no one but the Athenians believed. At Salamis, he paid tribute to the Aeginetans, who surpassed the Athenians as effective fighters. But at Plataea he noted that it was an Aeginetan who suggested to Pausanias that he mutilate the body of Mardonius, and although there was a number of fake tombs on the battlefield, it was the tomb of the Aeginetans that he singled out by name as a fraud. He was cynical about Phocian patriotism,[21] and yet was not unkind to Argos, which had medized with less excuse than Thebes.[22]

He cited the case of Athens to show that *isegorie* (ie., an equal voice in public affairs) was a good thing, for while Athens was ruled by tyrants, she was no better than her neighbors; but once the Athenians had equality, and were free to speak out as they pleased, then everyone worked for himself, thereby increasing the power of the city as a whole.[23] Yet we should not conclude too quickly that Herodotus was an unqualified supporter of Athenian democracy. The *Old Oligarch* expatiated upon a not entirely dissimilar theme, that the Athenian *demos* was skillful at acting in its own self-interest. Both observed that the people worked well for their own gain.

The success of Aristagoras in involving Athens in the Ionian Revolt demonstrated another aspect of democracy that Herodotus found less admirable. The *demos* could be easily taken in by a smooth politician with specious arguments. Aristagoras made the same points in Athens that had failed to move King Cleomenes in Sparta: Persia was wealthy, and her soldiers would be easy to defeat. But he added a smidgen of the propaganda that Athens promoted in the early years of the Delian League, when

---

publication date between 431 and 425 B.C., and prefers a date before the death of Pericles, possibly before the plague (430 B.C.); cf. Martin Ostwald, *From Popular Sovereignty to the Sovereignty of Law* (Berkeley and Los Angeles, 1987), 182n.3, 188–91. There is a body of opinion that puts the pamphlet as early as the 440s: see G. W. Bowersock, "Pseudo-Xenophon," *HSCP* 71 (1966), 33–55.

[20] J.A.S. Evans, *GRBS* 5 (1964), 236n.24.

[21] Hdt. 8.94.1–4; 8.93.1; 9.78–79; 9.85.3; 8.30.

[22] Hdt. 7.148–52. On the other hand, B. M. Lavalle has instanced examples of anti-Argive bias: *LCM* 11.9 (1986), 150.

[23] Hdt. 5.78.

Athens claimed that the Ionians were her colonists.[24] Athens should protect Miletus, said Aristagoras, for she was her colony. Thirty thousand Athenians were led astray by this combined appeal to their greed and their imperial instincts, whereas Aristagoras' craftiness was unable to seduce King Cleomenes.[25] It seems that Herodotus saw both positive and negative points to Athenian democracy, and we do not know if he reached a final verdict, or what that verdict was.[26]

On the evidence that we have, we cannot show that Herodotus was the partisan of anyone. The modern supposition that he was the house historian of the Alcmaeonids rests on the fragile basis that he interrupted his account of Marathon for a long digression, which purports to be a defense of them against the charge of medism, and he concluded with the story that the mother of Pericles dreamed that she was delivered of a lion just before she bore Pericles. However, as Plutarch[27] was later to point out astutely, Herodotus might better have served the interests of the Alcmaeonids by saying nothing. Nor should we assume that the lions bore the same symbolic connotation in classical Greece as they did in the age of chivalry.[28] In fact, one other reference that may point to Pericles sounds a faintly critical note. Among the Lycians, he reported, if a male citizen, *even if he was the first man among them*, took a foreign wife or concubine, the children had no honor.[29] If that was written not long after Pericles carried his law restricting Athenian citizenship to persons born of two Athenian parents, it was merely an interesting observation aimed probably at an Athenian audience. But after Pericles lost his legitimate sons to the plague,

[24] Cf. J. J. Alty, *JHS* 112 (1982), 8. The Athenians used this argument against the Peloponnesians immediately after the victory at Mycale (9.106.3).

[25] Hdt. 5.97.2.

[26] Truesdell Brown, *AncW* 17 (1988), 99n.3, notes that Herodotus seems to have picked up "a certain antityranny fervor" on Athens (cf. 5.66), but it is inconsistent. It is perhaps apposite to remember that oligarchic propaganda portrayed Athens as a tyranny founded on sea power (cf. A. Momigliano, "Seapower in Greek Thought," *Secondo Contributo alla Storia degli Studi Classici* [Rome, 1961], 59–67), thereby using antityranny sentiment for antidemocratic purposes.

[27] *De Mal. Her.* 863A. The wheel has come full circle since Heinrich Stein (*Herodotus*[6] [Berlin, 1962], xxv) wrote that Herodotus referred to Pericles only once but "wie einen Gott." Now Robert Develin ("Herodotus and the Alkmaeonids," in John W. Eadie and Josiah Ober, eds., *The Craft of the Historian. Essays in Honor of Chester G. Starr* [Lanham, 1985] 125–39), argues that Herodotus was not dependent on the Alkmaeonids, and A. J. Podlecki ("Herodotus in Athens?" *Greece and the Early Mediterranean in Ancient History and Prehistory. Studies Presented to Fritz Schachermeyer on the Occasion of his 80th Birthday*, ed. K. H. Kinzl [Berlin, 1977], 246–65) argues that Herodotus was never in Athens.

[28] Cf. Aesch., *Agamemnon*, 717, where Paris is a "lion" and Aristophanes, *Frogs*, 1431–33, where Alcibiades is also compared to one. See also Fornara, *Herodotus*, 55–58; *con.* F. D. Harvey, "The Political Sympathies of Herodotus," *Historia* 15 (1966), 254–55.

[29] Hdt. 1.173.5.

he persuaded the Athenians to let him enroll his son by Aspasia as a citizen,[30] and the memory of that dispensation was still fresh when the *Histories* were published. In the light of it, this comment by Herodotus on Lycian custom has a subtle point that would not have been lost in Athens.

The best we can say is that Herodotus' attitude was independent. In that respect, he was like the oral bard, who moved from *panegyris* to *panegyris* and sought his audiences where he could find them. He assumed the universal perspective of the Homeric epic: a quality that had been lost by the lyric poets of the late archaic period who wrote to confer fame upon their patrons.[31] It is hard to believe that Herodotus had a patron, and we have no solid evidence that he ever did.

Yet the effort to assign Herodotus a parti pris has had a long history. In the ancient world he was charged with being anti-Theban, anti-Corinthian, probarbarian or simply mendacious, while in the modern world he has been labeled both pro- and anti-Athenian, antiwar, an apologist for the Athenian Empire, or merely equivocal. Every historian must be influenced by his milieu and his sources, and Herodotus was no exception. But it is one thing to understand the past in the light of the present, and quite another to compose with deliberate bias. Homer's bias is not a matter of dispute, although a little scholarly effort can demonstrate that his treatment of the Greeks and Trojans was not entirely evenhanded, and in that he was no doubt responsive to the outlook of his audience. Yet what was important for the epic poet was not to promote a parti pris, but to keep alive the memory and glory of great deeds of the past. It was an outlook that Herodotus shared. Somehow, like the epic poets, he was able to maintain a degree of independence as a researcher and a performer of historical *logoi* until his *Histories* were finally complete.

Aside from the *Histories* themselves, our sources for Herodotus' life are scanty. He was born in Bodrum, ancient Halicarnassus, and migrated to Thurii at an uncertain date. The *Souda* reports a sojourn in Samos. Beyond that, our reconstruction of his travels rests on inferences from the *Histories* themselves. However, there is extensive evidence that during his lifetime he gave oral performances of his "researches," either as recitations from memory (though not necessarily repeating himself word for word), or as readings from a written text.[32] The clinching testimony is the scornful ref-

[30] See Plutarch, *Pericles*, 37.

[31] Cf. Gregory Nagy, "Ancient Greek Epic and Praise Poetry: Some Typological Considerations," in John Miles Foley, ed., *Oral Tradition in Literature* (Columbus, Ohio, 1986), 89–102.

[32] The evidence is summarized by L. Canfora, *Belfagor* 26 (1971), 658–60. Cf. H. W. Parke, "Citation and Recitation: A Convention in Early Greek Historians," *Hermathena* 67 (1946), 80–92.

erence of Thucydides[33] to *logographoi* who were more interested in holding the attention of the public than in accuracy, for the gibe included Herodotus, and may have been directed chiefly at him, since it follows an attempt to correct Herodotus on two points.[34] The word *logographos* does not appear in Herodotus, whose term is *logios*, a "man versed in *logoi*": the designation comes from the world of the presocratics,[35] from a time before historical research was separated from other branches of learning and became a genre in its own right. Thus, Anacharsis the Scyth, who was included in some lists of the Seven Wise Men, is an *aner logios*, evidently the only one that the Pontic region had ever produced.[36] As it happens, Herodotus applies the term only to non-Greeks in the *Histories*, though we should not attach particular significance to that.[37] The emergence of the word *logographos* in the late fifth century to designate a "chronicler" probably means that by then, men versed in *logoi* of the past used writing as a matter of course. The unlettered oral memorialist, who relied solely on a trained memory, was obsolescent. Authors, whether they were natural philosophers, chroniclers, or sophists, produced texts which were copied and sold in the book stalls: Socrates in Plato's *Apology*[38] asserted that Anaxagoras' works could be purchased in Athens for a drachma per papyrus roll!

Yet the author still sought a wider audience by giving public readings, or, if we may extrapolate from the example of Protagoras in Plato's dialogue that takes its title from his name, they had someone read for them. Oral performance was still the most effective method of winning public recognition: that much we may conclude from Lucian's essay on Herodotus that relates how he headed straight for the Olympic Games where his talents could get maximum exposure, and gave a public reading there. But the process of adaptation to a largely written culture in Greece was as complete as it would ever be by the last quarter of the fifth century.[39]

Public performances still went on. Historians were to continue to give

[33] 1.21.1.

[34] 1.20.3.

[35] Cf. Alan B. Lloyd, *Herodotus, Book II. Commentary 1–98* (Leiden, 1976), 16–17. Aristotle was the first to use the word "history" in the modern sense to designate the genre that Herodotus launched: cf. Christian Meier, *Arethusa* 20 (1987), 41.

[36] Hdt. 4.46.

[37] Cf. Gregory Nagy, "Herodotus the *Logios*," *Arethusa* 20 (1987), 175–84; also Mabel Lang, 203–5; W. R. Connor, 255–66. Greek *logioi* are implied in the proem of the *Histories*, which is cast as a debate between Persian and Greek *logioi*, though the Greeks are not given a chance to speak. I cannot agree with Nagy that Herodotus was himself a *logios* except in the pre-Socratic sense of the word, for though he borrowed techniques from them and used them as sources, he seems rather to have measured himself against researchers in the Ionian tradition: cf. 2.15; 2.17.

[38] Plato, *Apology* 26, d–e.

[39] Cf. Bruno Gentili, *Poesia è Pubblico nella Grecia Antica, da Omero al V Secolo* (Roma, 1984), 3–30.

them long into the future. There was no sharp break with the past: witness Lucian's stay-at-home historian who read his "eyewitness" history of the war of Marcus Aurelius and Lucius Verus against the Parthians before a Corinthian audience. But the up-to-date *logios* used writing, and produced manuscripts, which he read, or had read for him, or conceivably used simply as a kind of mnemonic device as he lectured or made his recital, adding impromptu improvisations in the course of his performance, much as an instrumental musician of the sixteenth century might have done. It is likely that the Greek *logios* arrived at his own version of the particular segment of the past on which he claimed to be an authority, much as a *griot* of West Africa did: he traveled widely in his younger years, listened to older *logioi*, and responded to the interjections of his patrons and listeners as he performed, until, by a process of repetition and modification, he attained a version that satisfied him and served his purposes.[40] But by the mid-fifth century, oral *logioi* were giving way to chroniclers who produced written scripts, and while the generic term *logios* in the *Histories*, when applied to a memorialist, may still suggest a specialist who worked within the oral tradition, the specialist could be literate and, for that matter, even read from a script. In the fourth century, even the term *logographos* lost the connotation that Thucydides had given it, and was applied generally to speechwriters and other prosewrights.

However, well into the classical period, one might still have found grouped under the designation *logioi*, specialists who were oral memorialists relying for the most part on trained memories to narrate stories of the past. Pindar[41] referred to them in the same breath as *aoidoi*, who were singers of songs (*aoidai*), and both the *logioi*, whose forte was prose, and the singers of song had the same aim: to celebrate the achievements of both the heroes of myth and legend and the more recent, tangible figures from the past, for it is likely that they blurred the distinction between the two. Their purpose was to save their *erga* from oblivion, whether they were the exploits of war or the foundation of cities. This was the first aim that Herodotus assigned himself in his proem: "that time may not draw the color from what man has brought into being," to quote David Grene's apt turn-of-phrase, or to put it more prosaically, that the great achievements of hu-

[40] Cf. G. Innes, "Stability and Change in Griots' Narrations," *African Language Studies* 14 (1973), 105–18, esp. 118. Innes based his study upon versions of the legend of Sunjata, the most famous of the Manding heroes, who established himself as king of Manding or Mali around 1235. The *griots* from The Gambia described by Alex Haley (*Roots* [New York, 1976], 574–79) sometimes recited to music, and a performance was surrounded by a sense of occasion. Their main function today is that of professional minstrels.

[41] *Pyth.* 1.183; *Nem.* 6.75; cf. Nem. 6.31; 6.47–48, where Pindar speaks of *aoidoi* and *logoi* treasuring splendid deeds (*erga*). Cf. Lasserre, *QS* 4 (1976), 113–42. For *aoidoi*, see Alan J. B. Wace and Frank H. Stubbings, *A Companion to Homer* (London, 1962), 217–18.

man activity—the *erga* of mankind[42]—might not fade with time from the collective memory of men.

Pindar's *logioi* shared the same aim as the oral bards and rhapsodes, but their medium was prose, and although there was no such thing as a standard type of *logios*, the comparison I have made with the *griots* of West Africa is a defensible one. The *logioi* to whom Pindar referred were remembrancers who, in the preliterate period, stored in their memories the traditions that society thought it important to preserve, and with the coming of writing, they gave way unhurriedly to the new technology. Probably we should also distinguish the *logios* from the *logopoios*, though the distinction may have more to do with professed aim than actuality. Herodotus applied the term *logopoios* to Hecataeus of Miletus[43] and once to Aesop,[44] and he meant by it an author of *logoi*,[45] which were intended to satisfy a more critical audience than myths (*mythoi*),[46] even though they might be fiction, as Aesop's fables were.[47] The *logios*, on the other hand, was a man versed in *logoi*, and the subspecies of *logioi* whose forte was the remembrance of things past professed to impart traditions, even though he might have no single word-perfect version of the stories he told. Africanists warn us that among the *griots* and other oral memorialists in Africa, each performance is unique, and whatever they may claim, there is no such thing as a correct prototype.[48] The remembrancer creates the past that he professes to relate.

Nonetheless, oral performances may take place in contexts of intense interaction between the person holding the memory and his listeners, particularly when the latter are emotionally involved. Thus, recollections frequently recited before others, though individual to begin with, take on perceptions and feelings about the events described that are shared by the

---

[42] For the meaning of *erga* in the proem, see H. R. Immerwahr, "*Ergon*: History as Monument in Herodotus and Thucydides," *AJPh* 81 (1960), 261–90.

[43] 2.143.1; 5.36.2; 5.125.

[44] 2.134.3.

[45] Similarly, an epic poet was an *epipoios* (2.120.3), and Sappho a *mousopoios* (2.135.2).

[46] This follows the distinction between *logos* and *mythos* made by W. Burkert, *Structure and History in Greek Mythology and Ritual* (Berkeley and Los Angeles, 1979), 3, 145.

[47] I do not find in Herodotus any evidence of the later connotation of *logopoios* (and the verb *logopoiein*) as a fabricator of tales, cf. Thuc. 6.38.2. According to Photius (*Bibl.* 72, p. 35b) Ctesias called Herodotus a *logopoios*, with pejorative intent.

[48] Ruth Finnegan, "What is Oral Literature Anyway? Comment in the Light of Some African and Other Comparative Material," *Oral Literature and the Formula*, ed. Benjamin A. Stolz and Richard S. Shannon III, (Ann Arbor, 1976), 127–66; also, *Literacy and Orality. Studies in the Technology of Communication* (Blackwell, Oxford, 1988), 86–109, where she points out that in Pacific cultures a different pattern is commonly found: the oral poet deliberately composes his poem beforehand for important occasions, and recite a word-perfect version.

entire audience.[49] Thus, the stories that a *logios* narrated could develop into an articulation of group perceptions, and if his usual audience was a genos, they would become an expression of its family lore and history. *Logioi* could serve as spokesmen and defenders of the particular traditions and historical perspectives of various groups, and Herodotus seems to have imagined them playing that role in the proem of his *Histories*, for there he envisioned Persian *logioi* setting forth the *aitia* of the enmity between Persia and Greece as the Persians saw it. The Greek *logioi* are given no opportunity for rebuttal, but we may infer their existence.

An international debate of this sort between groups of *logioi* on the cause of the Persian Wars is highly improbable, but the idea could not have been completely outlandish to contemporary Greece. *Logioi* may well have acted as champions of various epichoric versions of common traditions, and since ancient traditions might be used to resolve everything from border disputes to questions of ritual, the sort of debate that Herodotus imagined could have arisen not infrequently, though with different protagonists and on other matters.

In Egypt, Herodotus found *logioi* with the best cultivated memories,[50] whereas in Scythia he knew only Anacharsis, and elsewhere in the Pontic regions, none at all.[51] The Scyths had traditions nonetheless, though they were meager; one that Herodotus reported dated their first king, Targitaeus, exactly one thousand years before the invasion of Darius.[52] Egypt was quite the opposite. "Those Egyptians who dwell in the arable part of Egypt most of all mankind cultivate the memory, and they are by far the most proficient at keeping records of any men I have tried."[53] In addition to the *logioi* with memories that were impressively trained, there were also ancient written records in Egypt: the priests could read the names of three hundred and thirty pharaohs to Herodotus from a king-list on a papyrus roll.[54] But nonetheless, he received the king-list as an oral transmission of

[49] Joseph C. Miller, "Introduction: Listening for the African Past," in *The African Past Speaks. Essays on Oral Tradition and History*, ed. Joseph C. Miller (Folkestone, 1980), 1–59, esp. 11. J. M. Foley, "The Traditional Oral Audience," *Balkan Studies* 18 (1977), 145–53, makes the point that the audience which an oral performer faced was often emotionally bound together by kinship or common experience, unlike modern mass audiences.

[50] Hdt. 2.77.1, cf. Virginia Hunter, *Past and Process in Herodotus and Thucydides*, 50–92. At p. 58, Hunter indicates that "memory" here should be taken as "records." However, I think that much of the information which the priests gave Herodotus came from oral tradition, and when they used a written source it was more as an *aide-mémoire* than as documentary evidence.

[51] Hdt. 4.46.

[52] Hdt. 4.7.1.

[53] Hdt. 2.77.1.

[54] 2.100.1. Donald B. Redford (*Pharaonic King-Lists, Annals and Day-Books*, SSEA Publications 4 [Mississauga, Ont. 1986], 215n.49) suggests that the "330" was a misinterpretation of the plural of "hundred" and of "ten" and that the idiom (literally "hundreds and

information, and it is unlikely that he took notes as he listened, for the names of these rulers could have meant little to him, and in any case—in an era before card files and xeroxes, when the writing materials available for note-taking were scant and cumbersome—a historian's best device for storing information was his memory. On that score, Herodotus was no different from an oral remembrancer himself.

We do have one instance where Herodotus describes his technique: his interpreter read him an inscription in "Egyptian letters" on the Great Pyramid and supplied an imaginative translation, which Herodotus (so he indicates) reproduced from memory.[55] Thus, when he was faced with three hundred and thirty names on a king-list, he fastened upon a few that he recognized, such as Nitocris, Moeris, and Sesostris. These he stored in his memory, and passed over the others as unimportant. Nowadays we would recognize this as a kind of information processing: a procedure whereby what is unfamiliar is placed within the context of the familiar. Herodotus used the time-honored research methodology of the *logios*, but the questions he asked, and the cognitive framework into which he put the answers he received, belonged to the intellectual world of Greece. He probed his sources for information like a Presocratic savant, even though in the end, the *Histories* he produced were a new species of intellectual achievement.

All of this suggests that, before the *Histories* were written down and published in its finished form, long passages existed in a prepublication state as oral history. This was the meaning of Thucydides' famous gibe, that he wrote a *ktema es aei*, whereas unnamed historians wrote what he denominates an *agonisma es to parachrema akouein*. We may safely infer that this was Thucydides' acknowledgment that his history was unusual: most historians of his day did compose for oral presentation, and hoped for applause. For that matter, the conventional translation of *agonisma es to parachrema akouein* as a "prize essay to be heard for the moment," has the wrong connotation: what Thucydides meant by an *agonisma* was a work to be read at an *agon*—for instance, at Delphi or Olympia, or at the Panathenaea in Athens—where an author might set up his booth and an audience would gather to hear him perform.[56]

---

tens") meant simply "a great many." On the other hand, A. B. Lloyd points out that the total is not implausible: *Historia* 37 (1988), 33–34.

[55] Hdt. 2.125.6–7. Thucydides (1.22.1) remarks on the difficulty of storing speeches word for word in his memory, and consequently the speeches he reproduced were an approximation of what was said. Plato, *Theat.* 142c–143c, supplies an example of note-taking, but that belongs to the fourth century.

[56] Cf. J. A. Davison, "Literature and Literacy in Ancient Greece," *Phoenix* 16 (1962), 141–56, 219–33, esp. 155. I know of no epigraphic evidence as early as the fifth century for recitals at panhellenic festivals by performers whom we would term historians, though their contemporaries might not. But for the late second century B.C., we have Ditt., *SIG*, 702, attesting the performance of Aristotheus of Trezene at Delphi. Cf. A. Momigliano, "The Historians of

If he had no patron, he would probably rely, like a professional sophist, on lecture fees. Herodotus asked for a fee from Corinth—so Dio Chrysostom reported—and Plutarch has relayed the tradition that the Thebans were niggardly and unwelcoming to Herodotus, whereas the Athenians gave him ten talents! Hence, Thebes suffered from the malignity of Herodotus, and Athens, by contrast, was favored.[57] Plutarch's report is garbled; he has cited the Athenian historian Diyllus from memory, overstated the fee for effect, and made Anytus, the prosecutor of Socrates, the secretary of the council when the payment was made! But Eusebius of Caesarea relates a similar story: in 445 B.C., the Athenian boule heard Herodotus recite and gave him a prize.[58] A fee or a prize is quite credible, though one of ten talents is not, and perhaps it increased Herodotus' willingness a smidgen to recognize that the steadfastness of Athens had, in fact, saved Greece. We can find instances that parallel Plutarch's report among African praise-singers who measure the warmth of their panegyrics by the rewards they receive.[59] But if we look at the *Histories* as a whole, it is not possible to demonstrate consistent bias. Herodotus seems to have maintained his independence.

There are still traces of audience reaction in the *Histories*. His reports of the fertility of the soil in Babylonia had encountered skepticism, he remarked, and consequently he would not tell how high millet and sesame grew there, although he knew. The report of the debate on the right constitution for Persia after the usurpation of pseudo-Smerdis was suppressed and was met with incredulity, which Herodotus acknowledged. Yet he asserted that it did take place, and he returned to the point later: Mardonius set up democracies in Ionia as part of the settlement after the Ionian Revolt, which proved it was quite credible that Otanes had spoken up for democracy in that remarkable debate.[60] It seems likely that Herodotus had found his listeners reluctant to believe that Persians could ever consider democracy as a form of government for themselves, for the conventional wisdom linked Persia to despotism. And in case a listener was curious

---

the Classical World and their Audiences: Some Suggestions," *ASNP* ser. 3, 8/1 (1978), 59–75, who is skeptical of the evidence for public readings of Herodotus and Thucydides, but admits it for later periods, where it is too abundant to be denied.

[57] Dio Chrysostom, *Orat.* 37.103; Plutarch, *De Her. Mal.*, 26.

[58] The report of Diyllus, if he is correctly cited, and of Eusebius cannot be reconciled. Anytus was still active in 386 B.C. when he was archon: Hans W. Helck, *Der Kleine Pauly, Lexicon der Antike* 1 (Stuttgart, 1964), col. 417; Legrand, *Hérodote* 1, 16–18.

[59] M. G. Smith, "The Social Function and Meaning of Hausa Praise-Singing," *Africa* 27 (1957), 26–45 describes how the praise poet might station himself at a public spot, call out the name of the person he intended to eulogize, and then sing praises of him using conventional themes; but if the reward was insufficient, he might continue with the same themes, using them to put his subject in an unfavorable light.

[60] Hdt. 1.193.4; 3.80.1; 6.43.3.

about which satrap had won the prize that Xerxes had promised for bringing the most splendid contingent to the army muster at Critalla, Herodotus anticipated the question by simply admitting ignorance.[61]

Elsewhere, Herodotus appears to invoke the judgment of a group of auditors. "We know this was the reason why Ephialtes went into exile," he wrote, or that the Danube is the "largest of any river we know."[62] Or there is the occasional explanatory note designed to anticipate a question from the audience: for instance, the daughter of Otanes, Phaedyme, got a chance to sleep with the magus Smerdis and discovered that his ears were missing because the polygamous Persians slept with their multiple wives in rotation. Thus, Pseudo-Smerdis was revealed as the magus whose ears Cyrus had once cut off for some offense. There is a conversational tone to the gloss, which explained what might otherwise be unclear to a Greek public, as Herodotus related what purported to be Persian history, but in reality, was a Greek folktale on a Persian subject.[63]

In fact, Herodotus' credo, that he must "say what is said" is probably also an example of his adherence to the rule of the public performer, thereby warding off any criticism. He reported the medism of Argos, but refused to vouch for it: yet he had to report what was said. He invoked the same principle for his Egyptian stories: let those Greeks who wished use them; he would put down what he had heard. Alongside these disclaimers, we have a number of instances where he claimed to know more than he would tell. He knew the Greeks who had plagiarized Egyptian beliefs about the transmigration of souls, but he would not name them, and he would omit the names of the Spartiates who died at Thermopylae, although he knew them.[64] These hints that further consultation might be worthwhile sound like the pitch of an oral performer who is advertising the mastery of his craft.

Similarly, his silences might tantalize. It would be unpleasant to say why the Egyptians depicted Pan in the same way as the Greeks, and he would not tell why the Egyptians sacrificed the pig to the moon and to Dionysos, although he knew.[65] These are probably vestiges of the prepublication life of the Egyptian *logos*, during which Herodotus could respond to the tastes

[61] For the promise: Hdt. 7.8.14. For the admission of ignorance: 7.26.2.

[62] Hdt. 7.214.2; 4.48.1; cf. C. Darbo-Peschanski, *Le discours du particulier*, 113–14.

[63] Hdt. 3.69.7; cf. A. Demandt, "Die Ohren des Falschen Smerdis," *Iranica Antiqua* 9 (1972), 94–101; Arnaldo Momigliano, *Alien Wisdom* (Cambridge, 1975), 131. Only in Greek iconography is the Persian king depicted with his ears covered, and hence the tale of the earless *magus* must have developed in a Greek context.

[64] Hdt. 7.152.3; 2.123.1; 2.123.3; 7.224.1. R. Ball, "Herodotus' List of the Spartans who died at Thermopylae," *Museum Africum* 5 (1976), 1–8, speculates that Herodotus may have included a list of Spartan dead at Thermopylae when he performed in the Peloponnesus or Magna Graecia, but omitted it elsewhere.

[65] 2.46.2; 2.47.2.

or the prudery of his audience, or provoke curiosity with the hint that he was constrained by some taboo. When publication eventually took place, it had the effect of freezing the text, but before that time, every oral performance offered an opportunity for interaction with the audience that listened to it.

There is no accepted boundary that separates a literate from a nonliterate culture, or for that matter, oral literature from its written counterpart.[66] Guessing the percentage of Greeks who could read and write at a given date will not help. There are many gradations of literacy, from the painful chirography and labored reading of the person who rarely encounters written texts to the proficiency of the habitual reader. The Greek mercenaries who scratched graffiti in 591 B.C. on the legs of the colossal statues at Abou-Simbel[67] in Egypt could at least write their names, though the Greek alphabets they used were not the same, and one wrote *boustrophedon*. In Herodotus' *Histories* there are many stories dating back to the archaic period that take for granted a widespread ability to read.[68] Reading and writing were familiar to most citizens in fifth-century Athens, and vase paintings showing figures in the act of reading appear with increasing frequency after the beginning of the century.[69] Goody and Watt, and Vanderpool before them,[70] have remarked perceptively that the institution of ostracism reveals the mindset of a literate society, for it assumed that at the very least, six thousand citizens could either write themselves or have easy access to someone who could write for them.[71] The qualification is important, for many voters cast *ostraka* that they did not inscribe themselves,[72] and simi-

[66] Cf. Finnegan, *Literacy and Orality*, 140–46.

[67] Marcus N. Tod, *A Selection of Greek Historical Inscriptions*[2] (Oxford, 1946), no. 4. The names are in various hands; one is *boustrophedon*.

[68] For examples, see Gianfranco Nieddu, "Alfabetizzazione e uso della scrittura in Grecia nel VI e V sec. a.c.," in *Oralità: Cultura, Letteratura, Discorso*. Atti del Convegno Internazionale, Urbino, 1980, ed. B. Gentili and G. Paioni, (Rome, 1985), 81–92.

[69] F. D. Harvey, "Literacy in Athenian Democracy," *REG* 79 (1966), 585–635; L. Woodbury, "Aristophanes' *Frogs* and Athenian Literacy," *TAPA* 106 (1976), 349–57; H. R. Immerwahr, "More Book Rolls on Attic Vases," *Antike Kunst* 16 (1973), 143–47.

[70] Jack Goody and Ian Watt, "The Consequences of Literacy," in Jack Goody, ed., *Literacy in Traditional Societies* (Cambridge, 1968), 27–68, esp. 42; Eugene Vanderpool, *Ostracism in Athens*, Lectures in Memory of Louise Taft Semple, ser. 2 (Norman, Okla. 1973), 215–50. Cf. D. J. Phillips, "Athenian Ostracism," in G.H.R. Horsley, ed., *Hellenika, Essays in Greek Politics and History* (North Ryde, N.S.W., 1982), 21–43.

[71] E. A. Havelock ("The Preliteracy of the Greeks," *The Literate Revolution in Greece,* 185–207) argues that the ability to write a proper name does not prove literacy, which I do not dispute. But the institution of ostracism did assume that every citizen had access to the use of the alphabet. Modern literate societies make a similar assumption, although the percentage of functional illiterates is frequently high.

[72] E.g., the *agrammatos agroikos* of Plut., *Arist.*, 7.7–8. Herbert Youtie, *HSCP* 95 (1971), 161–76 (= *Scriptiunculae*, Amsterdam, 1973, 611–26) pointed out that there are examples of village scribes in Hellenistic and Roman Egypt who were illiterate. This seems a contradic-

larly, many Greeks who were functional illiterates or "slow readers" acquired their knowledge of literary works—to say nothing of decrees and records inscribed on stone—by listening to someone else read them aloud.

Reading aloud was normal practice in the Greco-Roman world;[73] long centuries after Herodotus, St. Augustine in his *Confessions*[74] was to record how St. Ambrose had the unusual habit of reading silently, and speculated that one reason why he did so was that, if he read aloud, his text might suggest a question to a listener, and he would have to stop and explain. (However, St. Augustine thought it more likely that he was saving his voice.) It is clear that a literary composition could be both an oral and a written work at the same time, for it "spoke" to its "readers" as long as public readings remained the norm, or for that matter, as long as anyone reading aloud to himself did not object to a listener, who might on occasion interrupt.

Thus, if Herodotus maintained the persona of an oral historian, he was following contemporary convention: by way of analogy, we should note that the historians of Tudor England whose works might be more widely known aurally than they were by the printed word, maintained a similar persona and regularly addressed their readers directly.[75] But there is one distinction we can make. The public performer who read from a text had a correct version of his composition before him, which inhibited his freedom to improvise and adapt, whereas an unlettered *logios* had no fixed version of his composition, and he could make variations as he performed, though these would grow fewer with each recital. The completion of a written text marked the termination of the creative process that produced it. But for the purely oral memorialist, the creative process need never reach final completion.

The life of Herodotus spanned a period of transition. When he was born, the spoken word was still the normal way of transmitting and publishing *logoi* about the past. When he died, Greece had progressed as far into literacy as it was to go in the classical period. St. Augustine thought it remarkable that St. Ambrose read silently, but in fact, our first literary ref-

---

tion in terms, but it does underscore the fact that an illiterate who had access to services of someone with the necessary skills could function in a literate environment quite successfully.

[73] G. A. Kennedy, *The Art of Persuasion in Greece* (Princeton, 1963), 4.

[74] *Confessions*, 6.3.

[75] Immerwahr, *Form and Thought*, 6–7, made this point about Herodotus. For Tudor England, see D. R. Woolf, "Speech, Text and Time: The Sense of History and the Sense of the Past in Renaissance England," *Albion* 18 (1986), 159–83; cf. W. Nelson, "From 'Listen, Lordlings,' to 'Dear Reader,'" *University of Toronto Quarterly* 48 (1976), 110–24. Y. Gitay ("Deutero-Isiah: Oral or Written?" *Journal of Biblical Literature* 99 [1980], 185–97), makes a similar point about D-I: the question whether it is oral or written literature is not a proper one, for even written material was meant to be read publicly.

erence to silent reading is in the *Frogs*[76] of Aristophanes, produced at the Lenaean festival of 405 B.C. The historian still gave public readings, but the difference was that they generally were now readings rather than recitals without a text. The written word directed the spoken word, not vice versa.

A generation of scholars has examined the form and structure of Herodotus' *Histories* and there is little left to add, except to make the unsurprising observation that many of the patterns which have been identified as characteristic in Herodotus are to be found in the oral literatures of other cultures as well. For instance, the annular patterns familiar to classicists who call them "ring-compositions," and binary and trinary designs are all to be found in the ballads of Mrs. Brown (Anna Gordon) of Falkland, which were collected before 1759, when the region was largely nonliterate.[77] There is an artless artfulness about the structures of oral literature that Herodotus shares. They allow the oral performer the freedom to digress, and even to digress a second or third time within his first digression, and yet never lose the main thread of the subject, for he continues to work within a pattern familiar both to himself and to his listeners.

Yet, Herodotus, notwithstanding his beginnings as an oral performer, did eventually produce a written record of his researches, and it was a work of such size and complexity that it marked its author as no mere *logios*, even though he may have shared techniques with the breed, and his achievement had the result of establishing history as a new genre. Hecataeus of Miletus had made a start. He carried over into the field of myth and legend some of the skepticism of Xenophanes. The introduction of his *Genealogies* reflects his effort to differentiate himself from the general run of *logioi*: "I write these matters as they seem to me to be true. For the *logoi* of the Greeks are many and absurd, it appears to me."[78] Herodotus stayed off Hecataeus' turf,[79] but nonetheless he was his intellectual legatee, and in Egypt we find him following literally in Hecataeus' footsteps. Hecataeus had introduced a new concept that took root. We can recognize his influ-

---

[76] 52–54. This is the common interpretation of this passage, though it might possibly refer to reading aloud with no audience present. *Frogs* 1084 also refers to the great number of *hypogrammateis* in Athens. Cf. R. Weil, "Lire dans Thucydide," *Le Monde Grec*, ed. Jean Bingen, Guy Cambier, and Georges Nachtergael (Brussels, 1975), 162–68.

[77] David Buchan, "Oral Tradition and Literary Tradition: The Scottish Ballad," in *Oral Tradition and Literary Tradition: A Symposium.* (Odense, 1977), 56–58; cf. Axel Obrik, "Epische Gesetze der Volksdichtung," *Zeitschrift für Deutsches Altertum* 51 (1909), 1–12, trans. Alan Dundes in *The Study of Folklore* (Englewood Cliffs, N.J., 1965), 131–41. For a discussion of the guideposts by which Herodotus directs his reader through his narration, see Mabel L. Lang, *Herodotean Narrative and Discourse* (Cambridge, Mass., 1984), 1–17.

[78] *FGrHist.* 1 F 1. A. Momigliano draws the comparison with Xenophanes: *Atti della Accademia della Scienze di Torino* 96 (1971), 95–105.

[79] That is the implication of 6.54–55.

ence in the declaration of Herodotus' contemporary, Antiochus of Syracuse, whom Dionysius of Halicarnassus[80] quotes: "Antiochus the son of Xenophanes has written the following account of Italy, which comprises all that is most credible and clearly true of the ancient *logoi*." Hecataeus had introduced a conception of historical truth that was based on rational judgment and research.

To be sure, there was a concept of a "truth" before Hecataeus, one that was based upon supernatural inspiration. Hesiod had denounced the lies of poets, and Homer himself had pretended to speak the truth.[81] But the concept of Hecataeus went further: what was true were *logoi* that could survive critical scrutiny, and however subjective a criterion that may have been, it meant that not all epichoric traditions were equally acceptable. While it might still be the duty of the memorialist to transmit oral reports, or as Herodotus[82] put it, *legein ta legomena*, he should also exercise judgment. Some traditions were more credible than others, and it was those which withstood rational criticism that the memorialist should accept as true. Herodotus went a step further. In the proem to the *Histories*, he turns his back on the speculations of the *logioi* on the causes of the Greco-Persian war that took them back into the unverifiable realm of myth, and stated simply that he would begin with Croesus, the man he *knew* to be the first to do wrong to the Greeks.[83]

Schadewaldt[84] argued years ago that here Herodotus was jettisoning myth and legend, which he distinguished sharply from history, but we must not overstate the case. Rather, he was staking out an area in time where his research method could produce knowledge, and wherein an explorer of the past could produce his results with the confident statement, "I know." Herodotus[85] used the word *mythos* only twice in the *Histories*, but it is clear what he meant by it: what was mythical was what could not be corroborated by reasonable evidence within human grasp. Thus, he rejected the myth of the river Ocean as a fiction of Homer. Yet as the memory of the past ascended through the generations, it blended with legend and myth, to which the Greeks accorded a space that was removed in time from the present day, but not entirely removed from reality.[86] Between the two

---

[80] *Roman Antiquities*, 1.12.3.

[81] H. Strasburger, *Homer und die Geschichtsschreibung* (Heidelberg, 1972), 21–25; F. Lasserre, *QS* 4 (1976), 117.

[82] 7.152.3.

[83] Hdt. 1.5.3.

[84] W. Schadewaldt, "Die Anfänge der Geschichtsschreibung bei den Griechen," *Die Antike* 18 (1934), 144–68; cf. C. Darbo-Peschanski, *Le discours du particulier*, 24.

[85] 2.23; 2.45; cf. A. E. Wardman, "Myth in Greek Historiography," *Historia* 9 (1966), 403–13.

[86] Cf. Paul Veyne, *Les Grecs ont-ils cru à leurs mythes?* (Paris, 1983), 28–38. *Pace* Veyne, I

spaces of historical and mythical time, there was no sharp boundary. Even Thucydides, whose criteria for authenticity should have excluded myth, subjected the legend of the Trojan War to rational analysis and used it as a source for his *Archaeology*. Herodotus did not classify all mythology with fiction. But it was not an area where his research method could yield satisfactory results. He differed both from Hecataeus, whose lineages in his *Genealogies* began with gods, and who advanced no further toward the contemporary world than the Dorian invasion, and from his coevals, Pherecydes of Athens and Hellanicus of Lesbos, whose chronicles included local legends about foundations of cities, and pedigrees of gods or heroes that received cult there.[87] Herodotus placed all of that beyond the limits of his research. For him, Croesus marked off a terrain within which a researcher could acquire historical knowledge by questioning informants, and distinguish traditions founded on sound evidence from those that could not be corroborated.

Thus, the reign of Croesus marked the beginning of the segment of the past that he sought to explore. He could say of Croesus, "*Ton de oida autos proton.*" "*I know* him to have been the first to have begun wrongful acts against the Greeks." This is the voice of a narrator who controls his evidence, and claims expert knowledge on the basis of it. Historical time, to be sure, was a continuum that stretched back into the past until it meshed with the world of myth and legend; but beyond Croesus, it became increasingly difficult for a researcher relying on human judgment to state confidently, "*I know.*" A poet might claim inspiration, but for Herodotus, that would not do. He wore the persona of a master of human knowledge based on verifiable traditions, and his medium was prose.

Herodotus makes the division again between the terrain of myth and human knowledge when he refers to Polycrates of Samos: he was the "first of the Greeks we know to make plans to be master of the sea," except for Minos and anyone else before him. But Polycrates was the first of "what we call the human race."[88] He belonged to a span of time beginning a little more than three generations earlier in the Greek world, wherein valid historical knowledge could be established by asking questions and making rational judgments, and it is probably no coincidence that modern collec-

---

do not think that the acceptance which the Greek accorded their myths differs greatly from that which a convinced Christian or Jew might accord the Book of *Genesis*.

[87] Hecataeus included, *inter alia*, the Deucalion legend: *FGrHist* I, F.13–16. Cf. W. von Leyden, "Spatium Historicum," *Durham University Journal* 42, n.s. 11 (1949–50), 89–104, esp. 90–92.

[88] 3.122.3. Cf. P. Vidal-Naquet, "Temps des dieux et temps des hommes," *Revue de l'histoire des religions* 157 (1960), 55–80 (now in English translation: *The Black Hunter*, Baltimore, 1986, 39–60). Herodotus, however, still felt free to include a digression upon Minos (7.170–71), even though he might consign him to *les temps des dieux*.

tors of oral history find that remembered traditions grow hazy and inaccurate beyond three generations, unless an organized effort is made to preserve them. But within the terrain that he marked out for himself, Herodotus sought to assume the persona of an expert whose knowledge was based on research: he "knew" the customs used by the Persians; Gyges was the first barbarian whom "we know" to send gifts to Delphi; the Satrai were never subjects of anyone, "as far as we know"; he does *not* know that there is a river Ocean. The defeat that the Messapian Iapygians inflicted on the Tarentines was the greatest disaster that "we know."[89] His product can be described by the eighteenth-century term *histoire morale*:[90] it went beyond a simple account of what happened, to embrace ethnology and geography as well. But throughout, Herodotus presented himself as an authority who knew and invited his audience to share his knowledge. He had command of the evidence.

All of this brings us eventually to the question of Herodotus' sources. Granted that his *Histories* had a prepublication life, and that Herodotus spent an indeterminate portion of his career as a combination of memorialist, and public lecturer as well as researcher in the tradition of Ionian science, he still had to find sources for his data, and that was a massive undertaking for a work as ambitious as his *Histories*. Where did he, and Hecataeus before him, find their information?

There was nothing in Greece comparable to the records of the ancient Near East, which were a byproduct of well-organized, bureaucratic kingdoms and temples.[91] Josephus, drawing the contrast, made the point that the Greek states neglected to keep records of events: "Even among the Athenians, who are by reputation autochthonous and care for learning, we find that nothing of the sort existed, but the oldest of their public records are the laws concerning homicide written for them by Dracon."[92] In 1843, an inscription was found of Dracon's law; it was inscribed in 409–408 B.C. from a copy kept by the archon *basileus*, presumably in the Royal Stoa.[93] Dracon takes us back to the late seventh century, and marks the beginning of written law in Athens.[94] In Sparta, according to the tradition, Lycurgus

[89] Hdt. 1.131.1; 1.140.1; 1.14.2; 7.111.1; 2.23; 7.171.

[90] Cf. Michele Duchet, "Discours ethnologique et discours historique: le texte de Lafitau," *Studies on Voltaire and the Eighteenth Century* 152 (1976), 607–23.

[91] F. Jacoby, *Atthis* (Oxford, 1949), 176–96; R. Drews, *Basileus. The Evidence for Kingship in Geometric Greece* (New Haven, 1983), 55–56.

[92] *Contra Apionem*, 1.21.

[93] Cf. Ronald S. Stroud, *Drakon's Law on Homicide* (Berkeley, 1968), 2–8, 28–34.

[94] Cf. John V. A. Fine, *The Ancient Greeks. A Critical History* (Cambridge, Mass., 1983), 100–104. Cf. the experience of Iceland, where in the winter of 1117, a committee set up by the National Assembly undertook the task of reorganizing and codifying the laws of Iceland, which for the most part had been preserved orally by lawspeakers until then: Peter Foote,

not only did not write down his laws himself; he prohibited anyone from doing so,[95] which, if true, would date him to a period when written law codes were already coming into being elsewhere in Greece, for it can be assumed that an action is never prohibited that would never take place. But in general, Josephus was right. The interest in redintegrating historical records and organizing archives dates to the fifth century, particularly to the latter part of the fifth century. Athens set up an archon-list in the *agora* (ca. 425 B.C.)[96] and Hippias of Elis published a list of Olympic Victors using local traditions, which Plutarch[97] considered untrustworthy. Hellanicus of Lesbos did the same for the Carneian Victors and the priestesses of Hera at Argos. Toward the end of the century, Athens converted the old Bouleuterion in the *agora* into an archive, thereby indicating that she felt the need to organize her records, and required room for them.[98]

In the same century, the logographers were at work. Dionysius of Halicarnassus provides the evidence, disputable though it may be. "Now ancient historians flourished in great numbers and in various places before the Peloponnesian War, including Euagon of Samos, Deiochus of Cyzicus, Bion of Proconnesus, Eudemus of Paros, Democles of Phygela, Hecataeus of Miletus, Acusilaos of Argos, Charon of Lampsacus and Amelesagoras of Chalcedon. Those who lived prior to the Peloponnesian War and down to the time of Thucydides were Hellanicus of Lesbos, Damastes of Sigeum, Xenomedes of Ceos, Xanthus of Lydia and many others."[99] These men wrote down epichoric traditions, and as Dionysius explained, their guiding principle was to neither subtract nor add to them: they put down even silly theatrical tales. They evidently held to the code of the *logios* summed up in the words *legein ta legomena*. They should perhaps be called not historians in the sense that Herodotus was one, but *logioi* who, at some point in their

---

"Oral and Literary Tradition in Early Scandinavian Law," in *Oral Tradition and Literary Tradition: A Symposium* (Odense, 1977), 47–55.

[95] Plutarch, *Lyk*. 11.1–3; *Mor*. 227b; cf. Douglas M. MacDowell, *Spartan Law* (Edinburgh, 1986), 3–5; Terence A. Boring, *Literacy in Ancient Sparta* (Leiden, 1979), 25. However, the rider to the "Great Rhetra" was written down by kings Polydoros and Theopompos: Plut. *Lyk*. 6.9–10. P. A. Cartledge, *JHS* 98 (1978), 35, calls Lycurgus' prohibition "doubtless apocryphal and inevitably 'Lykurgan.' " Still, he argues that literacy in Sparta was thinly spread, and "deep literacy" was the preserve of an elite "operating at the highest level of the state." (p. 37).

[96] *M-L*, no. 6.

[97] *Numa*, 1.4.

[98] Ernst Posner, *Archives in the Ancient World* (Cambridge, Mass., 1972), 102–10; A. L. Boegehold, "The Establishment of a Central Archive at Athens," *AJA* 76 (1972), 23–30. Before the establishment of a central archive, official documents written on boards or papyrus were scattered in the offices of the various magistrates.

[99] *On Thucydides*, 5 (trans. W. K. Pritchett, Dionysius of Halicarnassus, *On Thucydides*, Berkeley, 1975, 3); cf. Arnaldo Momigliano, "Greek Historiography," *History and Theory* 17 (1978), 1–28.

careers, produced texts of their recitals, and thus became chroniclers whose scripts were their *erga*. Herodotus quoted only one of them, Hecataeus of Miletus, whom Dionysius grouped (perhaps unfairly) with the others, since he tried to do more than merely "say what was said": he sought to distinguish traditions he considered absurd from those that were sound. As for the others whom Dionysius listed, the failure of Herodotus to mention them need not mean that he never encountered any of them or heard them perform,[100] but if he did, it is not likely that he distinguished them from other *logioi* who practiced their craft without producing a written version.

So the sort of contrast we make between oral and written history is a modern one, and anachronistic when applied to the fifth century B.C. All these lost chroniclers whom Dionysius lists must have produced texts that were initially meant to be read aloud, and they were quite as likely to have communicated their researches with each other orally as in written form. The most efficient way to learn from a chronicler was to listen to a public performance of his composition.

So the vexing question of whether or not Herodotus used these shadowy figures whom Dionysius listed (to say nothing of others whom he did not), would not be solved even if we did have secure publication dates for their works, for we cannot assume that he was unacquainted with them before the texts were available to read. The work of a chronicler who recited before an audience might already be in the public domain long before a script of it was ready for sale in the book stalls. Even after it was available to read, it might nonetheless continue to be better known as an oral work.

What is more pertinent to ask is what sort of help the author of a large, complex work like the *Histories* might have had from these relatively unambitious chroniclers. If Hecataeus' *Periegesis*, which embraced both Europe and Asia, took up only two papyrus rolls in the library of Alexandria, he must have been much briefer in his treatment of Egypt than Herodotus, who has been accused of wholesale borrowing from him by critics both ancient and modern.[101] How much could Herodotus have found in Hecataeus to borrow? He provided Herodotus with a frame of reference when he visited Egypt, but it seems likely that Hecataeus, who was known to Herodotus from a written text and was the only prose writer he cited, was useful to him more as a model than as a source.

The sources Herodotus commonly cites purport to be epichoric and

---

[100] Hecataeus is an exception: Herodotus was born too late to hear him give a public performance, and must have read his works himself. The latest treatment of traveling savants is Truesdell Brown, "The Greek Exiles: Herodotus' Contemporaries," *AncW* 17 (1988), 17–28.

[101] Cf. Truesdell Brown, "Herodotus in Egypt. (1) The Country," *AncW* 17 (1988), 77–87, esp. 77–79; Legrand, *Hérodote* 1, 58–61.

oral. They are commonly introduced with a prefacing phrase such as: "The
Athenians say," "The Carthaginians say," "I am telling you what the Lib-
yans say," or the like. At other times, the preface is simply: "It is said," or
"The story has it." There are more than three hundred such citations: Jacoby takes up two columns listing the instances.[102] Four times he mentions
individual informants by name.[103] In addition, he cites informants such as
the priests of Hephaestus at Memphis and the priests at Heliopolis and
Thebes whom he consulted to corroborate a story that he was told at Memphis, or the scribe at the temple of Neith at Sais.[104] He supplies the names
of the three priestesses at Dodona whom he consulted on the origin of the
oracle there.[105] But in general, his epichoric traditions come from anony-
mous informants, and Herodotus presents himself as a disinterested researcher motivated by intellectual curiosity, who collected and compared
evidence from a variety of local groups, each with a set of traditions that
apparently met the approval of the group as a whole. At least, he distinguished no divergent opinions within these groups.[106] Having collected
these various local traditions, he collated, verified, and amplified them by
cross-checking, matching them whenever he could to the surviving evidence.

Let us take an example where four selected traditions are interwoven and
attested by monuments. Alyattes of Lydia carried on a war against Miletus
inherited from his father, until in the twelfth year of it, the Lydians acci-
dentally burned the temple of Athena of Assesos. Shortly thereafter,
Alyattes fell ill, and Delphi refused him an oracle until the temple was re-
built. Herodotus attributed that much of the tradition to the Delphians.
But the Milesians had an addition that involved the tyrant of Corinth, Periander, who informed the tyrant of Miletus of the reply that Delphi had
given Alyattes. Thus, the Milesian tradition confirmed that of Delphi, and
filled out the story. The mention of Periander allowed Herodotus to digress upon his court poet, Arion, and his adventure with a dolphin, and
this tale is identified as a Corinthian tradition that was corroborated by
Lesbos.[107] Surviving monuments added authenticity: there was a bronze
figure of a man on a dolphin at Taenarum that commemorated Arion; at
Delphi there was a silver bowl dedicated by Alyattes to commemorate the

[102] *RE*, Suppl. 2, cols. 398–99; Catherine Darbo-Peschanski, "Les 'Logoi' des autres dans
les 'Histoires' d'Hérodote," *QS* 22 (1985), 105–28.

[103] 3.55.2; 4.76.6; 8.65; 9.16.1.

[104] 2.3.1–2; 2.28.1.

[105] 2.55.3. Herodotus also consulted the Dodonans connected with the shrine.

[106] Cf. H. Verdin, "Notes sur l'attitude des historiens grecs à l'égard de la tradition locale,"
AnSoc 1 (1970) 183–200.

[107] 1.19–24.

recovery of his health, and there were two temples of Athena of Assesos built by Alyattes to replace the one he had burned.

Let us take another example which involves three interlocking epichoric traditions.[108] The story of how the colony of Cyrene was founded, began with a Spartan tradition that related how the Minyans, driven out of Lemnos, came as refugees to Sparta and were at first accepted; then they grew arrogant and the Spartans were about to exterminate them when Theras, who was leading a colony to Thera, took some of them as colonists. Once the colony was founded at Thera, it seems that Spartan tradition about it had nothing to add. For the next episode, the foundation of Cyrene by Thera, the main source seems to have been the epichoric tradition of Thera. The traditions of Cyrene agreed with those of Thera except on one point: Cyrene had a different story to tell about Battus: the Theraeans made him a prominent citizen of Thera and a descendant of the Minyans, while Cyrene told a folktale that described how Battus' mother had narrowly escaped her stepmother's designs upon her life. The story of Cyrene's founding touched at one point on a Samian story of how Colaeus of Samos reached Tartessos, and this tale was corroborated by a great bronze vessel dedicated in the temple of Hera at Samos, which was bought with a tithe of Colaeus' profits. Three epichoric traditions bound together in a time sequence, and a Samian story anchored to a temple dedication make up this foundation legend.

But that is not all, for the Minyans were tied to the legends of Jason and the Argonauts, and Theras, whose line went back to Cadmus, was the grandfather of Aegeus who founded the Spartan clan of the Aegeidae, and thus there was a checkpoint with a family tradition. In essence, by means of cross-reference and rough genealogical reckoning, Herodotus attempted to place these traditions within the framework of historical time.[109]

We have another example of interlinked traditions in the story of Dorieus, the unfortunate half brother of King Cleomenes of Sparta. The Sybarites claimed that Dorieus, while on his voyage to plant a colony on Segestan territory in Sicily, heeded a call from Croton for help against Sybaris, and had a hand in its capture. The Crotoniates claimed that no foreigner had helped them against Sybaris except for Callias, a soothsayer from Elis belonging to the Iamid clan of hereditary seers. The Sybarites pointed to a shrine honoring Athena of Crathis which they said Dorieus founded after the capture of Sybaris. The Crotoniates, to corroborate their tradition, pointed out that no allotments of land had been given in their

[108] 4.145–58.

[109] Cf. E. R. Leach, "Primitive Time-Reckoning," in C. Singer, E. J. Holmyard, A. R. Hall, *A History of Technology* 1 (Oxford, 1954), 110–27, esp. 114–15.

territory to Dorieus or his descendants, whereas the allotments that were given to Callias and his descendants were still in existence. Both traditions could cite surviving evidence, and Herodotus declined to choose between them.[110]

Behind this technique, there lay an important assumption. It was that identifiable groups such as the Persians, Spartans, Theraeans, Milesians, and the like, possessed traditions that could be defined as uniquely theirs. These groups were usually ethnic groups, city states, or tribes. There were family and clan traditions as well: Herodotus cited one belonging to the Gephyraeans which claimed that they came from Eretria, but Herodotus thought otherwise.[111] Taken as a whole, however, the evidence for his use of family archives is sparse. There are no specific references to "Alcmaeonid archives," though the belief that Herodotus used them has become almost canonical among modern *quellenforschers*. He does, however, mention one attempt he made to tap family tradition: in Sparta, he interviewed Archias at his home about his grandfather who had distinguished himself in the Lacedaemonian assault on Polycrates,[112] and this may be taken as evidence that he did consult family traditions when he found them. But generally, he treated what he learned from individual sources as extra details that fleshed out the traditions belonging to groups, variously designated as "the Samians," "the Spartans," and the like.

The model, therefore, that Herodotus assumed was one where there existed a great number of epichoric traditions which might amplify, corroborate, or compete with each other, and the task that Herodotus undertook was to mediate among them, reporting what was said, noting congruence when he found it, and expressing skepticism when he considered it warranted. Not all epichoric traditions were of equal value. Herodotus approached them with the confidence of an authority, willing to state his opinion in some instances and withholding judgment in others. The persona of an oral historian who performed in public demanded that he present himself as a savant who possessed expert knowledge of past events, and possibly the demands of his profession led him to imply that he had direct access to more epichoric sources than he did. In the non-Greek world, his access must often have been second- or thirdhand. But the question that must concern us is this: is such a model credible? Was there any organized effort in the world that Herodotus knew to preserve epichoric traditions?

From that question, it is a short step to the next one: did Herodotus find the equivalent of oral "archives" among the various groups he names as

[110] 5.43–45.
[111] 5.57.1–2.
[112] 3.55.1–2.

sources, and if so, did such a tradition represent a consensus that the group possessed about its past? And how reliable would such group traditions be, if they did exist? Archaic Greece does not provide enough evidence to give a clear answer, but we may look elsewhere for analogies.

THE NATURE OF ORAL TRADITION

The search for analogies can take us far afield. The history of Iceland provides a well-documented case of the codification of oral law.[113] Before the laws were written down, they were kept in the trained memories of law-speakers who conveyed them in language that moved in well-oiled grooves, but was not set to music, like information kept in verse form. Genealogies, important both for establishing social relationships and for chronology,[114] were preserved in a number of ways. Serbo-Croatian villagers may remember their ascendants for eight or nine generations—from the founder of the clan to the present—by reducing their genealogy to poetry within the bardic tradition.[115] In Ireland before the seventeenth century, there was a class of bard, the *senchaid*, that specialized in pedigrees which they recited,[116] and the *griots* of Mali in Africa learned their genealogical lists in the form of a rapid chant: Niane[117] has noted that nine times out of ten, when a Manding memorialist is asked to repeat a genealogy slowly, he loses the thread and makes mistakes. The litany of names in meter is a variety of literature as old as Homer's Catalogue of Ships, which is essentially a list of the Greek contingents and leaders that assembled at Aulis to sail to Troy, nine years before the events described in the *Iliad* took place. The meter was essential for the preservation of the catalog.

The thesis of Jack Goody that listing as such is not a mental process natural to oral cultures does not argue against the authenticity of all lists, for even he must concede that oral catalogs do occur in preliterate cultures, such as genealogies recited in ritual situations, or words for food and ani-

---

[113] Cf. n.94. See also E. Paul Durrenberger, "Stratification without a State: The Collapse of the Icelandic Commonwealth," *Ethnos* 53 (1988), 239–65.

[114] David Henige, *Oral Historiography* (London, 1982), 97–102; also, *The Chronology of Oral Tradition* (Oxford, 1974), 3–26.

[115] Barbara Kerewsky Halpern, "Genealogy as Oral Genre in a Serbian Village, *Oral Traditional Literature. A Festschrift for Albert Bates Lord*, ed. John Miles Foley (Columbus, Ohio, 1981), 301–21.

[116] G. L. Huxley, *Greek Epic Poetry from Eumelos to Panyassis* (London, 1969), 192; cf. J. H. Delargy, "The Gaelic Story-Teller. With Some Notes on Gaelic Folk-Tales," *Proceedings of the British Academy* 31 (1945), 177–221, esp. 180. "*Seanchai* (also *seanchasai*) is applied as a rule to a person, man or woman, who makes a speciality of local tales, family-sagas, or genealogies, social-historical tradition, and the like, and can recount many tales of a short realistic type about fairies, ghosts, and other supernatural beings." Delargy is speaking of the twentieth century.

[117] D. T. Niane, *Recherches sur l'Empire du Mali au Moyen Âge* (Paris, 1975), 8n.2.

mals.[118] Even in societies where writing is available, but literacy is restricted, the old methods of preserving genealogies may live on, as long as pedigrees are important for defining family status. Some Gaelic-speaking Scottish families who settled in Nova Scotia preserved their family trees by a simple expedient: the head of the house gathered the boys together after Sunday Mass and had them recite their ancestors' names for up to twenty-one generations,[119] and in Iceland, the genealogies of the Scandinavian settlers on the island were preserved orally until Ari Thorgilsson entered them in the *Landnamabok* which he compiled in the twelfth century. These were lists kept for a purpose: pedigrees are signposts for social relationships. Thus, Lord Macaulay remarked that, while English esquires of the seventeenth century were unlettered, they knew the genealogies and coats of arms of all their neighbors. This is a significant point to consider when we assess the verity of family traditions: a family might magnify its own past, but neighboring families lacked any similar motive for pretense, and hence to some degree they served to keep family traditions honest. It was Macaulay, too, who noted one of the characteristic inaccuracies of oral tradition: its inflation of statistics—even intelligent men accepted wildly exaggerated estimates of the population of England in 1685.[120] Herodotus' reckoning of the size of Xerxes' army is an unrecognized parallel.

Long before Milman Parry began to collect the modern oral poetry of Yugoslavia, Fr. J.-F. Lafitau in 1724 reported that among the Iroquois, a professional singer (with occasional relief from an assistant) would sing songs in archaic style about the heroic deeds performed in the past, at the feast given to celebrate a young hunter's first kill.[121] These were apparently oral bards with special training, who took apprentices in order to pass on their skills and erudition. There are examples of nonliterate societies setting up schools for formal training in oral traditions, and they are as far apart as Peru, Ireland, Polynesia, and precolonial Africa.[122] It is, indeed, Africa that provides the greatest wealth of information, including some suggestive analogies for our purposes.

[118] Goody (*Domestication of the Savage Mind*, 74–111), argues that arranging things in a list is a mode of classifying them, and that this sort of classification is extraordinary in oral conditions. Genealogies, however, are kept for practical purposes, not from any simple desire to preserve information: cf. J. Vansina, *Oral Tradition as History* (Madison, 1985), 178–85. However, Goody's argument does affect lists such as the archon list set up in the Athenian *agora* about 425 B.C. (*M-L* 6). Such a register could not be the product of an illiterate society, if his theory is right.

[119] James McGivern, "The Beckoning Past," *Imperial Oil Review* 63/4 (1979), 24–27.

[120] *The Works of Lord Macaulay*, ed. Lady Trevelyan, 1 (London, 1879), 221–22, 251.

[121] Fr. Joseph François Lafitau, *Customs of the American Indians Compared with the Customs of Primitive Indians*, trans. William N. Fenton and Elizabeth L. Moore, 1, (Toronto, 1974), 318–19.

[122] Jan Vansina, *Oral Tradition. A Study in Historical Methodology* (Chicago, 1965), 31–34.

Alex Haley's *Roots* has recently brought public attention to the *griots* of The Gambia, but in fact, most societies in Africa made an organized effort to record their traditions which, in the absence of writing, were transmitted orally. They became a chain of testimonies passed on by word of mouth from generation to generation, and preserved by conscious effort, for without it, memories grow faded after three generations.[123] History was kept by remembrancers, who might go under various labels. In the hierarchical societies of precolonial West Africa, the *griots* served as living archives. Each princely family had its *griot* to preserve its traditions, and it was from among his *griots* that a king chose the tutor for his children. The social upheavals caused by colonization followed by decolonization have reduced the status of the *griots*, and they have retreated to the villages, where Alex Haley found his; but at one time, they functioned as hereditary remembrancers of the traditions of their kingdoms.

They learned their craft not merely from their fathers, but from extensive traveling to listen to other *griots*.[124] In Nigeria, the Yoruba town of Ketu had an official called the *baba elegun* whose duty it was to know the town's traditions by heart, and to recite them at the coronation of each new ruler. The office was hereditary in the Oyede family, where the traditions were passed from father to son.[125] In Mali, each village had a *griot* who was the village historian: he held, so to speak, the village "chair" of history. He chose and saw to the training of his successor, whose education might take several years and entail a tour of the Manding villages to learn from famous memorialists. One village in particular, Keyla (near Kaba, the seat of the emperors of Mali), developed a reputation as a center of *griot* education, and attracted *griots* from far afield.[126]

Similar officials who stored records in their memories and might suffer punishment if they made mistakes, could be found at the courts of most African kings. Rwanda, which was a caste society headed by a king (the *Mwami*) until 1961, when a republic was proclaimed, had genealogists, who could recite catalogs of kings and queen mothers; memorialists, who stored in memory the important events of each reign; rhapsodes who could recite the panegyrics of the kings; and finally, the *abiiru*, the preservers of the secrets of the dynasty, who, unlike the other groups of experts, formed

[123] Vansina, *Oral Tradition* (1965), 21–30; also "Once Upon a Time: Oral Tradition as History in Africa," *Daedalus* 100 (1971), 442–68; also, *Kingdoms of the Savanna* (Madison, 1968).

[124] Djibril Tamsir Niane, *Soundjata, ou l'épopée Mandingue* (Paris and Dakar, 1960), 5–11, 150–53; also, *Recherches sur l'Empire du Mali au Moyen Âge* (Paris, 1975), 7–33; Jack Goody, *The Interface between the Written and the Oral* (Cambridge, 1987), 101–9; Innes, *African Language Studies* 17 (1973), 117–18.

[125] Vansina, *Oral Tradition* (1985), 37.

[126] Niane, *Recherches*, 8–11.

a hereditary caste.[127] Not infrequently, the remembrancers were persons entrusted with ritual duties: among the Ovimbundu, it was the gravekeepers of the kings who preserved royal traditions.

Relics and mementos might serve as mnemonic devices in Africa as elsewhere:[128] among the Ashanti of Ghana, for instance, the keeper of the king's stool had to know the stool's history. All these historical tales were in a sense official; they were recited by specialists on ceremonial occasions and were transmitted within particular social groups, whose interests they served.

Thus, the general history of a tribe, which was usually the history of the ruling house when there was one, served the interests of the tribe as the tribe perceived it. There were also traditions handed down by families and clans which leaned to some extent in favor of the kinship groups that preserved them, and there were religious traditions too, connected with myths and ritual formulas. There were also private traditions: the sort of popular lore and individual recollections with which Macaulay fleshed out his picture of seventeenth-century England. But the recording of private traditions was relatively slipshod. They possess the advantage of being less subject to official distortion,[129] but they have a kindred variety of bias: they tend to put the source of the tradition, whether an individual or group, in a favorable light.

Social structure has an enormous influence not only upon the manner by which traditions are preserved, but also upon their shape. In Burundi, traditions were brief, unlike those of neighboring Rwanda, for they were recited at informal gatherings where everyone wanted to have his say. In Rwanda, by contrast, where a professional reciter was expected to entertain his patron for a whole evening, traditions might be deliberately lengthened.[130] The great Tutsi families of Rwanda, who held their fiefs from the *Mwami*, liked listening to tales about the exploits of past kings, and their preferences gave professional reciters who looked for favors an

[127] The college of *abiiru* (singular *mwiiru*) was made up of hereditary experts who guarded the secrets of royal ritual and taboo, and carried them out. See Lucy Mair, *African Societies* (Cambridge, 1974), 170–71; Vansina, *Oral Tradition* (1985), 36–39; id., *Oral Tradition* (1965), 78–80.

[128] M. T. Clanchy, *From Memory to Written Record. England, 1066–1307* (London, 1979), 21–28, notes the use of objects (e.g., swords) as mnemonic devices in medieval England. Hdt. 8.120 provides an analogy: two gifts of Xerxes to the Abderites were evidence that Xerxes took the overland route back to Asia and did not embark on ship at Eion on the Strymon.

[129] Cf. Claude-Helene Perrot, "De la richesse au pouvoir: les origines d'une chefferie du Ndenye (Côte d'Ivoire)," *Cahiers d'Études Africaines* 61–62 (16), 173–87 who shows how the official oral history of the chiefdom of Yakessa, recited on ritual occasions, differed significantly from a private tradition that she learned from a neighboring chief.

[130] Vansina, *Daedalus* 100 (1971), 446.

incentive to learn them. But Rundi society was more fluid. Historical accounts might be told by a person sitting in a circle sipping beer, and his auditors would break in with their contributions. There was no time for long recitals, and thus in Burundi, history was told in tales, songs, and proverbs.

Moreover, a literary genre might impose conventional requirements upon a reciter. Vansina[131] reports a recitation by a young Rundi of some verses in praise of himself, where he named the enemies he had killed with his lance or bow. When questioned, he admitted freely that he had not killed anyone, but that he was following the conventions of his poetic genre: the *amazina* that he had recited was a type of poem where one had to boast of mighty deeds, real or imaginary. Mythopoeic motifs, conventional language, and the etiquette of the genre might all warp the historical accuracy of the data. But in no case was historical accuracy the prime consideration. The *logoi*[132] of these tribes, to use a Greek term, were made up of what they chose to remember.

It could be a conscious choice made by community decision. Vansina reported that among the Kuba people of Zaire, who have a passion for history, the criterion of historical truth is consensus, and official traditions are not recited before the consensus have been tested and affirmed in a closed-door meeting of the appropriate council. To the Kuba, "to believe" is "to agree," and consequently, tradition is founded on agreement and can be changed in the same way, and a new "historical truth" established by consensus.[133] The Kuba are perhaps an extreme case of history made by community decision, but the tendency is common. Among the Igbo of Nigeria, J. N. Onije reported a dispute between the elders of the tribe and later immigrants who felt that the elders' version of tribal history undermined their standing in the community. Privately, the immigrants admitted that the elders were right, but the question at issue was not historical accuracy but the status that traditions could bestow upon individuals and groups within the tribe.[134]

Vansina's experience with the Kuba is relevant here. In 1957, he produced a dissertation which analyzed Kuba traditions in detail at every level:

[131] Vansina, *Oral Tradition* (1965), 89–90.

[132] Ibid., 141–82. Vansina classifies African oral literature as follows: 1) Formulas, including didactic and ritual formulas; 2) Poetry, official or private, including historical, panegyrical, religious, and personal poetry; 3) Lists, including genealogies; 4) Tales, dealing with general, local, or family history, myths, including aetiological myths, tales of artistic merit and personal recollections, which, by their nature, were transmitted without external control. See also Vansina, *Oral Tradition* (1985), 79–83.

[133] Jan Vansina, *The Children of Woot. A History of the Kuba People* (Madison, 1978), 18–19.

[134] "The Ngwa-Igbo Clan of Southeastern Nigeria. An Oral Overview," *Oral History Review* 9 (1981), 65–84.

family, clan, village, chiefdom, and kingdom.[135] Twenty years later he re-examined his data in the light of later research and concluded that a great deal that he had taken as history was fiction. The Kuba legends of tribal origins and migrations represented a fabrication of the past. These traditions of the Kuba, which he had taken from an official spokesman who had rehearsed them first with the chief and all the notables, were official history, and represented what the leaders of the community had chosen to regard as true. This is consensual history with a vengeance, and the process of creating history by consensus can take place with particular ease in a purely oral context, for no documents survive from the past to bear witness to earlier interpretations that might introduce a discrepant note. But we should not imagine that this operation of recreating the past in order to put the present in an appropriate light is found only in nonliterate socie-ties. It is a common feature of much historical writing produced for pop-ular consumption. History textbooks written for schools can usually fur-nish examples.[136]

Time was calculated by sociological data: regnal lists, length of time since a notable event such as the founding of a village, and, not least, ge-nealogies. For the Kuba, the past consisted of three periods: the period of origin, followed by the period of migration, and finally the contemporary period, a static time without change. They did not think in terms of his-torical development. For the Alur there were two periods in the past: first, mythical time, before their ancestors migrated across the Nile, and second, historical time after they had made the crossing.[137] But the two periods need not be completely separate—Bronislaw Malinowski reported that among the Trobriand Islanders, mythical and historical time existed side by side.[138] Genealogies are found everywhere: societies with hereditary rul-ers almost always recorded time in terms of the reigns of kings, which served to represent generations,[139] and even when reigns overlap, they of-ten appear as consecutive. Darius' Bisitun Inscription provides an example of this latter tendency, for there Darius named nine ancestors of the Achae-menid House ruling before him, without indicating that in part, they ruled in parallel lines.[140]

[135] "Comment: Traditions of Genesis," *Journal of African History* 15 (1974), 317–22. See also Vansina, *Oral Tradition* (1985), 95–96.

[136] See J.D.Y. Peel, "Making History: The Past in the Ijesha Present," *Man* 19 (1984), 111–32.

[137] Vansina, *Oral Tradition* (1965), 100–102; also, id., *The Children of Woot*, 20.

[138] *Argonauts of the Western Pacific* (London, 1950), 300–301.

[139] We should separate genealogies from true king-lists, which arrange the names of the kings in correct sequence, give the length of each reign, and note gaps between reigns: cf. Redford, *Pharaonic King-Lists*, 1–2, 62–64. The king-list validates the dynasty, whereas ge-nealogies buttress family status.

[140] Henige, *Chronology of the Oral Tradition*, 42–46; J.A.S. Evans, *Canadian Journal of Oral History* 4/2 (1980), 11–12.

However, the purpose of genealogies was not so much to measure time as to establish social relationships, and consequently pedigrees (particularly family lineages uncontrolled by royal remembrancers) have a certain spurious exactitude. Goody and Watt[141] report the case of the Tiv in Nigeria, who could recite genealogies going back some twelve generations to eponymous ancestors when the early British colonial administrators first made contact with them. But when, forty years later, the Tiv were confronted with the genealogies that these administrators had written down, they said the written record was wrong. Their pedigrees were now different. Lineages formed the basis of the Tiv political system, and if they were to serve their purpose adequately, they could not be static. Even lines of descent could rest upon consensus within the group.

There was also a very natural process at work whereby unimportant names fell off the genealogical list and eminent persons found their way onto it. Memories lapse, and the urge to enhance the standing of the family is rarely absent. Yet, when the African kingdoms encountered writing, pedigrees were often among the first records to be written down,[142] which indicates that the group carried on the process of altering its lineages unaware, and unconsciously adjusted them to the new historical truth, all the while accepting the accuracy of the list.[143]

We have been looking at structured African societies, where formal oral performances by specialist historians are the rule. The Bobangi of the Zaire (formerly the Congo) River basin present a different picture. They are an individualistic, mobile population who live primarily by fishing and trade, and their way of life militates against closely-knit kinship groups. Each village possesses a headman who rules by virtue of being the most powerful trader, not because of any hereditary or ritual claims, and there is no central political organization. The Bobangi have no specialist "remembrancers." Their oral traditions are simply recited around their camp fires, and stories are remembered only so long as they have some relevance, after which they are forgotten, except perhaps by a few people with exceptional memories.

[141] Jack Goody, ed., *Literacy in Traditional Societies*, pp. 31–32; Laura Bohannan, "A Genealogical Charter," *Africa* 23 (1952), 301–15; cf. Ruth Finnegan, *History and Theory* 9 (1970), 198–99.

[142] D. H. Jones, *Journal of African History* 11 (1970), 162. When Sultan Njoya of Bamum in the Cameroons invented a script, the first items to be written down were the royal chronicle, the law code, and the local pharmacopoeia: Engelbert Mveng, *Histoire du Cameroun* (Paris, 1963), 235–36.

[143] David Henige, " 'The Disease of Writing': Ganda and Nyoro Kinglists in a Newly Literate World," in Joseph C. Miller, ed., *The African Past Speaks* (Folkestone, 1980), 240–61, casts doubt on the accuracy of purely oral king-lists: his examination of the king-list of Buganda, which once was accepted as reliable, tends to bear out Jack Goody's argument (see n. 118) that making accurate lists is a mental activity belonging to literate societies. See Vansina, *Oral Tradition* (1985), 178–85.

The stories are generally brief, taking from ten minutes to half an hour to recite, and genealogies rarely reach back further than four generations.[144]

Thus, precolonial Africa provides a variety of models for the researcher in the field of oral history. At one end of the spectrum, we have societies where tribal groups retained oral records of the past by assigning the task of remembrance to specialists, who stored them in trained memories, and passed them on to the next generation of specialists. Some of these experts would count as oral poets, but others kept in their memories what we would recognize as historical documents. The history they retained involved a choice of what to remember, and the criterion was not a concept of unbiased historical accuracy. Rather, what was omitted was what was not perceived as relevant to the community, or what might cast doubt upon present behavior. The creation of a historical tradition involved less a haphazard loss of memory than a conscious choice of what to remember, and it could be renovated by degrees like an old building, and brought up to current fashion. Yet the selection process often did not succeed in consigning all irrelevant stories to oblivion, and family traditions sometimes recorded information that did not reflect well upon the ruling dynasty or the community as a whole.

Thus, the historical tradition of the group was not monolithic. Even when there was a general consensus, reconsideration at a later date could alter the "historical truth" about the past. But for our purposes, the definition of epichoric tradition is important: it represents a local group's view of its own past, and it was frequently maintained by trained specialists whose profession it was to store records in their memories and to pass them on to successors who would do likewise.

At the other end of the spectrum, we have the model of the Bobangi, for whom history was the unorganized recollections of the past. In this model, the immediate past is well known, and the remote past, particularly if it is identified with a heroic age, is the substance of myth and saga; but between the two, there is usually a period of varying length where historical data are scanty. This knowledge gap is a feature of all nonliterate societies to some extent, but particularly those without hereditary ruling houses.

How well do these models fit archaic Greece? The Greek states did possess officials called "remembrancers." Aristotle, naming the essential officials for a *polis*, is witness: "Fifthly there is the office which keeps the records that have to be made of contracts made between private persons, and of law-court decisions; and this same office ought also to be the place for the registration of prosecutions and the introduction of suits. (Sometimes this office is also divided, and in some places, a single supreme office covers

---

[144] Robert W. Harms, "Bobangi Oral Traditions: Indicators of Changing Perceptions," in J. C. Miller, ed., *The African Past Speaks*, 178–200.

them all.) The officials are called Keepers of the Sacred Records (*hierom-nemones*), Controllers (*epistatai*), Recorders (*mnemones*) and other such names."[145] A *mnemon* is a "remembrancer," and although one would expect *mnemones* in Aristotle's day to be literate, the name implies a time when they relied on their memories. They served as registrars of property and contracts,[146] but it seems that they could act as arbiters in property disputes as well—a role analogous to that of the *histor* in Homer.[147] Their command of information gave them a degree of importance: an inscription from Halicarnassus shows that they could act upon occasion as guardians of disputed property.[148]

A recent discovery on Crete of a bronze mitra with an archaic inscription dating to about 500 B.C., sheds an interesting light on the position of "remembrancer." It sets forth the rights and privileges of one Spensithios, who was to be *poinikastes* and *mnemon* of an unnamed city in the Lyttos-Afrati area, and his descendants after him. Spensithios was the master of Phoenician letters for a *polis*, and a keeper of records, which he probably published, when called upon to do so by giving a public reading of them.[149] The position of *mnemon* is found elsewhere on Crete as well,[150] and the fact that it is hereditary need not surprise us: in a nonliterate society, the most efficient way of preserving the continuity of traditions was to preserve them within families.[151] But the office of *poinikastes*, which is coupled with that of *mnemon*, introduces a new element. The probable meaning of the term is "a specialist in Phoenician letters." In a society which was still to a large degree unlettered, Spensithios was a master of the new technology. He could write, and in the settlement of disputes, written records

---

[145] Pol. 6.8: 1321b, 38–39; trans. T. A. Sinclair, Penguin Classics (Harmondsworth, 1951, rev. ed., 1957).

[146] Egon Weiss, *Griechisches Privatrecht auf Rechtsvergleichender Grundlage* 1 (Leipzig, 1923, repr. Hildesheim, 1965), 252–54; id., *RE* 15.2; (Stuttgart, 1934), cols. 2261–64.

[147] Iliad, 18.50, 23.486; cf. Luigi Piccirili, *Gli Arbitrati Interstatali Greci* (Pisa, 1973), 261–65.

[148] M-L, no. 32.

[149] Lilian Jeffery and Anna Morpurgo-Davies, *Kadmos* 9 (1970), 118–54; A. E. Raubitschek, *Kadmos* 9 (1970), 154–55. Raubitschek comments that poinikazein kai mnamoneuein surely means "record and recite," i.e., the *poinikastes* both recorded public documents and read aloud texts recorded in the past. This was also the function of the "scribe" in Athens.

[150] R. Descat ('Aux origines de l'*oikonomia* grecque," *QUCC* 28 [1988], 103–9) makes the interesting observation that at Aesch. *Agamemnon*, 155, where *menis* (i.e., Clytaemnestra) is given the qualification of *mnamon* (remembrancer of the royal house), the image is taken from the function of the mnemon in cities. Royal houses and clans might have remembrancers too, and the metaphor is a natural one.

[151] Cf. the Homeridai, still the leading performers of Homer at the beginning of the fifth century, though they had virtually lost that distinction by the end of the century, when Greece had become a literate society; H. T. Wade-Gery, *The Poet of the Iliad* (Cambridge, 1952), 19–21; Wace and Stubbings, *Companion*, 219.

had something of the finality of written law. Scribes possessed status in archaic Greece. Three such individuals in Athens during the latter part of the sixth century were commemorated by dedicatory statues on the Acropolis: seated figures holding wax tablets on their laps.[152] Yet, if we may draw an analogy from the African kingdoms, oral and written traditions probably coexisted over a considerable period of time, and the guardians of oral traditions gave way only reluctantly to the new literacy.

But we are still left with our question. Granted that the Greek states had remembrancers who at one time relied on trained memories for keeping records. Granted, too, that temples had *hieromnemones*, so that temple dedications acted as mementos in a very practical way: they served as mnemonic devices that would keep fresh memories about their donors in the minds of the *hieromnemones*. And we must grant, too, that there were families of specialists such as the Homeridai, claiming to be Homer's kinsmen; the Talthybiadai, hereditary heralds of Sparta; and the Iamidai of Elis who were famous seers. There were also priestly families that maintained the records of their genealogies with care: the Eteobutadai in Athens deposited a copy of theirs in the Erechtheion.[153] But Greece lacked the well-organized, divine-right monarchies that we find in Africa, and the priestly families notwithstanding, there was no professional priesthood capable of authenticating a select tradition,[154] though undoubtedly there were many priests and priestesses quite ready to give opinions on questions put before them. Thus, a great deal of what Herodotus found must be counted as unorganized recollections, family lore, and tales surrounding various state or family cults.

Even the folktale telling how Perdiccas the Temenid founded the Macedonian royal house, for which Herodotus is our earliest source,[155] betrays the marks of its transmission. The royal house of Macedon sacrificed to a river that flooded and prevented the crossing of the horsemen whom the king of Macedon had sent in pursuit of Perdiccas and his brothers, thus saving them from capture. The tale explained the sacrifice. Thus, the founding legend of the dynasty was linked to a ritual of the royal house, and yet it does not seem to have been the official tradition of the house with the stamp of dynastic approval, for Euripides produced a play at the Macedonian court in which the founder of the house was named not Per-

[152] Humfry Payne, *Archaic Marble Sculpture from the Acropolis*[2] (New York, 1951), 47.
[153] Plutarch Vit. X Or. 843 E.
[154] As there was in Judaea: cf. A. Momigliano, *ASNP* 8 (1978), 70–71.
[155] 8.137–39; Ap. Dascalakis, "L'Origine de la Maison Royale de Macédoine et les Legendes Relatives de l'Antiquité," *Ancient Macedonia. Papers Read at the First International Symposium, Thessaloniki, 21–29 August, 1968*, ed. Basil Laourdas and Ch. Makaronas (Thessaloniki, 1970), 155–61; Eugene N. Borza, "Athenians, Macedonians, and the Origins of the Macedonian Royal House," *Hesp. Suppl.* 19 (1982), 7–13.

diccas, but Archelaus. The king who was Euripides' patron also bore the name Archelaus, and perhaps the intention of the emendation was to flatter. However, if the story that Herodotus reproduced formed part of the approved oral traditions of the dynasty, analogous to what might have been found among the ruling houses in Africa, it is not likely that liberties which Euripides took with it would have been received without objection. An Africanist might class Herodotus' story as an aetiological myth, combined with a legend concocted to lend status to the ruling clan. But it is unlikely that he would recognize it as a morsel of official dynastic history based on venerable traditions preserved by remembrancers. We cannot demonstrate that Macedon had anything that would correspond to that.

Sparta should have provided a favorable milieu for remembrancers, for it had two royal houses, and Spartiate society had some resemblance to that of the Tutsi in Rwanda before the revolution of 1963. Sparta clearly had organized epichoric traditions: Herodotus cites the pedigrees of both royal houses, which are king-lists of sorts. But genealogies are a common feature of kingships, and in any case, the pedigrees that Herodotus reproduces may have been taken from Hecataeus' *Genealogies*. Their ultimate origin, however, would be records of the dynasties themselves, and their function would be that of most royal genealogies: they served to organize the past into an appropriate relationship with the present, and they lent legitimacy to the royal house.[156]

Once, in his tale of Lycurgus, Herodotus cites specifically Lacedaemonian tradition for the source of the Spartan *agoge* in Crete.[157] He cites Spartan tradition again for the foundation of Thera, for the reason why Sparta had two royal houses, for why Cleomenes went mad, and for the story of Sperthias and Bulis, which brought him down to the Peloponnesian War.[158] But Herodotus cross-checked against other epichoric traditions when he could: for instance, he gave the Argive explanation of Cleomenes' madness more space than the Spartan one. Moreover, he verified the stories he heard with the evidence of monuments when he found them.

Some of the data that Herodotus collected actually centered on monuments, such as dedications in temples, and when this was the case, his sources may have been *hieromnemones*, who knew their history and interpreted any inscriptions that they might bear.[159] In any case, it is clear that

---

[156] Cf. Claude Calame, "Le récit généalogique Spartiate: la représentation mythologique d'une organization Spartiate," QS 13 (1987), 43–91.

[157] 1.65.

[158] 4.150.1; 6.53.1; 6.84.1; 7.137.1.

[159] For example, at Delphi and at the temple of Ismenian Apollo at Thebes, it was probably *hieromnemones* who imparted to Herodotus his knowledge of Croesus' dedications (1.51–52), and in the latter temple, a *hieromnemon* also interpreted the "Cadmaean" letters that he saw engraved on three tripods (5.59–61).

the dedications served as mnemonic devices. The fetters that the Lacedaemonians had brought to bind the Tegeans, and with which they had themselves been bound when the Tegeans worsted them, were to be seen in
Herodotus' day in the temple of Athena Alea at Tegea, and the bronze
krater which the Lacedaemonians intended as a gift for Croesus had found
its way into the temple of Hera at Samos. A duplicate of the breastplate
that the pharaoh Amasis intended for the Spartans, and which the Samians
also stole, was in the temple of Athena at Lindus on Rhodes. The story of
how the Samians saved the three hundred Corcyraean boys whom Periander was sending to Alyattes to be castrated, was connected with a festival
at the temple of Artemis which was still celebrated with the same ritual in
Herodotus' day. These all appear to be local traditions that focused on
dedications that survived in temples, or on rituals.

There should also have been family traditions in Sparta to consult, but
Herodotus specifically cites only one: he interviewed Archias in the Pitanate deme, and got a morsel of family tradition: his father was named Sa-
mius because his grandfather, Archias, had died like a hero at Samos. This
does not amount to much: Archias' family history seems to have been suit-
ably laconic. The "history" of his grandfather, Archias, was only a brief
heroic tale that explained his father's name. But the citation does show that
Herodotus cross-checked and amplified epichoric traditions with family
memories when he could.

Herodotus cited an aetiological legend that explained the origin of Sparta's double monarchy, and this story may have been the explanation approved by the kings themselves in Herodotus' day. More tantalizing is the
information that the kings appointed the *Pythioi* who were the official messengers to Delphi, and that they also safeguarded the prophecies which
were received, sharing knowledge of them with the *Pythioi*.[160] This must
mean that the kings kept an archive (or possibly two separate archives) that
preserved oracles, and perhaps some other records as well, and if this was
an ancient privilege extending back into the preliterate age, then at one
time the kings must have had specialists with trained memories in charge
of their collections, who might bear comparison with the *abiiru* of
Rwanda. Thus, the oracle which foretold that Sparta would either fall victim to Xerxes or lose a king, which (Herodotus believed) persuaded Leonidas to make his stand at Thermopylae, was received from Delphi by the
kings through their agents, the *Pythioi*. If the oracle was a fabrication, it
was indeed a royal one.[161]

The evidence suggests that the royal houses made some organized effort

---

[160] Hdt. 6.57.2; cf. Pericles B. Georges, "Saving Herodotus' Phenomena. The Oracles and
the Events of 480 B.C." *Classical Antiquity* 5 (1986), 14–59, esp. 31–37.

[161] However, the legend of Leonidas may owe more to folktale than to any royal source. It
sounds suspiciously like the self-sacrifice of the mythical king of Athens, Codrus.

to preserve their traditions, and the great families preserved legendary material that contributed to their prestige: the clan of the Aegidae, as we have seen, had a contribution to make to the foundation legend of Thera. When Charon of Lampsacus wrote his chronicle of the kings and ephors of Sparta, based on Spartan sources, we may be reasonably sure that he found traditions that met the approval of the royal houses and the ephorate. But Herodotus' interview with Archias leaves the impression that family traditions were less interested in the relatively recent period that Herodotus marked out as his historical space than they were in the legendary past.

On the whole, Sparta seems to have been closer to the model of Burundi than of Rwanda; like the Rundi, the Spartans seem to have had no consensual tradition that bore the mark of official approval, but rather songs in praise of brave men,[162] apothegms, jests about those who had fallen short of the heroic ideal, and stories, which could, upon occasion, represent conflicting perspectives within the ruling class. For instance, King Cleomenes, son of Anaxandrides, who is first introduced to us in the *Histories* as a man of integrity whom Maeandrius of Samos could not bribe, has become deranged when Herodotus relates the traditions of the royal family about him.[163] His reputation had no doubt suffered from the resentment of his half brothers (the sons of Anaxandrides' first wife, whom Cleomenes had displaced), one of whom was to succeed him. But the pejorative judgment on Cleomenes, even with the backing of the royal house, failed to win complete consensus, and his portrayal reveals a mixture of unflattering and favorable recollections.

The memory of Thermopylae seems to have been partly preserved by apothegms. The bravest of the Spartans there, Dieneces, was remembered for various sayings, one of which Herodotus[164] quotes. There was a good supply of private traditions, but Herodotus gives no grounds for positing a consensual version of the battle in Sparta, much less an official one.

However, the Spartans had an appetite for history. They were a receptive audience for recitals of pedigrees and tales of the past. For that we have the attestation of Hippias of Elis, who explained his success in Sparta as a traveling lecturer. The Spartans liked nothing better than hearing about the genealogies of men and heroes, the founding of cities and, in short, the whole study of the past.[165] But the emphasis seems to be upon the legendary past. Yet, not surprisingly, the Spartans cherished the memory of brave men, like Aeimnestus, who killed Mardonius at Plataea,[166] and later died himself in the Helot Revolt, along with three hundred Spartiate *hippeis,*

[162] Cf. Plut., *Lyk.* 18, 3–4.
[163] 3.148; 5.41–42.
[164] 7.226–27.
[165] Plato, *Hippias Major*, 285 B.
[166] 9.64.3.

and they preserved the names of the bravest warriors in battle. Their exploits were the subjects of encomiastic songs at festivals, and probably, too, *logioi* recounted their great deeds before their peers in the *syssitia*.

What of Athens? The general belief that Herodotus tapped records of aristocratic Athenian families probably has some truth to it, but we should not overemphasize their value. His digression on the Alcmaeonids that interrupts his account of Marathon,[167] with its expressed judgment that they were the real liberators of Athens from the tyranny, sounds like a story with an Alcmaeonid source. Or at least the Alcmaeonids may well have been its ultimate source, for its political value, which would have been significant in the first quarter of the fifth century, was much diminished by the last quarter. On the other hand, his treatment of the conspiracy of Cylon, with its bold statement that blame fell upon the Alcmaeonids for the murder of the conspirators, contrasts with the longer, more circumspect account in Thucydides, and could hardly have been welcome to the *oikos* at the start of the Peloponnesian War, when Sparta tried to use the family curse against Pericles![168] The story of the murder of Miltiades' father, Cimon, could have come from a Philaid family tradition, which was tied to Cimon's tomb. It attested hostility with the Pisistratids, which the Philaids liked to remember. But at the same time as Herodotus reports this hostility, he reveals that the Pisistratids had treated Miltiades well![169] It seems clear that there was a free market of traditions in Athens, and Herodotus picked and chose without feeling under obligation to celebrate or flatter.

To give a case in point: the first citation of Athenian tradition tells how the Alcmaeonids bribed the Pythia to urge the Spartans to rid Athens of her tyranny.[170] The Spartans dispatched a force under Anchimolius to do the Pythia's bidding, but it was annihilated. The episode ends with the detail that Anchimolius' grave was at Alopecae in Attica. If we apply the criterion that family tradition usually forgets data that does not put the family in a good light, then this tale which recounts the deliverance of Athens strikes one sour note: the Alcmaeonids, who claimed to be liberators, had suborned Delphi to inveigle Sparta into intervention. That was a feature with an odor of sacrilege. But however unflattering a family might find a tradition to be, it was powerless to suppress it in an open society like that of Athens, where other families might choose to remember it.

But in this case, the expulsion of the tyrants gave rise almost

---

[167] Hdt. 6.123–31.

[168] Hdt. 6.123; cf. Thuc. 1.126–27. See Mabel Lang, "The Kylonian Conspiracy," CP 62 (1967), 243–49; cf. C. Hignett, *A History of the Athenian Constitution to the End of the Fifth Century* (Oxford, 1952), 2–3, who notes correctly that with the exception of Cylon, oral tradition in Athens had little to report before Pisistratus.

[169] Hdt. 6.103; 6.39.1; cf. Hignett, *History of the Athenian Constitution*, 326–31.

[170] Hdt. 5.63.1.

immediately[171] to another competing tradition, which received a degree of official sanction: Harmodius and Aristogeiton were commemorated by a public monument and their descendants had hereditary privileges. The story that made them tyrannicides held its own so well against the written version of Herodotus and Thucydides that the Parian Chronicle, erected in 264–263 B.C., reads under the year 511–510, that Harmodius and Aristogeiton killed Hipparchus, who is identified as his father's successor as tyrant. Yet Thucydides[172] claimed that the Athenians were well aware that it was not thanks to the tyrannicides but to Spartan intervention that Hippias was expelled. But the tradition of tyrannicides more than held its own.

The Alcmaeonids could neither claim undisputed credit as liberators of Athens, nor expunge from the record the tale of how they corrupted the Pythia, since it was in the public domain which they could not control. Athens was a society of plural traditions variously preserved, which provided cross-references and restricted the power of any family or clan to deform history to its benefit. In any case, the tale of bribery at Delphi was not entirely a liability, for though it made the Alcmaeonids appear unscrupulous, it also established them as anti-Pisistratid, and the Spartans as bumblers. But it seems clear that the overriding concern of Herodotus was to tell a good story, and not to choose traditions that flattered, or vice versa.

Finally, there was the tomb of Anchimolius, which acted as a mnemonic device. A field worker interviewing a local informant on the purport of the tomb might have obtained a story that started with the bribery of the Pythia and concluded with the death of the unfortunate Spartiate: the sort of tale centered on a monument that, centuries later, Pausanias was to collect on his tour of Greece from local storytellers whom he called *exegetai*.[173] This was folk-memory in the public domain, which Herodotus might gather by asking questions; it belonged to no "family archive." In fact, the designation "family archive" probably overstates the reality: the evidence seems to suggest that family and clan traditions in Athens consisted simply of genealogies, anecdotes, private recollections about family members, tales surrounding family shrines and tombs, and myths about eponymous heroes.

The picture that emerges is of a mosaic of epichoric and family traditions, sometimes complimenting, sometimes competing with each other, and within a *polis*, various groups, such as families, clans, or even political clubs might have traditions of their own which interacted in much the same way. A *polis* might give official sanction to one particular tradition, as Athens attempted to do by granting the descendants of the tyran-

---

[171] Cf. Charles W. Fornara, "The Cult of Harmodius and Aristogeiton," *Philologus* 114 (1970), 155–80.

[172] 6.53.

[173] Cf. Paul Veyne, *Les Grecs ont-ils cru à leur mythes?* 28.

nicides special privileges, but such efforts could be only partially successful if there was a strong competing tradition. The standard way of winning consensus was by much retelling: an epichoric tradition that stood the test of time, and could be retold in its own locale without fear of contradiction, attained credence. Within its own home area, it became true.

Public monuments, and the establishment of festivals and rituals were instruments by which a group might ensure the permanence of its tradition, and champions of competing traditions might use such mnemonic devices as evidence.[174] But we must not underestimate the influence of the *logioi* in shaping tradition. The recitations of these oral performers took place under conditions of interaction between the performer and the group that made up his audience, and, if we may borrow from the African model, the result of repeated performances and amendments was that the performer and his audience eventually reached a consensus on what the correct tradition was. Thus, the story of the past that a *logios* told might be a composite tale, adroitly avoiding what might be distasteful to members of the group, but showing no such tact toward outsiders. The *logios* not only transmitted epichoric tradition; he played a role in shaping it as well, for by retelling it, he helped bring it to the point where it could be put forward confidently as *the true* tradition that the group forming his audience held of the past.[175]

Some *logioi* must have found patrons among the great families, just as the praise-poets did, and have contributed to the shaping of their family traditions. Pherecydes had a relationship of this sort with the Philaid clan, to which Miltiades belonged:[176] the fact that he used writing marked him as a *logios* who moved with the times, but probably did little to affect his status. Once a family or clan tradition won consensus within its own group, it became the official history of the clan or family; but outside its group it remained a private tradition, forced to compete with others.

The same competition could be found among states: within one state, the citizens might reach a consensus on a story for reasons that had nothing to do with historical accuracy. They might, for instance, accept a tradition that increased the prestige of their own *polis*, or denigrated a rival one, and the fact that neighboring states rejected it would not affect their allegiance to it. One example of such a tradition touches Salamis: the Athenians agreed that at the battle, the Corinthians fled until they encountered mysterious boatmen who told them that the Greeks were winning, whereupon they reversed direction. The Corinthian tradition, however, had it that

[174] Cf. Hdt. 5.44–45: the Sybarites adduced a temple said to have been founded by Dorieus to prove that he had helped the Crotoniates when they took Sybaris.

[175] The remarks of Paul Veyne on "vulgate tradition" as "historical truth" are particularly pertinent: *Les Grecs ont-ils cru à leurs mythes?* pp. 17–27.

[176] Cf. Kurt von Fritz, *Die Griechische Geschichtsschreibung* 1 (Berlin, 1967), 83.

their fleet fought valiantly,[177] and the rest of the Greeks agreed, which is a good reason to doubt the Athenian tale.

Here is a tradition that may have been pure fiction, or possibly some unexplained incident lay behind it. But whatever the grounds for it may have been, it fitted an interpretation of the battle that gratified the Athenians in the latter half of the fifth century, when Corinth had become bitterly hostile. This tradition clearly achieved a degree of consensus among Athenians for political reasons. But the observation is still true that in an open society such as existed in Athens, it was not easy for official traditions to take root, particularly if they wandered too far from the truth. The story of the Corinthian poltroonery at Salamis would probably have been forgotten once the political situation changed, except for the fact that Herodotus put it into writing.

We are left with a hypothesis. It is that archaic Greece had prose memorialists as well as oral poets, and that these memorialists retained historical data in trained memories, which they passed on to successors, who not infrequently were their own descendants. They operated on a lower literary plane than the poets, and for the most part sought their audiences within individual *poleis* and received appropriate rewards: though we know of no official historians like the *baba elegun* in the Nigerian town of Ketu, cities did remunerate poets at public expense and could have done the same for *logioi*.[178]

Some were no doubt patronized by clans or *phylai*. In any case, they were in a position to help shape the traditions of a community as well as to record them, for though Thucydides[179] complained that people accepted stories of the past uncritically, the audience was not passive. There was a degree of interaction between the *logios* and the listener, and from it, an epichoric tradition that represented a consensus would result. But it was not always a stable consensus, and it faced challenges from personal recollections and other local traditions.

The first of these faded sharply after three generations. A field-worker in classical Greece would have found that once he delved beyond the memory span of three generations (which for practical purposes is no longer than one hundred and twenty-five years), recollections of the past grew thin and selective until he reached the heroic age. At this point, poetic imagination took control of the data, and the investigator would have to proceed with the caution that Jan Vansina learned he had to apply to Kuba traditions of

---

[177] Hdt. 8.94.

[178] Cf. pseudo-Herod. *Vita Homeri*, 12–13, which describes how the council at Kyme considered, but rejected, a motion to maintain Homer. The story is probably apocryphal, but it shows that public maintenance of *aoidoi* was not altogether unusual, and *logioi* might have received similar treatment.

[179] 1.20.1.

genesis. Local traditions that centered around monuments were a different matter. They could be purely fictional. An isolated monument without a legible inscription is a mythopoeic catalyst. For that matter, myths could gather around natural phenomena, such as rock formations. But not every monument was an unreliable commemorative, and within the temple precincts of Greece there was a host of dedications, as well as *hieromnemones* whose business it was to know something about them. The tangible *erga* of the past acted as mnemonic devices that helped preserve recollections which epichoric traditions might otherwise have let slip into oblivion.

The situation of the *logios* specializing in the traditions of a community must have evolved in a new direction once *logioi* began to give recitals at panhellenic festivals. Lucian implies that Herodotus was the first to do this at Olympia, and he may have been right as far as the Olympic Games are concerned. But there were other interstate festivals in Greece, and one might imagine that contests of *logioi* appeared at Ionian or Dorian *panegyreis* earlier than at the panhellenic festivals. However, these interstate festivals meant that the *logioi* no longer performed merely within the context of the *oikos*, the *genos*, phratry, or *polis*, but within a panhellenic one. This internationalization must have been increased with the emergence of a new breed of *logioi* who were, for practical purposes, stateless, sometimes because they were, in fact, exiles, sometimes because they moved from *polis* to *polis* in search of audiences. Thus, there developed a breed of *logioi* who were more than remembrancers of a city or a clan. Like the *aiodoi*, they toured, seeking audiences and financial rewards where they could, possibly even, like the *aoidoi*, wearing special costumes to attract attention as they performed.[180]

Inevitably, some *logios* would perceive a demand for exotic *logoi*: Persian, Scythian, Egyptian, or others, and he would conceive of these according to the model with which he was familiar. They also would be based on Persian, Scythian, or Egyptian traditions, which the researcher might collect from local sources (or informants who claimed to know them) by using his ears, and check by using his eyes and his critical judgment. In Egypt, he would be impressed by the extraordinary span of historical time, and the well-trained memorialists that he found; in the Pontic regions and Scythia, by contrast, he would find little, for Herodotus knew only one Scyth who merited the designation of *logios*. Scythia had traditions of the past nonetheless, but they were thin, and Herodotus did not accord them the respect that he gave those of Egypt: he related the Scythian tradition of genesis, for instance, only to reject it.[181]

---

[180] For the special costume of the aoidos, see Hdt. 1.24.5; Plato, Ion, 535d. Cf. Morrison, *Durham University Journal* 10 (1948), 58n.21.

[181] 4. 5–12.

The next development came with the Persian Wars. The staple subjects of the *logioi*, like those of the poets, drew heavily upon the legendary past, which was the common heritage of the Greeks. But the war with Persia rapidly acquired a standing in literature equivalent to mythology: Phrynichus and Aeschylus made it the subject of tragedy, and we hear of several epics, including one by Herodotus' uncle or cousin, Panyassis. Like the Trojan War, the Persian Wars affected all of Greece. But they fell within historical space. Witnesses could be interviewed, and questions asked and answered. The *logios* who made the Persian Wars his subject could do more than repeat legends. He could analyze the struggle itself, and with this change of purpose, he became an explorer and investigator of the past rather than a mere reporter of tradition.

Writing did not cause an abrupt change. Nevertheless, Plato's verdict on the new technology was right: those who acquired it ceased to train their memories and grew forgetful.[182] They came to rely upon writing to recollect historical data. The shadowy chroniclers listed by Dionysius of Halicarnassus as well as others he did not list, whose names have survived along with a few fragments, were *logioi* who gave public performances of their *logoi* based on epichoric traditions that they had mastered to please their patrons. The stimulus that led them to preserve their data in writing may have arisen partly from a scarcity of successors with trained memories to carry on their craft for the next generation.

Herodotus may have read none of their works, except for those of Hecataeus, who was too famous to be overlooked and too early for Herodotus to have known him except through his books. But it is reasonable to suppose that he was aware of their activity and heard some of them perform. It is clear that he did not work in a vacuum.

It appears that the African model provides some useful parallels, but we should apply them with caution. Even when we find social structures that have analogies in Africa, the manner in which oral traditions were transmitted and preserved could be markedly different. Within Greek states there could be dominant traditions, and within social groups there could be a degree of consensus that *logioi* helped to shape by their public performances. But Greece was not fertile soil for official traditions to take root and the transmission of historical data was not highly organized. The *mnemones* whom Aristotle named, retained in their memories (and later in writing) contracts and property records and the like: information of practical value to society, which must have included a good deal that might count as history, but it was not their purpose to retain an organized record of the past. The *hieromnemones* attached to temples could give some account of temple property, and when their data was accurate, it must have been valu-

---

[182] *Phaedrus*, 275 a–b.

able. Delphi could comment upon and amplify *logoi* that involved its oracles, but the temple does not seem to have kept an archive of them. Delphi was a rich source, but it owed its wealth of traditions to the fact that so many figures from the past had left memorials there. The priestesses of Zeus at Dodona, whom Herodotus cited by name, could tell him about the legendary beginnings of the oracle, but what they had to tell was not a tradition of any antiquity; it seems to have been merely a fifth-century rationalization.[183]

Family traditions did not give a connected account of the past. They were strong on genealogies and heroic tales of legendary ancestors, but of less help within the historical space that Herodotus had marked out for himself. It all seems rather haphazard. Nevertheless, one point emerges clearly. It is that a field-worker of Herodotus' day could have found in Greece a great variety of recollections and traditions which could be identified as the property of a group, and most often the group was a locality or a *polis*. The immediate past had no panhellenic, vulgate tradition. What there was instead was a mosaic of epichoric traditions of unequal value, which could be put together into a coherent whole, and checked against other evidence such as personal recollections, monuments, and even inscriptions. All this could be placed within a framework of relative chronology. Moreover, when Herodotus surveyed the non-Greek world, he recognized, or thought he recognized, the same model.[184]

HERODOTUS AS FIELD-WORKER

I have suggested that Herodotus conceived of the story of the past as a narrative made up of a great many discrete traditions that paralleled and amplified each other, and that he made it his business to seek them out and examine them. I have proposed one technique that he followed: he listened to other memorialists perform. He also sought out informants and asked questions, and the questions one asks go far to shape the answers one receives. The modern field-worker who gathers oral data is equipped with tape recorders and notebooks, and he has a short list of useful manuals to tell him how he should conduct his interviews. The questions he asks, and the manner in which he puts them can do much to shape the information that he receives. He approaches his informant as an outsider with his own mindset; he processes the data that he obtains within his own frame of reference, and usually he publishes his results with a specific public in mind. It may be his fellow researchers in the academic world, or perhaps

[183] Lloyd, *Commentary*, 2, 253–54.

[184] Cf. Oswyn Murray, "Herodotus and Oral History," *Achaemenid History*, 2, *The Greek Sources, Proceedings of the Groningen 1984 Achaemenid History Workshop*, ed. Heleen Sancisi-Weerdenburg and Amelie Kuhrt (Leiden, 1987), 93–115, esp. 108ff.

the trade book market, but whatever it is, it can exercise a subtle influence on the configuration of what Herodotus would have called "the public display" of the field-worker's researches. The published work, which is the final result, is a piece of literature; and literature, to quote Northrop Frye,[185] "belongs to the world man constructs, not to the world he sees; to his home, not his environment." It is shaped by the author's own mindset, which in turn is molded by the literature he has read or heard.

This "research" that Herodotus published was literature that differed from epic, which also recollected the past, and belonged to the world that man constructs. As Aristotle[186] was to express it a century after Herodotus, history deals with what actually took place at a certain time for one people or more, and with how they happened to behave toward each other, whereas poetry had to do with universal truths. Aristotle capped the definition of history for the ancient world, though he had an advantage which Herodotus did not, for by the fourth century, history was established as a genre. Nonetheless, the research of Herodotus dealt with human deeds and achievements remembered by his sources. Behind the sources were facts that should be capable of verification.

To recover the past, Herodotus had his eyes, his ears, and his judgment. The eye is more trustworthy than the ear, as Candaules remarked to Gyges,[187] but the researcher does not always have a choice. I have already suggested one way that Herodotus gathered his information: he listened to other *logioi* expounding epichoric traditions. New *logoi* were shaped out of old ones. Herodotus' sources were only partly raw data that he collected with his queries. Some part of his data had already received a literary configuration.

The oracles that Herodotus reports are a case in point. He cited a number of them; the longest are the two that the Pythia gave the Athenian *theopropoi* in 481 B.C., the second of which refers cryptically to a "wooden wall" that would not be captured.[188] The oracles are an integral part of the story; they serve as prelude to the introduction of Themistocles, and there is every reason to believe that they have a basis in fact. It would be odd if Athens did not consult Delphi on the eve of Xerxes' invasion. But we can be reasonably sure that Delphi never delivered the two twelve-line stanzas that Herodotus quotes, or for that matter, any other of the metrical oracles that appear in the *Histories*.[189] The Pythia made replies in verse only in folktales.

---

[185] *The Educated Imagination* (Toronto, 1963), 8.
[186] *Poetics*, 1459a23; cf. Christian Meier, *Arethusa* 20 (1987), 41–42.
[187] Hdt. 1.8.2.
[188] Hdt. 7.140–41.
[189] Joseph Fontenrose, *The Delphic Oracle: Its Responses and Operations, with a Catalogue of*

Where did Herodotus get his verse oracles? The answer may be that the oracles he quotes had already received a conventional reworking into metric form by *logioi* and *aoidoi* before Herodotus incorporated them into his *Histories*. The story that Athens consulted Delphi before Xerxes' invasion is likely enough to be authentic, and the twelve-line stanzas that Herodotus quoted may report the tenor of the reply correctly. The first oracle simply advised the Athenians to run away; the second, which may have added some cryptic reference to Salamis, advised them to board their ships and sail away. It was realistic advice. But, retold by the *logioi*, it became the two oracles in verse that served to introduce Themistocles into Herodotus' story. The Pythia's replies had already been shaped to fit the conventions of the *logioi* before the story reached Herodotus, who had no wish to diminish its popular appeal by an excess of accuracy.

Thus, the oracles appear in the *Histories* in verse because the literary conventions of the *logos* demanded it, and the audience that might listen to the tale expected it. Are they forgeries? Not at all. The principle that the *logioi* employed was one which Thucydides adapted for his own use when he composed the speeches that appear in his work. "I have found it difficult to remember the precise words used in the speeches which I listened to myself, and my various informants have experienced the same difficulty; so my method has been, while keeping as closely as possible to the general sense of the words that were actually used, to make the speakers say what, in my opinion, was called for by each situation."[190] The replies of the Pythia in the *Histories* of Herodotus are appropriate for the occasion. Yet they must meet the requirements of literary convention. Therefore, they are presented in meter. They belong to the past that the *logioi* and *aoidoi* constructed, not to the past of historical facts and documents.

Egypt provides another sort of case study that shows Herodotus the researcher at work in the field. The first ninety-eight chapters of the second book are based (so Herodotus[191] claimed) on *opsis, gnomē*, and *historiē*: his eyes, his judgment, and his investigations. He owed his contacts, it seems clear, to the descendants of those Greek and Carian mercenaries whom Psammetichus had settled at Stratopeda, and Amasis had moved to Memphis: from the Egyptian children whom Psammetichus had given them to educate had sprung the guild of interpreters that Herodotus found in Egypt.[192] Egypt was not a tabula rasa. The priests whom Herodotus met were accustomed to Greeks asking questions, and they were happy to ac-

---

Responses (Berkeley, 1978); cf. Michael Herzfeld, "Divining the Past," *Semiotica*, 38 (1982), 169–75.

[190] Thuc. 1.22. trans. Rex Warner (Penguin Classics, Harmondsworth, 1954).

[191] 2.99.1.

[192] Hdt. 2.154. Cf. in general, T. S. Brown, "Herodotus Speculates about Egypt," *AJPh* 86 (1965), 60–76.

commodate another Greek who was trying to put this strange, exotic country into familiar terms.

The sixteenth- and seventeenth-century explorers of the New World provide an instructive parallel. The marvels that they reported had lived in the collective imagination of Europe long before the New World was discovered. Walter Raleigh told of a race of headless men in Guiana, and Jacques Cartier reported that an Indian told him of people living in the north who did not eat, and others who had only one leg.[193] Montaigne, who wrote an essay on cannibals, knew the problems of obtaining evidence from witnesses who tried to explain a new culture in terms of another, more familiar one: the New World in terms of classical antiquity. He had a witness who had lived more than a decade in the Americas, and had taken part in the abortive attempt of the French to plant a colony in Brazil. "This man that I had was a plain, ignorant fellow," he wrote, "and therefore the more likely to tell the truth: for your better bred sort of men are much more curious in their observation, 'tis true, and discover a great deal more, but then they gloss upon it, and to give the greater weight to what they deliver, and allure your belief, they cannot forebear a little to alter the story; they never represent things to you simply as they are, but rather as they appeared to them, or as they would have them appear to you, and to gain the reputation of men of judgment, and the better to induce your faith, are willing to help out the business with something more than is really true, of their own invention."[194]

For Herodotus, there was double jeopardy. First, it is reasonably clear that his Egyptian interlocutors were prepared to accommodate his questions, and perhaps gloss upon their information, like Montaigne's "better bred sort of men." He was not the first Greek they had encountered. Second, the questions he asked were those that would interest a Greek audience. He had read Hecataeus before he came to Egypt, he knew the speculations of Anaximander about the Nile, and he used his borrowed knowledge to shape his questions. As a young man, he himself had shared the weltanschauung of the Ionian savants. Last, the Greeks regarded Egypt not as a "New World" but as an ancient one where men like Pythagoras and Solon had found wisdom. What were the sort of questions that Herodotus asked?

One—the first that appears in the Egyptian *logos*—had to do with the experiment of Psammetichus which showed that the Phrygians rather than the Egyptians were the most ancient race of men. He queried the priests of Ptah at Memphis about this, and apparently priests at Heliopolis and Thebes as well. The question seems to have been something like: "Which

[193] Lafitau, *Customs of the American Indians*, 1, 63–64.
[194] *The Essays of Michel de Montaigne*, trans. Charles Cotton, 1 (London, 1911), 217.

version of this story the Greeks tell about Psammetichus is right?" The priests chose a version that showed Psammetichus acting in the spirit of scientific inquiry. He was more Presocratic philosopher than pharaoh.

Then there was the geological formation of the Nile Valley. Herodotus asked if the Nile Valley was originally a gulf of the sea, filled in by the silt brought down by the river. The priests agreed with this theory. They also gave him some information about the height of the Nile floods, which he used to demonstrate that the silting action was raising the level of the land, so that in his own day, higher floods were necessary to inundate the arable area than had been the case in the past, and eventually the inundation would become impossible. Then Egypt would revert to desert and the Egyptians would starve. But Herodotus was too anxious to fit the evidence into his hypothesis. The measurements that the priests gave him were for the crests of the flood in different places, but he took them for measurements at different periods in time.[195]

Then he asked why the Nile flooded, and he got no satisfactory reply. But he specified one interlocutor, who told him a legend about deep springs where the Nile had its source, between two mountain peaks called Crophi and Mophi. Herodotus found it incredible, and no wonder. But the interlocutor was the *grammatistes ton hieron chrematon* at the temple of Neith, whom the Greeks identified with Athena, at Sais—the "clerk of the sacred money." He was almost certainly the same official as the *hierogrammateus* whom we find in the temples of Ptolemaic Egypt, in charge of recording the temple revenues, and ranking under the high priest, the prophet, and *stolistes*, but nonetheless important in the priestly hierarchy.[196] In processions, he walked with a book in his hand, for he was in charge of the profane knowledge of the priesthood. The temple library would have been under his supervision, for temples did have libraries (in Athens, by contrast, Euripides was the first to have a private library), and thanks to the chance survival of one belonging to the crocodile god Sobek in the Fayum, dating from the first century B.C. to the fourth century A.D., we have some idea of their contents.[197]

Two points emerge, however. First, Herodotus' informant in this in-

---

[195] 2.10–14, cf. Alan B. Lloyd, *Commentary*, 2, 70–73. Detlev Fehling, *Die Quellenangabe bei Herodot. Studien zur Erzählkunst Herodots* (Berlin and New York, 1971), 25–27, connects this passage with 7.128–30, on the geology of the mouth of the Peneus River. Both are attempts to find rational explanations for perceived geological change, but otherwise the two passages are independent.

[196] Walter Otto (*Priester und Tempel im hellenistischen Ägypten* [Leipzig and Berlin, 1905], 77) placed the *hierogrammateus* in the upper order of the priesthood. Cf. J.A.S. Evans, YCS 17 (1961), 183–84, 190–91.

[197] Redford, *Pharaonic King-Lists*, 227. Redford's chapter on Manetho (pp. 201–30) is important for the light it throws on the sort of historical sources an Egyptian priest commanding demotic could uncover in Ptolemaic Egypt. He also used oral tradition.

stance was not a low-ranking priest. He was, in fact, the member of the temple hierarchy most capable of answering his questions: the man in charge of the library and the temple traditions. Second, what the amiable priest told him was a legend connected with the *Hapi*-festival at Silsila,[198] somewhat garbled by him, perhaps, and further garbled by Herodotus who did not understand it. The *hierogrammateus* was the priest in the hierarchy most likely to be familiar with the temple library, and have access to the kind of information Herodotus wanted to find. Yet it appears that he drew on oral traditions to give Herodotus his answer. Herodotus thought he was joking. But it was popular belief in Egypt that the Nile sprang from the earth, and the *hierogrammateus*, anxious to satisfy this importunate Greek and to maintain his own reputation as an expert, embroidered it only slightly.

We must not imagine that the priests had accurate historical records which they could readily consult with the ease of a modern researcher with a catalog at his disposal. At Memphis the priests read him a king-list from papyrus scrolls, which shows that some temples did possess lists approximating the Royal Turin Canon.[199] But that was no chronicle, and the names meant nothing to Herodotus, though it appears that his interpreter made a valiant attempt to translate some of them into Greek equivalents. What this incident shows is that in Egypt there was documentary evidence behind the oral traditions that Herodotus received, but he still had to probe the unknown from the standpoint of what he knew, and that meant that he had to find checkpoints in the Greek past against which to correlate these unfamiliar royal names. His first secure correlations were with Heracles and the Trojan War, though he believed that he found evidence of the still earlier visit of Perseus to Egypt. For Egyptian history before Perseus, there were no points of reference.

However, the questions he put betray his mindset. Did the gods come from Egypt to Greece? Yes. How was it that there was no trace of the hero Heracles, the son of Amphitryon, in Egypt, though the Egyptians worshiped Heracles as a god? A blind alley. At the shrine of the "foreign Aphrodite," whom Herodotus guessed to be Helen of Troy, he asked what happened to Helen. The priests replied with a romance that showed a nice comprehension of what would interest a Greek audience, which they pre-

---

[198] W. Spiegelberg, *The Credibility of Herodotus' Account of Egypt*, trans. A. M. Blackman (Oxford, 1929), 17–18. The Egyptian "Hymn to the Nile," which may go back to the Middle Kingdom, begins, "Hail, to thee, O Nile, that issues from the earth." *ANET*², 372–73.

[199] Hdt. 2.100.1; cf. Fehling, *Die Quellenangaben*, 54–59; N. K. Weeks, "Herodotus and Egypt: Discerning the Native Tradition in Book II," *Ancient Society* 7 (1977), 25–34 = G.H.R. Horsley, ed., *Hellenika. Essays on Greek Politics and History* (North Ryde, N.S.W., 1982), 63–68.

sented as part of their own indigenous tradition.[200] It is clear that Herodotus found informants who were not only cooperative and willing to please, but claimed knowledge based on traditions more ancient than any known in Greece. Thus, on the question of the Trojan War, he thought the Egyptians more trustworthy than Homer, for they had preserved an eyewitness account from Menelaus himself as part of their local history!

Sometimes he betrays his method. With some satisfaction he states that he himself concluded on the basis of cultural similarities that the dwellers in Colchis were Egyptians before he heard the suggestion from anyone else, and he tested his theory by questioning both the Colchians and the Egyptians.[201] The Colchians could tell him more about their Egyptian background than the Egyptians themselves; however, the Egyptians took the theory seriously and surmised that some soldiers of Sesostris must have settled in Colchis, thereby satisfying their interrogator. Herodotus' procedure here involved two steps: first, he framed his theory, and then he tested it on both the Egyptians and the Colchians. Both gave Herodotus the answers he found satisfactory.

Yet he was determined not to be gullible. The priests at Sais showed him twenty great wooden statues of naked women, and told him that they were the concubines of Mycerinus. Herodotus suspended judgment. They also told him that the statues of Mycerinus' servant girls had their hands lopped off to commemorate their betrayal of Mycerinus' daughter to her father, who fornicated with her, as a result of which she hanged herself and her mother punished the perfidious servants by cutting off their hands. The hands, Herodotus noticed, were lying at the feet of the statues, having simply broken off. The pyramid of Mycerinus was not built by the famous courtesan Rhodopis; that was an unfounded story of some Greeks, but Herodotus knew his audience, and included a digression on Rhodopis anyway. He stood on the shore of the Lake of Moeris, and accepted the report that in the center of it stood two great pyramids with colossal seated figures on top, but he was skeptical when he was given to understand that the lake basin had been excavated. Where was the earth that was dug out? His informants explained, and Herodotus accepted the explanation because he remembered a report of something similar happening in Nineveh.[202]

[200] Hdt. 2.50; 2.43; 2.112–19.

[201] Hdt. 2.104–5; cf. Fehling, *Die Quellenangaben*, 15–17.

[202] Hdt. 2.130–31; 2.134–35; 2.149–50; cf. J.A.S. Evans, "Herodotus and the Problem of Lake Moeris," *Classical World* 56 (1963), 275–77. O. Kimball Armayor (*Herodotus' Autopsy of the Fayum: Lake Moeris and the Labyrinth of Egypt* [Amsterdam, 1985], 20–36) attempts to revive the theory of Gertrude Caton-Thompson and E. W. Gardner ("Recent Work on the Problem of Lake Moeris," *Geographical Journal*, 73 [1929], 20–60; id., *The Desert Fayum*, [London, 1934]), that Herodotus' lake of Moeris did not exist, and gives an unreliable and incomplete summary of modern geological research on the Fayum. The latest survey work does not support Caton-Thompson and Gardner. See Barbara Bell, "Climate and the History

Occasionally, we get glimpses of him struggling with this foreign language, sometimes with a modicum of success. A "good man" in Egyptian was a *piromis*; Herodotus was close enough.[203] The two rock carvings in Ionia that Herodotus thought represented Sesostris (and not Memnon, as others imagined), were supposed to bear inscriptions in hieroglyphics, which he quoted, and they do have authentic Egyptian echoes dating back to the eleventh dynasty,[204] thus betraying an Egyptian origin for the tale, however bogus it may be. The brief excursus on the Lake of Moeris confuses the name of the village of Gurob with a regnal name of Amenemhet III: a mistake that bears the marks of a local tradition of some antiquity.

However, the replies he received to his questions were based on the oral traditions and legends of Egypt, with an admixture from Greek mythology that his interlocutors had learned by contact with the Greek world. Temple libraries might be repositories for all manner of texts, but annals and king-lists were in the minority, and even these must have contained mythological tales.[205] But the Egyptian priests did not normally search their libraries for facts about the past. To do that, they must first have acquired the conception of history which Aristotle held: that it dealt with what men had actually done in the past, and was not merely what an individual or a group cared to remember. There is no reason to think that they would have recognized Aristotle's concept, much less that they had a perception of history that would satisfy a modern academic. A great deal of the wisdom that the priests imparted to Herodotus in Egypt must be classed as oral tradition that continued to flourish even though it was vested in a caste of literate specialists: written texts and oral tradition existed side by side.[206]

---

of Egypt: The Middle Kingdom," *AJA* 79 (1975), 223–69; Angela P. Thomas, *Gurob: A New Kingdom Town: Introduction and Catalogue of Objects in the Petrie Collection* 1 (Warminster, 1981); Rushdi Said, Claude C. Albritton, Fred Wendorf, Romuald Schield, Michal Kobusiewicz, "Remarks on the Holocene Geology and Archaeology of the Northern Fayum Desert," *Archeologia Polonia* 13 (1972), 7–22. The size of the lake in the Old Kingdom is disputed, but may have stood at 12 m. above sea level. In the Middle Kingdom it rose to 18 m.

[203] Hdt. 1.143; cf. P. Montet, Eternal Egypt (Mentor Books, New York, 1968), 326. Herodotus' unilingualism has often been noted: cf. Meyer, *Forschungen*, 1, 192–95. Hdt. 1.139 is often taken as proof of his incompetence in Persian, for all Persian names do not end in a sibilant as he claims in this passage: only the i- and u-stems in the nominative do. However, our knowledge of the actual pronunciation of Old Persian is limited, and the practice of Ctesias, who should have known, supports Herodotus. It is possible that the Greeks believed they heard a sibilant pronounced at the end of Persian names with an a-stem as well: cf. J. M. Cook, *The Persian Empire* (London, 1983), 44–45. Herodotus was interested in foreign languages, and perhaps had a "Berlitz Phrase-Book" knowledge of some of them.

[204] 2.106; cf. Redford, *Pharaonic King-Lists*, 148n.94.

[205] Redford, *Pharaonic King-Lists*, 215–25.

[206] Jack Goody describes a parallel situation in India, where the recitation of the Vedic texts (the sacred writings of the orthodox Hindus) was confined to the Brahman caste, literate

Persia supplies a parallel. There cannot be much doubt that there were documents behind three of the most famous passages in the *Histories* that deal with Persia: the satrapy list, the description of the Royal Road, and the Persian army and navy lists.[207] If we accept Jack Goody's argument that creating lists and tables of this sort is not a mental process natural to oral societies, then the ultimate model for these passages should be documents drawn up by the Achaemenid bureaucracy. But as Murray[208] has pointed out, these are not documents in the modern sense: they are not verbatim reproductions of written records that are represented as authentic. Though they may have begun as written records, they have been assimilated to the oral tradition, and in the case of the army and navy lists, the model, though a somewhat distant one, is the Catalogue of Ships in the *Iliad*.

Or let us take another example: the usurpation of the Magi. Somewhere behind the story that Herodotus relates is the written account that we find at Bisitun, which was published throughout the Persian Empire. But what Herodotus gives us has the form and motifs of a folktale.[209] The official account had already been transformed before it reached Herodotus, in whose hands it attained its final shape. Herodotus—to cite Murray again— "had access, not to an official royal version of Persian history, but to variants of it current in the high aristocracy: paradoxically it was always easier for Greeks to make contact with the ruling classes in the Persian Empire than with the imperial bureaucracy."[210] It was oral tradition that he could tap, not written sources.

In his treatment of the non-Greek world, the chief task for Herodotus was to put alien traditions and an alien way of life into terms that the Greeks could understand.[211] He looked for mirror images of things Greek which he could put into context with what was familiar: for that reason, he was always impressed when he saw in Egypt customs which were the opposite of those in Greece. In Egypt, the women ran the shops; the men did the weaving, and they threaded their looms in a manner unlike the

---

specialists who communicated orally: "Oral Composition and Oral Transmission: The Case of the Vedas," in Gentili and Paioni, eds., *Oralità, Letteratura, Discorso*, 7–17; id., *The Interface between the Written and the Oral*, 110–22. Hieroglyphic writing was confined to the priesthood during this period, and in practice, demotic must also have been largely confined to it as well, since the language of administration was Aramaic.

[207] 3.89–97; 5.52–53; 7.61–98.

[208] Murray, "Herodotus and Oral History," 109–10.

[209] Cf. E. J. Bickerman and H. Tadmor, "Darius I, Pseudo-Smerdis and the Magi," *Athenaeum* 56 (1978), 239–61. See n.70.

[210] Bickerman and Tadmor, *Athenaeum* 56 (1978), 111.

[211] Cf. Hartog, *Mirror*, 61–111; Corcella, *Erodoto e l'analogia*, 68–74. Eighteenth-century descriptions of the New World provide an interesting parallel: see Roger Mercier, "Image de l'autre et image de soi-meme dans le discours ethnologique au XVIII siècle," Studies in Voltaire and the Eighteenth Century 154 (1976), 1417–35.

Greek weavers. Egyptian men carried loads on their heads; the women, on their shoulders. Priests shaved their heads; in Greece they let their hair grow long. The Egyptians practiced circumcision; elsewhere, men retained their foreskins except those who had learned circumcision from the Egyptians.[212] These antitheses, which made Greece the basis of comparison, allowed Herodotus, and his audience, to relate to this foreign country that was Egypt.

But the opposition was never insuperable. Egypt was too great a source of things Greek for that, such as her gods, the ancestors of the Spartan royal houses, and the oracle of Zeus at Dodona. Egypt preserved the true account of the Trojan War. Egyptian wisdom, which possessed an antiquity that made Greece seem tyronic, elucidated the traditions of the Greek heroic past, as well as the science that the Ionian thinkers had conceived. And though none of the other *nomoi*-sections are developed at such length as the Egyptian one, we may observe similar principles there too: the Persian eating customs are contrasted with the Greek, and the Persian burial customs are antithetical.[213]

How remarkable his approach was is apparent when we compare him with the explorers and ethnographers of the sixteenth to eighteenth centuries, who had to adapt to the influx of new data from the Americas, which had just been discovered. They, for instance, took for granted that the native Americans were recent immigrants: an assumption that fitted their Eurocentric outlook and saved the verity of the Noah's Ark legend. Marc Lescarbot speculated that Noah had put his shipbuilding skills to use and had colonized the Americas during the three hundred and fifty years he lived after the Flood. Father Joseph de Acosta speculated that the American Indians were descendants of the Jews, while Hugo Grotius preferred a Scandinavian origin. And Lafitau thought the Lycians were the ultimate ancestors of the Iroquois, though unlike the Colchians who obligingly remembered something of their Egyptian origins when questioned by Herodotus, the Iroquois could think of only some old traditions of migration from the west to lend frail support to Lafitau's theory.[214]

By contrast, Herodotus was open-minded and latitudinarian. His conceptualization was Greek (how could he help it?), but whereas the European explorers made the New World conform to the conceptual patterns of the Old, Herodotus respected the integrity of Egypt. It is remarkable how frequently he eschewed a Graecocentric viewpoint. One passage in-

[212] 2.35–36.

[213] Hdt. 1.133; 1.140.

[214] See Margaret T. Hodgen, *Early Anthropology in the Sixteenth and Seventeenth Centuries* (Philadelphia, 1964), 295–349; Clarence J. Glacken, *Traces on the Rhodian Shore. Nature and Culture in Western Thought from Ancient Times to the end of the Eighteenth Century* (Berkeley, 1967).

forms the Greeks that the Egyptians called those who did not speak their tongue "barbarians," which was a mirror image of a Greek usage thrown back at them.[215] He may call attention to the greater wisdom of Egypt. The Greeks told silly tales about Psammetichus' experiment that supposedly proved the Phrygians were the oldest race of men; that the Egyptian calendar was better than the Greek; that the Greek sense of the past was minimal compared to the Egyptian[216] and that the gods originally came to Greece from Egypt, and not merely the gods but their names as well.[217] Even Homer stood revealed as an unreliable source for the Trojan War when he was compared to the Egyptian priests.[218]

To conclude: Herodotus framed his questions within a Greek conceptual world. He was a field-worker researching epichoric traditions that were usually oral, which he in turn would transform into a series of *logoi* for a Greek audience. His informants seem to have been as well-qualified to answer his questions as any Greek could hope to find in the fifth century B.C., and they were willing to satisfy his curiosity as best they could. He faced the double hazard of the field-worker: the need to use familiar concepts to probe an unknown world, and informants who wanted to please. Yet he put Egypt within the realm of otherness and allowed her *nomoi* an integrity of their own. Whereas the sixteenth- and seventeenth-century anthropologists attempted to integrate the New World into their own hierarchy of values, Herodotus presented the Egyptians as divergent and at times antithetical; he felt a degree of satisfaction when he found an Egyptian custom to be the inverse of a Greek one, for such instances let him give his Greek audience reference points by showing it a mirror image of the world with which it was familiar. Neither here nor, for that matter, in any *logoi* on non-Greeks is there any attempt to measure the peregrine world against a superior standard of values belonging to the Greeks. It was polarity, not inferiority, that Herodotus considered worthy of remark in alien cultures.

The approach that Herodotus used in Egypt was the same one he used when he investigated all epichoric traditions. The difference is that in the *Aegyptiaca* we see it on a grand scale. He acted upon the assumption that he could put together a *logos* on Egypt by using his familiar methodology: he sought out the *logoi* of the country, and tested them against the evidence of his eyes, using his judgment. He was impressed at finding in Egypt *logioi* with memories better trained than anywhere else, but he also found written records there of far greater antiquity than he encountered elsewhere. It is

---

[215] 2.158.8; cf. Christian Froidefond, *Le Mirage égyptien dans la littérature grecque d'Homère à Aristote*, (Aix-en-Provence, 1971), 117.

[216] Hdt. 2.2; 2.4; 2.143.

[217] Hdt. 2.43; 2.50.

[218] Hdt. 2.113–20; cf. Truesdell Brown, "Herodotus in Egypt. (2) The People," AncW 17 (1988), 89–98, esp. 93–95.

easy to criticize him for failing to cope with them. But an abundance of written sources must have been a completely new experience for him, and in the case of Egypt, these sources, written in hieroglyphic or demotic, had to be read to him by the appropriate priests and interpreted by translators before he could comprehend them.

These written sources had to be reduced to an oral form before he could use them, and in the last analysis, Herodotus was probably no less dependent on oral traditions in Egypt than he was elsewhere. Unfortunately, we do not know what an Egyptian priest, even an upper-level one, thought about Egypt's past in the fifth century B.C., or what sort of oral traditions he might have purveyed. Perhaps Herodotus had it right.

From Oral Research to Written History

Sir Isaiah Berlin, in his essay on Count Tolstoy, *The Hedgehog and the Fox*, dredges up a fragment of Archilochus which he uses to make a point. "The fox knows many things, but the hedgehog knows one big thing." These words serve as a metaphor for one of the sharpest differences that divide researchers into groups: there are the "foxes," whose thoughts move on many levels and seize upon a vast variety of experiences without trying to fit them into any all-embracing pattern, or system. Then there are the "hedgehogs," who relate everything to a single central vision: a universal organizing principle in terms of what they perceive as significant. Berlin counted Herodotus as a "fox" along with Shakespeare, Aristotle, Montaigne, and a few others. Plato, Lucretius, and Hegel are numbered among the "hedgehogs." Thucydides remains unclassified.

Herodotus was undoubtedly a "fox." He had, to be sure, a luxury that modern historians are denied: "history" was as yet undefined, and consequently none of his contemporaries could tell him that he was really a geographer, an ethnologist, or an anthropologist, and a historian only as an afterthought. Arguments along those lines had to await the departmentalization of knowledge. In the world in which Herodotus was born, a *logios* was merely a man versed in *logoi*, and the *logoi* might embrace many subjects and experiences. No one had separated the study of man's past from the study of mankind in general. Herodotus began as a "fox" who had experienced many things, and the simile is particularly apt, for like a fox, he threaded his way through a great number of traditions with a certain degree of cunning.

Yet at some point, Herodotus began to develop certain characteristics of a hedgehog. His *Histories* still show the fox at work, but they have developed a plan and a central preoccupation.[219]

The one followed from the other, and I think it was the central preoc-

[219] Cf. Hdt. 1.95, where he refers to his plan, and 4.30.1, where he indicates that digressions are a part of his overall plan.

cupation that came first. But let us look first at the general plan. Not the formal structure, which has been the subject of a number of studies in the last twenty-five years, but rather the overall organization of the material. At the end of the *Histories* is the *Medika*: Xerxes' invasion. It begins with Xerxes announcing his expedition, vacillating, and then, after a warning dream, making up his mind, and it ends with Xerxes back at court, where he had started, involved in the affair of Masistes' wife. Before the *Medika*, there are two divisions. The first commences with Croesus, and after his fall, the design that Herodotus set for himself took him next to Cyrus and the rise of imperial power in Asia. Each new aggression of Persia is preceded by a rehearsal of the geography and *nomoi* of the quarry, except for the Lydian *nomoi*, which are described after the fall of Croesus, though still at the point where Lydia became part of the Persian Empire. The section ends with Darius' expedition against the Scyths, which brought the Persian Empire into Europe as far as Macedon. Darius yoked the Bosporus and overstepped the boundary of Asia with impunity.

And then, after the Scythian expedition, there was a moment of peace. The Ionian Revolt starts a new section that ends with the battle of Marathon. There the Greeks for the first time lost their fear of the Persians, and the Persians their reputation for invincibility.

Thus, the schema of the *Histories* falls into three divisions. First comes a section on the growth of an aggressive empire in Asia, which succeeded and consolidated other aggressive empires: the Assyrians, the Medes, and, most important for the Greeks, the Lydians. It concludes with an unsuccessful expedition against the Scyths in Europe. The next phase treats the involvement with Greece, beginning with the revolt of Ionia. The Ionians vacillated, their leaders were inadequate, and when they did find one such as Dionysius of Phocaea who knew what was needed for victory, they were unwilling to cooperate with him. The section ends with another setback for Persia at Marathon, where the Athenians did choose to be free, and were the first to confront the Persians unafraid. The final section is the story of Xerxes' invasion. Persia was on its way to universal empire. Greece was left as the major obstacle. The section concludes with Persia's final defeat, and the *status quo ante Croesum* was restored.

What then, was the central idea that cemented these sections together? Herodotus made an oblique reference to it, when he wrote at the end of his proem that he would deal alike with small and great cities, for those that were once great had become small, and vice versa. His subject was the vicissitudes both of cities and empires, and the rise and fall of imperial power. He was the first historian to articulate the idea of the succession of empires: a concept that was to be much developed after him, so that it became virtually unrecognizable.[220] For Herodotus, the imperialism of

220 Cf. A. Momigliano, "Biblical Studies and Classical Studies: Simple Reflections upon Historical Method," *ASNP* ser. 3, 11 (1981), 25–32.

Asia at the expense of the Greeks started with Croesus, but he was only a precursor, an advance man for the Persian Empire. The Persians had succeeded the Medes, who, under their king, Cyaxares, had conquered the Assyrians, and under the father of Cyaxares, Phraortes, had made the Persians their vassals. Persia was the last of a catena of Asian empires, and the most successful. Her predecessors had not conquered Babylon, Lydia, nor Egypt as far as Herodotus was aware, for he knew nothing of the Assyrian invasion of Egypt. But Persia did, and under Darius, her imperial advance brought her into Europe. Xerxes had little choice but to carry on, but what Darius had done with some measure of success[221] brought disaster on his son. Finally, in 479 B.C., Persian imperialism was stopped. The segment of man's past that Herodotus chose to research reached an end.

And what then? Athens took over the hegemony from Sparta and established a tribute-paying empire of her own. By the time the *Histories* were complete, Greece was polarized into two centers of power at war with each other. How and why imperial power rose and fell became questions of changed significance. At any rate, Herodotus looked back on his scattered experiences and considered the time ripe to fit them into a study that demonstrated the growth and concentration of imperial power and its eventual decline.

Of course, Herodotus must have had more than one motive for putting his researches in order toward the end of his life and publishing them. He had made public displays of his researches by recitals and readings; the finished, written *Histories* would be his final public display. The book trade was burgeoning, and he would take advantage of it. He was doing what other researchers into the past had done or would soon do, for the works of Xanthus of Lydia and Antiochus of Syracuse must have been closely contemporary or possibly even earlier; Pherecydes probably was. Certainly Herodotus was immediately followed by a flood of historians whose names have survived along with a few fragments of their work. He was the giant, but the rest cannot all be classed as pygmies.

But the *Histories* were different. Herodotus went far beyond the local chronicle. His subject was the aggression of imperial Persia against *to Hellenikon*: the "Greek entity," marked by a common tongue, common blood, and shared gods, festivals, and holy places.[222] He followed in the footsteps of the *logioi*, who concentrated on epichoric traditions and reproduced "what was said" with a minimum of critical evaluation. But he subjected their *logoi* to the investigative techniques developed by the Ionian scientists (also called *logioi*) and he organized them around a central theme and vision that he considered appropriate for his contemporary world. His sub-

---

[221] The Scythian expedition was a setback rather than a disaster. Darius' venture into Europe brought Thrace into his empire, and reduced Macedon to a protectorate.

[222] Cf. Hdt. 8.144.4.

ject was the rise and fall of empire and the nature of the compulsion that regulated the imperial destiny.

We cannot say what he would have thought, had he seen the conclusion of the Peloponnesian War, which ultimately sustained what Collingwood[223] identified as the sound principle of the poets: that certain antecedents normally resulted in certain consequents, and that excess in one direction led to excess in another. But the polarities were different: not luxury against poverty, or the *nomos* that commands an imperial monarch to expand against the *nomos* that commands free men to resist conquest. The defeat of Athens would not have easily fitted the model for the rise and decay of empires that Herodotus established for Persia. And yet it was, I think, the beginning of the Peloponnesian War that crystallized his thinking, and changed him from a *logios* working within the oral tradition into a historian, and the founder of a new genre.[224]

[223] R. G. Collingwood, *The Idea of History* (Oxford, 1946), 22–23.

[224] Cf. J. Cobet, "Herodotus and Thucydides on War," *Past Perspectives*, ed. I. S. Moxon, J. D. Smart, and A. J. Woodman (Cambridge, 1986), 1–18.

BIBLIOGRAPHY

Adams, S. M. "Salamis Symphony: The *Persae* of Aeschylus." In *Studies in Honour of Gilbert Norwood. Phoenix*, edited by M. White, 46–54. *Suppl. I*. Toronto, 1952.

Adkins, A. *Merit and Responsibility*. Oxford, 1960.

Alty, J. "Dorians and Ionians," *JHS* 102 (1982), 1–14.

Armayor, O. K. *Herodotus' Autopsy of the Fayum: Lake Moeris and the Labyrinth of Egypt*. Amsterdam, 1985.

Avery, H. C. "Herodotus' Picture of Cyrus," *AJPh* 93 (1972), 529–46.

Balcer, J. M. *Herodotus and Bisitun. Problems in Ancient Persian Historiography. Historia Einzelschrift* 49 (1987).

Ball, R. "Herodotus' List of Spartans who died at Thermopylae," *Museum Africum* 5 (1976), 1–8.

Barnes, J. *The PreSocratic Philosophers*, I. London, 1979.

Bell, B. "Climate and the History of Egypt: the Middle Kingdom," *AJA* 79 (1975), 223–69.

Bernadete, S. *Herodotean Inquiries*. The Hague, 1969.

Bichler, R. "Die 'Reichsträume' Herodots. Eine Studie zu Herodots schöpferischer Leistung und ihrer quellenkritischen Konsequenz," *Chiron* 15 (1985), 125–47.

Bickerman, E. J., and H. Tadmor, "Darius I, Pseudo-Smerdis and the Magi," *Athenaeum* 56 (1978), 239–61.

Boegehold, A. L. "The Establishment of a Central Archive at Athens," *AJA* 76 (1972), 23–30.

Bohannan, L. "A Genealogical Charter," *Africa* 23 (1952), 301–15.

Boring, T. A. *Literacy in Ancient Sparta*. Leiden, 1979.

Borza, E. N. "Athenians, Macedonians, and the Origin of the Macedonian Royal House," *Hesperia* Supplement 19 (1982), 7–13.

Bowersock, G. W. "Pseudo-Xenophon," *HSCP* 71 (1966), 33–55.

Brown, T. S. "Herodotus in Egypt. (1) The Country," *AncW* 17 (1988), 77–87.

———. "Herodotus in Egypt. (2) The People," *AncW* 17 (1988), 89–98.

———. "The Greek Exiles: Herodotus' Contemporaries," *AncW* 17 (1988), 17–28.

Buchan, D. "Oral Tradition and Literary Tradition: The Scottish Ballad." In *Oral Tradition and Literary Tradition: A Symposium*. Odense, 1977.

Burkert, W. *Structure and History in Greek Mythology and Ritual*. Berkeley and Los Angeles, 1979.

Butcher, S. H., trans. *Aristotle's Theory of Poetry and Fine Art*[4]. London, 1907, repr. New York, 1951.

Calame, C., "Le récit généalogique Spartiate: la représentation mythologique d'une organization Spartiate," *QS* 13 (1987), 43–91.

Canfora, L. "Il 'ciclo' storico," *Belfagor* 26 (1971), 653–70.

Cartledge, P. "Literacy in the Spartan Oligarchy," *JHS* 98 (1978), 25–37.

Caton-Thompson, G., and E. W. Gardner. "Recent Work on the Problem of Lake Moeris," *Geographical Journal* 73 (1929), 29–60.

———. *The Desert Fayum.* London, 1934.

Clanchy, M. T. *From Memory to Written Record.* England, 1066–1307. London, 1979.

Cobet, J. *Herodots Exkurse und die Frage der Einheit seines Werkes, Historia Einzelschriften* 17. Wiesbaden, 1971.

———. "Herodotus and Thucydides on War." In *Past Perspectives* edited by I. S. Moxon, J. D. Smart, and A. J. Woodman, 1–18. Cambridge, 1986.

Coleman, R. "The Role of the Chorus in Sophocles' *Antigone*," *PCPS* 18 (1972), 4–27.

Collingwood, R. G. *The Idea of History.* Oxford, 1946.

Cook, J. M. *The Persian Empire.* London/Melbourne/Toronto, 1983.

Corcella, A. *Erodoto e l'analogia.* Palermo, 1984.

Cotten C. (trans.) *The Essays of Michel de Montaigne*, I. London, 1911.

Dandamaev, M. A. *Persien unter den ersten Achämeniden (6. Jahrhundert v. Chr.).* Wiesbaden, 1976.

Darbo-Peschanski, "Les 'Logoi' des autres dans les 'Histoires' d'Hérodote," *QS* 22 (1985), 105–28.

———. *Le discours du particulier. Essai sur l'enquête hérodotéene.* Paris, 1987.

Dascalakis, Ap. "L'origine de la maison royale de Macédoine et les legendes relatives de l'antiquité." In *Ancient Macedonia. Papers read at the First International Symposium*, edited by B. Laourdas and Ch. Makaronas, 155–61. Thessaloniki, 1970.

Davison, J. A. "Literature and Literacy in Ancient Greece," *Phoenix* 16 (1962), 141–56, 219–33.

Dawe, R. D. "Some Reflections on *Ate* and *Hamartia*," *HSCP* 72 (1967), 89–123.

Delargy, J. H. "The Gaelic Story-Teller, with some notes on Gaelic Folk-Tales," *Proceedings of the British Academy* 31 (1945), 177–221.

Demandt, A. "Die Ohren des Falschen Smerdis," *Iranica Antiqua* 9 (1972), 94–101.

den Boer, W. "Themistocles in Fifth-Century Historiography," *Mnemnosyne* ser. 4, 15 (1962), 225–37.

de Romilly, J. *Thucydides and Athenian Imperialism.* Translated by P. Thody. Oxford, 1963.

———. "La vengeance comme explication historique dans l'oeuvre d'Hérodote," *REG* 84 (1971), 314–37.

de Sanctis, G. "Il *logos* di Creso," RFIC, ser. 2, 15 (1936), 1–14.

Descat, R. "Aux origines de l'*oikonomia* grecque," *QUCC* 28 (1988), 103–9.

Detienne, M., and J.-P. Vernant. *Cunning Intelligence in Greek Culture and Society.* Translated by J. Lloyd. Hassocks, Sussex, 1978.

Develin, R. "Herodotus and the Alkmaeonids." In *The Craft of the Historian. Essays in Honor of Chester G. Starr*, edited by J. W. Eadie and J. Ober, 125–39. Lanham, Mass., 1985.

Dewald, C. "Women and Culture in Herodotus' *Histories*." In *Reflections on Women in Antiquity*, edited by H. F. Foley, 91–125. New York, 1981.

————. "Practical Knowledge and the Historian's Role in Herodotus and Thucydides." In *The Greek Historians*, edited by M. H. Jameson, 47–63 (Raubitschek *Studies*). Saratoga, Calif., 1985.

Drews, R. "Herodotus' Other *Logoi*" *AJPh* 91 (1970), 181–91.

————. *The Greek Accounts of Eastern History*. Cambridge, Mass., 1973.

————. *Basileus. The Evidence for Kingship in Geometric Greece*. New Haven, 1983.

Dübner, Fr., ed. *Scholia Graeca in Aristophanem*, Paris, 1877, repr. Hildesheim, 1969.

Duchesne-Guillemin, J. "Religion et politique de Cyrus à Xerxes," *Persica* 3 (1967–68), 1–9.

Duchet, M. "Discours ethnologique et discours historique: le texte de Lafitau," *Studies on Voltaire and the Eighteenth Century* 152 (1976), 607–23.

Durrenberger, E. P. "Stratification Without a State: The Collapse of the Icelandic Commonwealth," *Ethnos* 53 (1988), 239–65.

Else, G. F. *The Origin and Early Form of Greek Tragedy*, Cambridge, Mass. 1965, repr. New York, 1972.

Emlyn-Jones, C. J. *The Ionians and Hellenism*. London, 1980.

Evans, J.A.S. "The Dream of Xerxes and the *Nomoi* of the Persians," *CJ* 57 (1961), 109–11.

————. "A Social and Economic History of an Egyptian Temple in the Greco-Roman Period," *YCS* 17 (1961), 143–283.

————. "Herodotus and the Problem of Lake Moeris," *Classical World* 56 (1963), 275–77.

————. "*Despotes Nomos*," *Athenaeum* 43 (1965), 142–53.

————. "The Settlement of Artaphrenes," *CP* 71 (1976), 344–49.

————. "What Happened to Croesus?" *CJ* 74 (1978), 43–60.

————. "Herodotus and Athens: The Evidence of the Encomium," *AC* 48 (1979), 112–18.

————. "Oral Tradition in Herodotus," *Canadian Journal of Oral History*, 4/2 (1980), 8–16.

————. "Notes on the Debate of the Persian Grandees in Herodotus, 3.80–82," *QUCC* 7 (1981), 79–84.

————. *Herodotus*. Boston, 1982.

————. "Herodotus and Marathon," *Florilegium* 6 (1984), 1–27.

————. "Candaules, Whom the Greeks Call Myrsilos," *GRBS* 26 (1985), 229–33.

————. "The Recent Prominence of Themistocles," *AJPh* 103 (1986), 382–84.

————. "The Medism of Pausanias," *Antichthon* 22 (1988), 1–11.

————. "The Story of Pythius," *LCM* 13/9 (1988), 139.

Fehling, D. *Die Quellenangabe bei Herodot. Studien zur Erzählkunst Herodots*. Berlin and New York, 1971.

Fine, J.V.A. *The Ancient Greeks. A Critical History*. Cambridge, Mass., 1983.

Finley, M. I. *The Ancient Economy*. London, 1973.

Finnegan, R. "Oral Tradition and Historical Evidence," *History and Theory* 9 (1970), 195–201.

————. *Literacy and Orality. Studies in the Technology of Communication*. Oxford, 1988.

Finnegan, R. "What is Oral Literature Anyway?" Comment in the Light of Some African and Other Comparative Material," in *Oral Literature and the Formula*, edited by B. A. Stolz and R. S. Shannon, 127–66. Ann Arbor, 1976.

Foley, J. M. "The Traditional Oral Audience," *Balkan Studies* 18 (1977), 145–53.

Fontenrose, J. *The Delphic Oracle: Its Responses and Operations, with a Catalogue of Responses*. Berkeley and Los Angeles, 1978.

Foote, P. "Oral and Literary Tradition in early Scandinavian Law." In *Oral Tradition and Literary Tradition: A Symposium*. (Odense, 1977), 47–55.

Fornara, C. W. "The Hoplite Achievement at Psyttaleia," *JHS* 86 (1966), 51–54.

———. "The Cult of Harmodius and Aristogeiton," *Philologus* 114 (1970), 155–80.

———. "Evidence for the Date of Herodotus' Publication," *JHS* 91 (1971), 25–34.

———. *Herodotus. An Interpretative Essay*. Oxford, 1971.

———. "Herodotus' Knowledge of the Archidamian War," *Hermes* 109 (1981), 149–56.

———. *The Nature of History in Ancient Greece and Rome*. Berkeley and Los Angeles, 1983.

Friedrich, W. H. "Der Tod des Tyrannen," *Antike und Abendland* 18 (1973), 97–129.

Froidefond, C. *Le mirage égyptien dans la littérature grecque d'Homère à Aristote*. Aix-en-Provence, 1971.

Frye, N. *The Educated Imagination*. Toronto, 1963.

Frye, R. N. *The Heritage of Persia*. Cleveland, 1963, repr. Mentor Books, New York, 1966.

———. *The History of Ancient Iran*. Munich, 1984.

Gentili, B. *Poesia è Pubblico nella Grecia Antica, da Omero al V Secolo*. Rome, 1984.

Gentili, B., and C. Cerri. *History and Biography in Ancient Thought*. Amsterdam, 1988.

Georges, P. B. "Saving Herodotus' Phenomena," *Classical Antiquity* 5 (1986), 14–59.

Gigante, M. *NOMOS BASILEUS*. Naples, 1956.

Gitay, Y. "Deutero-Isaiah: Oral or Written?" *Journal of Biblical Literature* 99 (1980), 185–97.

Glacken, C. J. *Traces on the Rhodian Shore. Nature and Culture in Western Thought from Ancient Times to the End of the Eighteenth Century*. Berkeley and Los Angeles, 1967.

Goody, J. "Oral Composition and Oral Transmission: The Case of the Vedas." In *Oralità, Letteratura, Discorso*, edited by B. Gentili and G. Cerri. Atti del Convegno Internazionale, Urbino, 1980. Rome, 1985.

———, ed. *The Domestication of the Savage Mind*. Cambridge, 1977.

Goody, J., and I. Watt. "The Consequences of Literacy." In *Literacy in Traditional Societies*, edited by J. Goody, 27–68. Cambridge, 1968.

Greenfield, J. G., and P. Porten. *The Bisitun Inscription of Darius the Great. CII* Pt. 1, 5. London, 1982.

Grene, D. "Herodotus the Tragedian," *Journal of Philology* 58 (1961), 477–88.

———, trans. *The History of Herodotus.* Chicago, 1987.

Guthrie, W.K.C. *A History of Greek Philosophy.* Vols. 1–3. Cambridge, 1969.

Haley, A. *Roots.* New York, 1976.

Halpern, B. K. "Genealogy as Oral Genre in a Serbian Village." In *Oral Traditional Literature. A Festschrift for Albert Bates Lord,* edited by J. M. Foley, 301–21. Columbus, 1981.

Harms, R. W. "Bobangi Oral Traditions: Indicators of Changing Perceptions." In *The African Past Speaks,* edited by J. C. Miller, 178–200. Folkestone, 1980.

Hart, J. *Herodotus and Greek History.* London, 1982.

Hartog, F. *The Mirror of Herodotus.* Translated by J. Lloyd. Berkeley, Los Angeles, and London, 1988.

Harvey, F. D. "Literacy in Athenian Democracy," *REG* 79 (1966), 585–635.

Havelock, E. A. *The Liberal Temper in Greek Politics.* New Haven, Conn., 1957.

———. *The Literate Revolution in Greece and its Cultural Consequences.* Princeton, 1982.

Hellmann, F. *Herodots Kroisos-Logos.* Berlin, 1934.

Henige, D. *The Chronology of the Oral Tradition.* Oxford, 1974.

———. *Oral Historiography.* London, 1982.

———. "The 'Disease' of Writing: Ganda and Nyoro Kinglists in a Newly Literate World." In *The African Past Speaks,* edited by J. C. Miller, 240–61. Folkestone, 1980.

Herington, J. *Poetry into Drama. Early Tragedy and the Greek Poetic Tradition.* Berkeley and Los Angeles, 1985.

Herzfeld, M. "Divining the Past," *Semiotica* 38 (1982), 169–75.

Hignett, C. *A History of the Athenian Constitution to the End of the Fifth Century B.C.* Oxford, 1952.

Hodgen, M. T. *Early Anthropology in the Sixteenth and Seventeenth Centuries.* Philadelphia, 1964.

Hoistad, R. *Cynic Hero and Cynic King. Studies in the Cynic Conception of Man.* Lund, 1948.

Homeyer, H. "Zu den Anfängen der griechischen Biographie," *Philologus* 106 (1962), 75–85.

How, W. W., and J. Wells. *A Commentary on Herodotus.* 2 vols. Oxford, 1928.

Humphreys, S. "Law, Custom and Culture in Herodotus," *Arethusa* 20 (1987), 211–20.

Hunter, V. *Past and Process in Herodotus and Thucydides.* Princeton, 1982.

Huxley, G. L. *Greek Epic Poetry from Eumelos to Panyassis.* London, 1969.

Immerwahr, H. R. "Aspects of Historical Causation in Herodotus." *TAPA* 87 (1956), 241–80.

———. "*Ergon*: History as a Monument in Herodotus and Thucydides." *AJPh* 81 (1960), 261–90.

———. *Form and Thought in Herodotus.* Cleveland, 1966.

———. "More Book Rolls on Attic Vases," *Antike Kunst* 16 (1973), 143–47.

Innes, G. "Stability and Change in Griots' Narrations," *African Language Studies* 14 (1973), 105–18.

Jacoby, F. "Herodotos." *RE*, Supplement 2, Stuttgart, 1913, 205–520.

———. *Die Fragmente der griechischen Historiker*. Berlin and Leiden, 1923–1958.

———. *Atthis. The Local Chronicles of Ancient Athens*. Oxford, 1949.

Jeffery, L., and A. Morpurgo-Davies. *"Poinikastes* and *poinikazein*. BM 1969. 4–2.1, A New Archaic Inscription from Crete," *Kadmos* 9 (1970), 118–54.

Jones, D. H. "Problems of African Chronology," *Journal of African History* 11 (1970), 161–76.

Kennedy, G. *The Art of Persuasion in Greece*. Princeton, 1963.

Kent, R. G. *Old Persian. Grammar, Texts, Lexicon.*[2] New Haven, 1953.

Knox, B. *Oedipus at Thebes*. New Haven, 1957.

Krischer, T. "Solon und Kroisos," *WS* 77 (1964), 174–77.

La Bua, V., "Sulla Fine di Creso," *Studi di Storia Antica offerti degli allievi a Eugenio Manni*. Rome, 1976, 177–92.

Lafitau, Fr. J.-F. *Customs of the American Indians Compared with the Customs of Primitive Times*, trans. by W. N. Fenton and E. L. Moore. Toronto, 1974.

Lang, M. "The Kylonian Conspiracy," *CJ* 62 (1967), 243–49.

———. *Herodotean Narrative and Discourse*. Cambridge, Mass., 1984.

Lasserre, F. "Hérodote et Protagoras: le débat sur les constitutions," *MusHelv* 33 (1976), 65–84.

———. "L'historiographie grecque à l'époque archaique," *QS* 4 (1976), 113–42.

Lateiner, D. "A Note on the Perils of Prosperity in Herodotus," *RhMus* 125 (1982), 97–101.

———. "Polarità: Il Principio della Differenza Complementare," *QS* 22 (1985), 79–103.

———. "Nonverbal Communication in the *Histories* of Herodotus," *Arethusa* 20 (1987), 83–107.

———. "Limit, Propriety and Transgression in the *Histories* of Herodotus." In *The Greek Historians*, edited by M. H. Jameson, 87–100 (Raubitschek *Studies*). Saratoga, Calif. 1985.

Lattimore, R. "The Wise Adviser in Herodotus," *CP* 34 (1939), 24–35.

———. "Aeschylus on the Defeat of Xerxes." In *Classical Studies in Honor of William Abbott Oldfather*. Urbana, 1943, 82–93.

———. *Story Patterns in Greek Tragedy*. Ann Arbor, 1965.

Leach, E. R. "Primitive Time-Reckoning." In *A History of Technology* I., edited by C. Singer, E. J. Holmyard, and A. R. Hall, 110–27. Oxford, 1954.

Legrand, Ph.-E. *Hérodote: I, Introduction*. Paris, 1932.

Lenardon, R. J. *The Saga of Themistocles*. London, 1978.

Leo, F. *Die Griechisch-Römische Biographie nach ihrer Literarischen Form*. Leipzig, 1901.

Lesky, A. "Grundzüge griechischen Rechtsdenkens. II *NOMOS*" *WS* n.s. 20 (1986), 5–26.

Levi, A. "The Ethical and Social Thought of Protagoras," *Mind* 49 (1940), 284–302.

Levy, E. *Athènes devant la défaite de 404*. Bibliothèque des Écoles Françaises d'Athènes et de Rome, Fasc. 225, Paris, 1976.

Lewis, D. M. "Persians in Herodotus." In *The Greek Historians. Literature and His-*

tory. Papers presented to A. E. Raubitschek, edited by M. H. Jameson, 101–17. Saratoga, Calif., 1985.

Lloyd, A. B. *Herodotus, Book II*. 2 vols. Leiden, 1975–76.

—. "Herodotus' Account of Pharaonic History," *Historia* 37 (1988), 22–53.

Lloyd, G.E.R. *Polarity and Analogy. Two Types of Argumentation in Early Greek Thought*. Cambridge, 1966.

Lloyd-Jones, H. *The Justice of Zeus*.[2] Berkeley and Los Angeles, 1971.

Macan, R. W. *Herodotus. The Fourth, Fifth and Sixth Books*. 2 vols. London, 1895.

MacDowell, D. M. *Spartan Law*. Edinburgh, 1986.

MacQueen, J. G. "The Assyrian *Logoi* of Herodotus and their Position in the *Histories*," *CQ* 28 (1978), 284–91.

Maddalena, A. *Interpretazione Erodotee*. Padova, 1942.

Mair, L. *African Societies*. Cambridge, 1974.

Malinowski, B. *Argonauts of the Western Pacific*. London, 1950.

Martin, V. "La politique des Achéménides. L'exploration prélude de la conquête," *MusHelv* 22 (1965), 38–48.

Mayrhofer, M. "Xerxes, König der Könige," *Almanach der Österreichischen Akademie der Wissenschaften*, 119 (1969), 158–70.

McDowell, D. M. *Spartan Law*. Edinburgh, 1986.

McGivern, J. "The Beckoning Past," *Imperial Oil Review* 63/64 (1979), 24–27.

McNeal, R. A., ed. *Herodotus, Book I*. Lanham, 1986.

Meiggs, R. *The Athenian Empire*. Oxford, 1972.

Meier, C. "Historical Answers to Historical Questions: The Origins of History in Ancient Greece," *Arethusa* 20 (1987), 41–47.

Mercier, R. "Image de l'autre et image de soi-même dans le discours éthnologique au XVII siècle," *Studies in Voltaire and the Eighteenth Century* 54 (1976), 1417–35.

Meyer, E. *Forschungen zur Alten Geschichte* I. Halle, 1892.

Miller, J. C. "Introduction: Listening for the African Past." In *The African Past Speaks. Essays on Oral Tradition and History*, edited by J. C. Miller, 1–59. Folkestone, 1980.

Momogliano, A. "Seapower in Greek Thought," *Secondo Contributo alla Storia degli Studi Classici*. Rome, 1961, 59–7.

—. "Storiografia su tradizione scritta e storiografia su traditizione orale: Considerazioni generali sulle origini della storiografia moderna," *Atti della Accademia della Scienze di Torino* 96 (1961–1962), 186–97, = A. Momigliano, *La Storiografia Greca*. Torino, 1982, 95–105.

—. *The Development of Greek Biography*. Cambridge, Mass., 1971.

—. *Alien Wisdom. The Limits of Hellenization*. Cambridge, 1975.

—. "Greek Historiography," *History and Theory* 17 (1978): 1–8.

—. "The Historians of the Classical World and their Audiences: Some Suggestions." *ASNP* 8 (1978), 59–75.

—. "Biblical Studies and Classical Studies: Simple Reflections upon Historical Method," *ASNP*, 11 (1981), 25–2.

Montet, P. *Eternal Egypt*. New York (Mentor Books), 1968.

Morrison, J. S. "An Introductory Chapter in the History of Greek Education," *Durham University Journal* 10 (1948–49), 55–63.

Murray, O. "Herodotus and Oral History." In *Achaemenid History II. The Greek Sources. Proceedings of the Groningen 1984 Achaemenid History Workshop*, edited by H. Sancisi-Weerdenburg and A. Kuhrt, 93–115. Leiden, 1987.

Mveng, E. *Histoire du Cameroun*. Paris, 1963.

Myres, J. L. "Herodotus the Tragedian." In *A Miscellany Presented to J. M. MacKay*. Liverpool, 1914, 88–96.

———. *Herodotus. Father of History*. Oxford, 1953.

Nagy, G. "Ancient Greek Epic and Praise Poetry: Some Typological Considerations." In *Oral Tradition in Literature*, edited by J. M. Foley, 89–102. Columbus, 1986.

——— "Herodotus the *Logios*," *Arethusa* 20 (1987), 175–84.

Nelson, W. "From 'Listen, Lordlings,' to 'Dear Reader,' " *University of Toronto Quarterly* 48 (1976), 110–24.

Newiger, Hans-Joachim, "Colpà e responsibilità nella tragedia Greca," *Belfagor* 41 (1986), 485–99.

Niane, D. T. *Soundjata, ou l'épopée Mandinque*. Paris/Dakar, 1960.

———. *Recherches sur l'Empire du Mali au Moyen Âge*. Paris, 1975.

Nieddu, G. "Alfabetizzazione e uso della scrittura in Grecia nel VI e V sec. a.c." In *Oralità: Cultura, Letteratura*, edited by B. Gentili and G. Paioni, Discorso. Atti del Convegno Internazionale, Urbino, 1980. Rome, 1985.

North, H. *Sophrosyne. Self-Knowledge and Self-Restraint in Greek Literature*. Ithaca, 1966.

Nyberg, H. S. *Historia Mundi III*. Munich, 1954.

Obrik, A. "Epische Gesetze der Volksdichtung," *Zeitschrift für Deutsches Altertum* 51 (1909), 1–12, repr. (in trans.) in A. Dundes, *The Study of Folklore*. Englewood Cliffs, 1965, 131–41.

Olmstead, A. T. *History of the Persian Empire*. Chicago, 1948.

Onije, J. N. "The Ngwa-Igbo Clan of Southeastern Nigeria. An Oral Overview," *Oral History Review* 9 (1981), 65–84.

Ostwald, M. *Nomos and the Beginnings of Athenian Democracy*. Oxford, 1969.

———. *From Popular Sovereignty to the Sovereignty of Law*. Berkeley and Los Angeles, 1987.

Otto, W. *Priester und Tempel im hellenistischen Ägypten*. Leipzig and Berlin, 1905.

Page, D. L. "An Early Tragedy on the Fall of Croesus," *PCPS* 188 (1962), 47–49.

Pagel, K. A. *Die Bedeutung des aitiologischen Momentes für Herodots Geschichtsschreibung*. Leipzig, 1927.

Parke, H. W. "Citation and Recitation: a Convention in Early Greek Historians," *Hermathena* 67 (1966).

———. "Croesus and Delphi," *GRBS* 25 (1984), 209–32.

Payne, H. *Archaic Marble Sculpture from the Acropolis*[2]. New York, 1951.

Pearson, L. "*Prophasis* and *Aitia*," *TAPA* 83 (1952), 205–23.

———. "Personalities in Greek History," *JHI* 15 (1954), 136–45.

Peel, J.D.Y. "Making History: The Past in the Ijesha Present," *Man* 19 (1984), 111–32.

Perisinakis, I. N. *I Ennoia tou Ploutou stin Istorie tou Irodotou*. Ioannina, 1987.

Phillips, D. J. "Athenian Ostracism," in *Hellenika. Essays on Greek Politics and History*. North Ryde, N.S.W., 1982, 21–43.

Piccirilli, L. *Gli Arbitrati Interstatali Greci*. Pisa, 1973.

Podlecki, A. J. *The Life of Themistocles: A Critical Survey of the Literary and Archaeological Evidence*. Montreal, 1975.

———. "Herodotus in Athens?" In *Greece and the Early Mediterranean in Ancient History and Prehistory*. Studies presented to Fritz Schachermeyer on the occasion of his 80th birthday. Edited by K. H. Kinzl, 246–65. Berlin, 1977.

Poghirc, E. "Homer și opera sa în Istoriile lui Herodot," *Studi Clasice* 19 (1980), 7–18.

Pohlenz, M. "*Nomos*," *Philologus* 97 (1948), 135–46.

Posner, E. *Archives in the Ancient World*. Cambridge, Mass., 1972.

Potscher, W. "Götter und Gottheit bei Herodot," *WS* 71 (1958).

Pouncey, P. R. *The Necessities of War. A Study of Thucydides' Pessimism*. New York, 1980.

Powell, J. E. *A Lexicon to Herodotus²*. Hildesheim, 1960.

Pritchett, W. K. *Dionysius of Halicarnassus: On Thucydides*. Berkeley and Los Angeles, 1975.

Raubitschek, A. E. "The Cretan Inscription BM 1969. 4–2.1: A Supplementary Note," *Kadmos* 9 (1976), 155–56.

Redfield, J. "Herodotus the Tourist." *CP* 80 (1985), 97–118.

Redford, D. B. *Pharaonic King-Lists, Annals and Day-Books*. SSEA Publications, 4. Mississauga, Ont., 1986.

Rohde, E. *Psyche*, trans. by W. B. Hillis. London, 1925, repr. New York, 1966.

Roisman, H. "*Ate* and Its Meaning in the Elegies of Solon," *Grazer Beiträge* 11 (1984), 21–27.

Said, R., C. C. Albritton, F. Wendork, R. Schield, and M. Kobusiewicz, "Remarks on the Holocene Geology and Archaeology of the Northern Fayum Desert," *Archaeologia Polonia* 13 (1972), 7–22.

Sansone, D. "The Date of Herodotus' Publication," *ICS* 10 (1985), 1–9.

Schadewaldt, W. "Die Anfängen der Geschichtsschreibung bei den Griechen," *Die Antike* 18 (1934), 144–68.

Schumpeter, J. *Imperialism and Social Classes*, trans. H. Norden. Oxford, 1951.

Sealey, R. "Thucydides, Herodotus and the Causes of War." *CQ* 7 (1957), 1–12.

Sebeok, T. A., and E. Brady. "The Two Sons of Croesus: A Myth About Communication in Herodotus," *QUCC* n.s. 1 (1979), 7–22.

Segal, C. "Croesus on the Pyre," *WS* n.s. 5 (1871), 39–51.

Sheffield, A. C. *Herodotus' Portrayal of Croesus: a Study in Historical Artistry*. (Diss., Stanford, 1973.)

Shipp, G. P. "*NOMOS* 'Law.' " Sydney, 1978.

Sinko, T. "L'historiosophie dans le prologue et l'épilogue de l'oeuvre d'Hérodote d'Halicarnasse," *Eos* 50 (1959–60), 3–20.

Smith, M. G. "The social function and meaning of Hausa praise-singing," *Africa* 27 (1957), 26–45.

Smith, S. *Babylonian Historical Texts Relating to the Capture and Downfall of Babylon*. London, 1924.

Snell, B. *The Discovery of the Mind*. Trans. T. G. Rosenmeyer. Cambridge, Mass., 1953, repr. New York, 1960.

Solmsen, F. "Two Crucial Decisions in Herodotus," Amsterdam, 1974.

Solmsen, L. "Speeches in Herodotus' Account of the Battle of Plataea," *CP* 39 (1944) 241–53.

Stein, H. *Herodotus*, I. Berlin, 1962.

Stier, H. E. *"NOMOS BASILEUS" Philologus* 83 (1927–28), 225–58.

Strasburger, H. *Homer und die Geschichtsschreibung*. Heidelberg, 1972.

Stroheker, K. F. "Zu den Anfängen der Monarchischen Theorie in der Sophistik," *Historia* 2 (1953/54), 381–412.

Stroud, R. S. *Drakon's Law on Homicide*. Berkeley and Los Angeles, 1968.

Thomas, A. P. *Gurob: A New Kingdom Town. Introduction and Catalogue of Objects in the Petrie Collection*, I. Warminster, 1981.

Tod, M. N. *A Selection of Greek Historical Inscriptions*, I. Oxford, 1946.

Trevelyan, Lady, ed. *The Works of Lord Macaulay*, I. London, 1879.

Vanderpool, E. "Ostracism at Athens," *Lectures in memory of Louise Taft Semple*, 2d Series. Norman, Okla. 1973, 215–50.

Vansina, J. *Oral Tradition. A Study in Historical Methodology*. Trans. H. M. Wright. Chicago, 1965.

———. *Kingdoms of the Savanna*. Madison, 1968.

———. "Once Upon a Time: Oral Tradition as History in Africa," *Daedalus* 100 (1971), 442–68.

———. "Comment: Traditions of Genesis," *Journal of African History* 15 (1974), 317–22.

———. *The Children of Woot. A History of the Kuba People*. Madison, 1978.

———. *Oral Tradition as History*. Madison, 1985.

Verdin, H. "Notes sur l'attitude des historiens grecs et latins," *AnSoc* 1 (1970), 183–200.

Veyne, P. *Les Grecs ont-ils cru à leur mythes?* Paris, 1983.

Vickers, B. *Towards Greek Tragedy*. London, 1973.

Vidal-Naquet, P. "Temps des dieux et temps des hommes. Essai sur quelques aspects de l'experience temporelle chez les Grecs," *Revue de l'histoire des religions* 157 (1960), 55–80; repr. *The Black Hunter*. Baltimore, 1986, 39–60.

von Fritz, *Die Griechische Geschichtsschreibung*. Vol. 1. Berlin, 1967.

von Leyden, W. "Spatium Historicum." *Durham University Journal* 11 (1949–50), 89–104.

von Voigtlander, E. *The Bisitun Inscription of Darius the Great, Babylonian Version*. *CII* Pt. 1, 2, i. London, 1978.

Wace, A.J.B., and F. H. Stubbing. *A Companion to Homer*. London, 1962.

Wade-Gery, H. T. *The Poet of the Iliad*. Cambridge, 1952.

Wallace, M. B. "Herodotus and Euboia," *Phoenix* 28 (1974), 22–44.

Walser, G. *Hellas und Iran*. Darmstadt, 1984.

Wardman, A. E. "Herodotus on the Causes of the Greco-Persian Wars: Hdt. 1–5." *AJPh* 82 (1961), 133–50.

Waters, K. H. *Herodotos the Historian*. Norman, Okla., 1985.

Weeks, N. K. "Herodotus and Egypt. Discerning the Native Tradition in Bk II." In *Hellenika. Essays on Greek Politics and History*. North Ryde, N.S.W., 1982, 63–68.

Weil, R. "Lire dans Thucydide." In *Le Monde Grec*, edited by J. Bingen, G. Cambier, and G. Nachtergael, 162–68. Brussels, 1975.

Weiss, E. *Griechisches Privatrecht auf Rechtsvergleichenden Grundlagen*, I. Leipzig, 1923, repr. Hildesheim, 1965.

West, W. C., III. "Saviours of Greece," *GRBS* 11 (1970), 271–82.

Westlake, H. D. *Individuals in Thucydides*. Cambridge, 1968.

Wiesehofer, J. "Kyros und die Unterworfenen Völker. Ein Beitrag zur Entstehung von Geschichtsbewusstsein," *QS* 26 (1987), 107–26.

Winnington-Ingram, *Sophocles. An Interpretation*. Cambridge, 1980.

Wood, H. *The Histories of Herodotus. An Analysis of the Formal Structure*. The Hague/Paris, 1972.

Woodbury, L. "Aristophanes' *Frogs* and Athenian Literacy," *TAPA* 106 (1976), 349–57.

Woolf, D. R. "Speech, Text and Time; the Sense of History and the Sense of the Past in Renaissance England," *Albion* 18 (1986), 159–83.

Youtie, H. "*AGRAMMATOS*: An Aspect of Greek Society in Egypt," *HSCP* 95 (1971), 161–76, repr. *Scriptiunculae*. Amsterdam, 1973, 611–26.

Zawadzki, S. "Herodotus' Assyrian History," *Eos* 72 (1984), 253–67.

INDEX

Ovimbundu, 116
Oyede family, 115

Pan, 101
Panathenaea, the, 99
Panyassis, 5, 131
Parian Chronicle, 127
Paris, 52
Parmenides, 5
Paros, 19, 31, 74, 78
Parry, Milman, 114
Parthians, 96
Pausanias, son of Cleombrotus, 4, 7, 11, 22, 41, 65, 66, 69, 72, 75, 80–84, 86, 88, 91, 127
Pelasgians, 19
Pelasgus, 36
Peloponnesian War, 7, 19, 21, 22, 26, 90, 91, 108, 123, 126, 146
Pelops the Phrygian, 14
Peneus River, 136n
Perdiccas the Temenid, 122
Periander, tyrant of Corinth, 72, 110, 124
Pericles, 7, 76, 81, 90, 93, 126; Periclean Athens, 84
Periegesis of Hecataeus, 109
Persepolis, 43
Perseus, 137
Peru, 114
Phaedyme, daughter of Otanes, 101
Phaleron, 10
Phaortes, 145
Pherecydes of Athens, 106, 128, 145
Philaids, 126, 128
Phocians, 92
Phoenicians, 30, 44
phonos, 29–30
Phrygians, 135, 142
Phrynichus, 4, 131
physis, 23, 24
physis and *katastasis*, 24
Pindar, 25
piromis, 139
Pisistratids, 11, 126
Pitanate deme, 124
Plataea, 66, 67, 80–84, 91; Plataeans, 91; battle of, 11, 12, 26, 27, 36, 65, 70, 79, 92, 125
Plato, 131, 143; *Apology*, 95; *Gorgias*, 25; *Laws*, 92

Plutarch, 43, 46, 93, 100, 108
poinikastes, 121
Polycrates, tyrant of Samos, 22, 48, 58, 71–73, 88, 106, 112
Polynesia, 114
polypragmosyne, 38
Pompeius Trogus, 51
Poseidon, 19
Potidaea, 19
Powell, J. E., 29, 29n, 47
praise-poets, 27, 100
Presocratics, 5, 20, 87n, 136
prophasis, 17, 19, 34, 84
Protagoras, 10, 24n, 95
Psammetichus, 134–36, 142
Psytalleia, island of, 79
Ptah, 135
Pythagoras, 135
Pythia, the, 31, 46, 126, 127, 133, 134
Pythioi, 124
Pythius the Lydian, 59

Raleigh, Walter, 135
retribution, 16
revenge, 15, 17, 21. *See also* vengeance
Rhodopis, 138
Rohde, Erwin, 34
Roots by Alex Haley, 115
Royal Road, 140
Royal Stoa, 107
Royal Turin Canon, 137
Rwanda, 115, 116, 123, 124, 125

Saint Ambrose, 103
Saint Augustine, 103
Sais, 110, 136, 138
Salamis, 62, 64, 75, 77–79, 91, 129; battle of, 10, 11, 14, 24, 26, 27, 35, 68, 73, 79, 85, 92, 128
Samos, 58, 94, 111; temple of Hera at, 111
Sandanis, 47–49, 72
Sardis, 13, 20, 32, 42, 48, 49, 58–62, 69
Satrai, 107
Schadewaldt, W., 105
Schumpeter, Joseph, 38, 39
Scylax of Caryanda, 43
Scythia, 6, 9, 17, 37, 38, 59, 98, 130
Scythian Expedition, 4, 9, 13, 14, 17, 18, 35, 59, 144
Scyths, 9, 17–19, 34, 59, 73, 98, 130, 144